# Becoming a Reflexive Researcher

*of related interest*

## Trauma, the Body and Transformation
**A Narrative Inquiry**
*Edited by Kim Etherington*
ISBN 978 1 84310 106 2
eISBN 978 1 84642 640 7

## Narrative Approaches to Working with Adult Male Survivors of Child Sexual Abuse
**The Clients', the Counsellor's and the Researcher's Story**
*Kim Etherington*
ISBN 978 1 85302 818 2
eISBN 978 0 85700 145 0

## Rehabilitation Counselling in Physical and Mental Health
*Edited by Kim Etherington*
ISBN 978 1 85302 968 4
eISBN 978 1 84642 322 2

## Counsellors in Health Settings
*Edited by Kim Etherington*
ISBN 978 1 85302 938 7
eISBN 978 1 84642 289 8

## Writing My Way Through Cancer
*Myra Schneider*
ISBN 978 1 84310 113 0
eISBN 978 1 84642 400 7

## Can You Read Me?
**Creative Writing with Child and Adult Victims of Abuse**
*Jacki Pritchard and Eric Sainsbury*
ISBN 978 1 84310 192 5
eISBN 978 1 84642 054 2

## Therapeutic Dimensions of Autobiography in Creative Writing
*Celia Hunt*
ISBN 978 1 85302 747 5
eISBN 978 0 85700 186 3

## Research in Social Care and Social Welfare
**Issues and Debates for Practice**
*Edited by Beth Humphries*
ISBN 978 1 85302 900 4
eISBN 978 1 84642 269 0

# Becoming a Reflexive Researcher

## Using Our Selves in Research

*Kim Etherington*

Jessica Kingsley *Publishers*
London and Philadelphia

Cover image 'Riding out the waves', and poems and paintings in Chapter 11 by Sue Law, used with permission from Sue Law.
Illustration on p.259 by Sarah Etherington, used with permission from Sarah Etherington.

First published in 2004
by Jessica Kingsley Publishers
73 Collier Street
London N1 9BE, UK
and
400 Market Street, Suite 400
Philadelphia, PA 19106, USA

*www.jkp.com*

**Library of Congress Cataloging in Publication Data**
Etherington, Kim.
  Becoming a reflexive researcher : using our selves in research / Kim Etherington.
    p. cm.
  Includes bibliographical references and index.
  ISBN 1-84310-259-5 (pbk.)
  1. Counseling—Research—Methodology. 2. Psychotherapy—Research—Methodology. 3. Psychology—Biographical methods. 4. Counselors—Psychology—Case studies. 5. Psychotherapists—Psychology—Case studies. I. Title.
  BF637.C6E765 2004
  150'.72—dc22

                                                    2004016275

**British Library Cataloguing in Publication Data**
A CIP catalogue record for this book is available from the British Library

ISBN 978 1 84310 259 5

Printed and Bound in Great Britain

*This book is dedicated to the memory
of our beloved daughter-in-law
Sarah Etherington.*

*I have learned to lose my way in this journey*

– Patti Lather in Lather and Smithies (1997, p.200)

# Acknowledgements

This book bears my name as author but there are many others who have contributed their time – a precious commodity indeed: time to meet and talk with me about becoming a reflexive researcher; time to read the transcripts of our conversations or drafts of the work; time to talk things through and give me feedback; or simply time to listen when I was unsure or needing to clarify my thinking out loud. These people have included Laurinda Brown, Michael Carroll, Carol Graham, Ali Leftwich, Shirley Margerison, Jane Speedy, Sheila Trahar and Sue Webb.

There are others who have contributed in a variety of ways: by giving me permission to use their work, excerpts from their dissertations and conference presentations, and pieces created especially for this book. These include Nell Bridges, Nigel Copsey, Sue Law, Ruth Leitch, Viv Martin, Peter Martin, Mel Rees, Catherine Thomas, Dori Yusef, and others who wish to retain their anonymity, but they know who they are.

There are numerous other people who have also contributed in less obvious ways: past and current students, previous research participants, clients and supervisees, all of whom have taught me so much, and many others who have encouraged and supported me throughout my own journey towards becoming a reflexive researcher, notably Tim Bond, Hazel Johns, John McLeod, Maggie Pettifer, William West. I am also indebted to Jessica Kingsley's publishing team, especially Amy Lankester-Owen, who has become a familiar ally on my various publishing journeys, and more recently, Leonie Sloman.

As ever, I am grateful to my family for their continuing inspiration and for the love, laughter and tears they bring into my life. Since this book was first printed we have been saddened by the death of our beautiful daughter-in-law Sarah Etherington who contributed the cartoon drawing of my dream at the end of the book: she was so pleased to have been part of the work and I felt honoured by her gift and enriched by her presence in my life. My thanks also go to Dave, my faithful friend, supporter and husband of more than 40 years, who has quietly worked away in the background, always willing to help with technical computer advice and listing references, as well as sustaining me with food, drink and reminders to rest when I become so engrossed that I am in danger of forgetting.

# Contents

# Preface

## In the Beginning is My Ending...

This book has come to represent my own journey as I travelled alongside others who appear within its pages. My stories are reflected in their stories and theirs in mine, and as we witnessed each other's stories our understandings were enriched, challenged and confirmed.

Stories are full and rich, coming as they do out of personal and social history. People live storied lives and tell stories of those lives, and as a researcher I have collected and re-presented parts of those lives in the hope that they will inform you about the process of becoming a reflexive researcher. I offer these stories in the hope that you can imagine ways to use them in your life or work. By entering into the narratives you may find new questions and hypotheses that lead you to further inquiries of your own. I seek to draw your attention to how these stories are contextualized within cultures, and how they might have changed over time.

The very act of forming stories requires us to create coherence through ordering our experiences, and provides us with an opportunity for reclaiming our selves and our histories. New selves form within us as we tell and re-tell our stories and when we write them down. When we use our own stories, or those of others, for research, we give testimony to what we have witnessed, and that testimony creates a voice (Frank 1995).

While researching this book I have sometimes felt like one of those people who run alongside a marathon runner for a few miles, giving encouragement and nurture. During this study I have received so much from 'running' alongside others on their research journeys: as their teacher, as their supervisor, as researcher, or as their colleague. They have been my community – my research community – and it is with them I have learned, played and experimented.

During this study I have been moved, surprised, excited, curious, and transformed by what people have told me. This is what can happen, at best, in community with others. I have also been troubled, anxious, angry, doubtful and bored at times, and wondered why on earth I started down this road. But I have learned from *all* of this.

On the pages that follow I have created a kind of 'community' – a community of voices of people I have met along the way: the voices of men and women seeking to use themselves more fully in their lives and work. It is my hope that you will discover within these pages something that will help *you* to feel part of this community, or perhaps something that will help you to create a community of your own – something that one of my participants, John McLeod, longs for:

## A community of researchers

If we can have,
somehow,
a sense of a community of researchers
(That's one of the places
I don't go very often
because I think that's impossible.
I don't enter that area of disappointment.)

But in terms of a notion of things changing,
like qualitative research being integrated into practice,
I think there have been times
in the history of therapy
when research has been different
if you look at Carl Rogers in the 50s,
a huge difference.
If you look at what was happening there…
there was a group of them engaged in practice together,
enquiry, research,
but I don't think any of us have got that.

But maybe there are other ways of doing it,
because Rogers was in Chicago
and all the other people were in Chicago,
because communication was harder then
but there's different ways of being in virtual community now.

But I do think that's an important part of it
and I don't really see how to make that happen
and I think it's really important.

And I mean,
you're making some of that happen
by getting different people's stories
and weaving them together
and perhaps being able then
to point to the threads of communication that are there,
but I think we need to do more than that,
somehow,.
as well.

It's important to have more of a *live* community
that other people can join
and that keeps growing.

Such a community could powerfully impact the field of qualitative research. Reflexive research may not be fully accepted or integrated into the mainstream yet, but maybe a collective voice will amplify these ideas and show the value of reflexive knowledge for those who strive to be more fully present in the research relationships they form. Laurel Richardson's words (quoted in Sparkes 1998), written over 13 years ago, spur me on:

> By emotionally binding together people who have had the same experiences, whether in touch with each other or not, the collective story overcomes some of the isolation and alienation of contemporary life. It provides a sociological community, the linking of separate individuals into a shared consciousness. Once linked, the possibility for social action on behalf of the collective is present, and, therewith, the possibility of social transformation. (Richardson 1990, p.26)

As you read this book I invite you to ask yourself about my own use of reflexivity. Have I been sufficiently transparent to help you judge the validity of this research and to help you answer the questions raised about the purposes, ethics, dilemmas and skills of reflexivity? And do you have enough understanding of the questions listed below in relation to yourself as reader, and myself as author?

- How has my personal history led to my interest in this topic?
- What are my presuppositions about knowledge in this field?
- How am I positioned in relation to this knowledge?
- How does my gender/social class/ethnicity/culture influence my positioning in relation to this topic/my informants?

# Part 1
# Bringing Theories Alive

# Chapter 1

# Introduction

This book is about a process of becoming – it implies movement, agency and continuity, rather than a striving to reach a state at which we have 'become'. It is based upon the notion that we are constantly changing and developing our identities, and that they are never fixed. As we grow through our professional lives we make different choices at different times, and this book is for and about those who are interested in choosing, or who have chosen, to tread the researcher pathway.

There are many good books nowadays about 'how to do research': books about methodologies, philosophies, theories, uses of skills and practices of research, and even about representing and writing research. Many of these books, while not directly related to my own field, nevertheless provide useful information and knowledge that I can apply to my research role. As someone who is involved with teaching counsellors about research methodologies and supporting them to produce dissertations at Masters and doctoral level, I frequently hear the complaint that many research books are difficult to read and seem to have little relationship to the reader's own lived experiences of undertaking research. Even mature academic researchers complain about the dearth of information about the process of becoming a researcher and the many aspects of life that this journey touches. So this book is a response to these comments.

Even less has been written that focuses on the personal experiences of social science practitioners who become *reflexive* researchers and, although I believe that aspects of this transition are particular to the field of counselling and psychotherapy, there are many that are also applicable to a whole range of practitioners whose work is focused on aspects of being human: medicine and related disciplines, law, anthropology, sociology, psychology, social work, mental health, education, disability studies, theology, to name a few. This book limits itself to stories about becoming a 'reflexive' researcher quite deliberately because it is this aspect that fascinates me and which has been paid little attention in research literature.

Some years ago my colleague Jane Speedy and I noticed how frequently MSc candidates would tell us about the transformations they were experiencing while undertaking the research module we were at that time teaching together (with input from other tutors). We began to anticipate these transformations, indeed almost to expect them as an outcome of this unit. Trainers at postgraduate diploma level have long recognized that people change and develop during their professional training – indeed if they do not then something seems sadly amiss.

Back in 1999 Jane and I delivered a paper at the research conference organized by the British Association for Counselling and Psychotherapy (BACP, then BAC) in which we focused on this phenomenon, and as a result of that I became intrigued to know more about *how* those transformations occurred (Speedy and Etherington 1999). About that time I became more aware of literature concerned with reflexivity and the use of self in research (Hertz 1997; Wosket 1999) and I undertook a reflexive research study in which I explored my practice with two ex-clients (Etherington 2000). In later reflective writing I examined how I had changed and developed through the process of conducting that study (Etherington 2001a) and during other studies that followed (Etherington 2001b, 2002a).

The research unit on the Masters course we teach at Bristol University seems to attract students who are interested in using reflexive methodologies. It would be disingenuous not to recognize that students are influenced by the methodologies used by us as their teachers and by the level of enthusiasm displayed in our teaching. However, I believe it goes beyond that.

Reflexive methodologies seem to be close to the hearts and minds of practitioners who value using themselves in *all* areas of their practices (including research) and who also value transparency in relationships. I am increasingly thinking that gender has a role to play in this. As I say in Chapter 2, reflexivity has been influenced by feminist approaches to research, and is closely in tune with women's ways of knowing.

## Using our selves in research

Having said that, it was a man, Clark Moustakas (1975, 1990) who described the stages of heuristic inquiry and introduced the concept of using 'self' as a major tool in the research process in psychological research (although a whole movement was emerging that supported reflexivity in research in the field of humanistic psychotherapy around this time). With his colleague Douglass (Moustakas and Douglass 1985) he described heuristic research, in its purist form, as a

> passionate and discerning personal involvement in problem solving, an effort to know the essence of some aspect of life through the internal pathways of the self… When utilized as a framework for research, it offers a disciplined pursuit of essential meanings connected with everyday human experiences. (Moustakas and Douglass 1985, p.39)

Valle and Mohs (1998, p.96) suggest that Moustakas developed heuristic research in reaction to the dominant worldview of his day:

His humanistic (or 'third force') approach was both a reaction to, and a progression of, worldviews that constitute mainstream psychology, namely behavioural–experimental and psychoanalytical psychology.

However, his views are nonetheless influenced by realist notions and 'essentialist' notions of 'self' – as we might expect for someone of his time in the history of psychological research.

Paradoxically these notions led Clements *et al.* (1998, p.122), in their description of 'organic research', to describe heuristic inquiry as 'masculine, theoretical, and inward focused'. So although many would view heuristic inquiry as valuing typically 'feminine' concepts, such as intuition, tacit knowing and 'felt sense' (as opposed to 'masculine' concepts such as logic, rationality and facts, that underpin positivist paradigms), these perceptions clearly depend on where one positions oneself at the time.

## My own pathway

In preparing this book I have thought a great deal about how I started down the researcher pathway and what has influenced my development since I began my counsellor training in 1987. In retrospect I was fortunate that my postgraduate Diploma included an expectation that we submitted a small research project on a subject of particular personal interest. During my initial counsellor training I was employed by social services as a community occupational therapist, visiting disabled people in their own homes to assess their daily living requirements. The need for emotional support was not even considered back then, but my experience of working in the field had shown me that there were a great many people with disabilities who wanted and needed to talk about how their lives, and their sense of self and identity, were impacted by their experience of disability. That recognition led me to train as a counsellor and guided my choice of topic for my first piece of research: *The Disabled Person's Act: the need for counselling.*

Students on that same Diploma nowadays are not required to undertake a research study, although they are expected to produce a major case study, which is approached in the spirit of research. I wonder though if the cost of separating research from professional training is that the research–practice gap has widened and that some practitioners lose sight at that stage of the possibility of taking the researcher pathway.

At that time I did not see myself as a 'researcher' but I *did* search the literature, conduct a small questionnaire survey of 26 disabled people and interview 8 volunteers in depth. Indeed, I now recognize that this *was* 'research' in its fullest, and even formal, sense. Back then, however, we had no training in methodology, methods or analysis, and my own view of research came from having been married to a biochemist since 1962: he wrote learned papers, presented them at international conferences, wore a white coat while he worked in his laboratory and used test tubes and spectrometers, and became excited about blobs on paper of which I could make no sense. This was what 'proper research' meant to me – so how could I see what I was doing as research?

Whether or not I had known it at the time, I became bitten by the research bug during that Diploma course and later plagued my tutor at the University to know when the first MSc in Counselling would commence, stating that my reason for wanting to do it was my interest in research. I was warned off at that point and told that research was not high on the agenda of the planned Masters, but rather an emphasis on training and supervision. However, early in 1990 I began the two-year course for an MSc in Counselling (Training and Supervision) and although there was very little formal research training on the curriculum then, we *were* expected to produce a dissertation. I engaged with excitement on a study that I now look back on as my first heuristic inquiry. It was a study of: *The Father–Daughter Relationship and its Impact on the Lives of Adult Women.*

Having successfully completed the MSc, my interest in research continued to flourish and grow. Concurrently, during these years, I had been experiencing several transforming relationships with therapists who had introduced me to my 'inner Child', who turned out to be full of curiosity and intelligence, and who had lain somewhat buried beneath layers of early childhood trauma. I had also discovered my 'Adult', who (much to my surprise) was capable of logical and rational thought, and my 'Parent', who was well versed in the art of critical analysis! At that time I was working as a trainer, counsellor and supervisor, and research questions arose every day out of each of these roles. As my confidence developed I realized that I might actually be able to explore some of these questions myself, not needing to depend entirely on what other people had discovered.

Towards the end of the time I was studying for my MSc I began to think about doing a PhD about male survivors of childhood sexual abuse. This was in the early 1990s when we, as a society, were able to accept and acknowledge the abuse of females by males, but the idea that males could also be victims of sexual abuse, or that females might be perpetrators, was relatively new and shocking. I discovered that very little was known about the subject of male sexual abuse, and anything that was known had come from the USA, or was based on research on clinical samples or known offenders.

So I decided to conduct my own in-depth study into the experiences of men who identified themselves as survivors of childhood sexual abuse. I wanted to hear and tell the stories of the 'man in the street', not convicted offenders or those who had been diagnosed within the mental health system, but the stories that had *not* been heard, told by the men themselves, in their own words. So I signed on to do a PhD and thus began a powerful, sometimes lonely, and transforming journey.

# Reflexivity

But what of reflexivity? At that stage I did not know the word, although I can see with hindsight how reflexivity had in fact become an important part of my process of learning and transformation. Reflexivity is a skill that we develop as counsellors: an ability to notice our responses to the world around us, other people and events, and to use that knowledge to inform our actions, communications and understandings. To be reflexive we need to be *aware* of our personal responses and to be able to make choices about how to use them. We also need to be aware of the personal, social and cultural contexts in which we live and work and to understand how these impact on the ways we interpret our world.

Over the past 15 years or so, with the challenges created by feminist and new paradigm research methodologies, the use of 'self' has become more and more legitimate in research. In my first study about disability I scarcely mentioned my self, except to indicate my professional interest in the topic of the disabled person's need for counselling. In my second research study on the father–daughter relationship I included a limited amount about my relationship with my own father because tutors actively encouraged us to locate our research question within ourselves. The fact that I had no intention of publishing made it possible to include myself at all. My PhD, a phenomenological study, also included selected parts of my own story, but bracketed off: I contextualized my self so that the reader could recognize my potential biases and how my previous knowledge of the phenomenon under exploration would inform the study – as would be expected in phenomenology.

More recently, reflexivity has become central to my work (Etherington 2000, 2001a, 2002b, 2003). This has been almost like a process of 'coming out' for me. In the early days I was so lacking in awareness that using reflexivity would have been impossible. Later I struggled between two conflicting ideas: on the one hand, during the MSc I was being encouraged to use my self as a powerful tool in my research, but on the other hand, I was still concerned that others would not consider my personal experience to be a legitimate source of knowledge. By the time I came to write up my PhD, I believed that even though it might be acceptable to use my self in the field of counselling, in the wider world of academia my subjectivity and reflexivity would almost certainly be seen as self-indulgent or narcissistic, and a contamination of 'objectivity' which was still the legitimate benchmark for 'good' research (Mykhalovskiy 1997).

In the late 1990s, having achieved my PhD, I conducted a study with two of my ex-clients in which I allowed myself full use of reflexivity (Etherington 2000). This was an exhilarating and terrifying experience. I now realize that, because by then I *had* a PhD (and the additional confidence its achievement had engendered in me), I was less concerned about the judgements of the 'academy' and more concerned with producing a book that was readable, engaging and informative; with the process of creating it; and in using methods that were in tune with my personal philosophy, worldview and ways of knowing, and which satisfied my ethical beliefs about conducting research.

Using reflexivity in my own research has meant I have had to find ways of being openly creative, and this has stimulated me to generate new ideas to help me avoid the research data being 'poured into a given theoretical mould' (Smyth and Shacklock 1998, p.6).

I have begun this book by telling you something of my own progress from practitioner to practitioner-researcher and academic, and as the rest unfolds I hope to develop this story further. However, I wanted to place my story *alongside* the stories of others who have also taken this pathway, and within the context of the development of counselling research in general. So I have had conversations with men and women who are at various stages along the way about their experience of becoming reflexive researchers: the Masters stage; the doctoral stage and the postdoctoral stage. They will, of course, be at new and different stages as you read their stories today.

## Development of research

Research practices have been changing and developing as postmodern thinking has blurred the boundaries between the disciplines of philosophy, psychology, theology, humanities, anthropology, sociology and literature. Counselling practices have also changed and developed, and in the process some fixed beliefs about psychological concepts of self and identity have been shaken. Narrative practices have challenged power relationships and opened our minds to think of those we help as co-researchers, and sessions as re-search rather than therapy (Bird 2000; Speedy 2001). Social constructionism has challenged modernist notions of truth and reality, and invited us to explore how meanings and identity are created through language, stories and behaviour, and to think about how we know what we know (McLeod 1997).

The principles that underlie my own thinking as I set out this book are based on notions of postmodernism and social constructionism: I value local stories and know the world as socially constructed. I am influenced by my training as a humanistic therapist and by feminist principles relating to equality and power. This book is not a poststructuralist account because the personal stories I tell have an individual as well as a social perspective. However, I am also influenced by some poststructuralist or non-structuralist thinkers, notably narrative therapy practitioners (Freedman and Combs 1996; Payne 2000; Speedy 2001; White and Epston 1990), and although some might say these ideas are impossible to hold together (Derrida 1981) I am still struggling to make sense of them in my own way.

Postmodernism is a term that is used in many different ways, generally related to 'inter-related dialogues in our current condition – and as many would say, a condition particularly characterizing post-industrial, information-based, global-ized economies' (Gergen 1999, p.195). Postmodernism is characterized by a sense of fragmentation, an erosion of the idea of a firm sense of self, a falling away of traditional values, and a loss of confidence in what have been called 'the grand narratives of the past' (*ibid.*) and the belief that those in power will lead us towards a better future. Social constructionism is part of this shift (Crotty 1998).

Social constructionism invites us to see the world and ourselves as socially constructed and challenges us to view grand narratives (including those of science and mathematics) as one of many discourses that are possible among others that have equal value. When we begin to view these discourses as social constructions we can begin to deconstruct fixed beliefs about their power and invite other ways of thinking. Freedman and Combs (2002) suggest that listening deconstructively begins with a 'not-knowing' attitude, which seems to me an ideal attitude for researchers who truly seek new knowledge, rather than trying to find knowledge that fits with, and reinforces, previously chosen theories about people and the world.

As an alternative method of inquiry, postmodernism invites other, often tentative, marginalized voices to be heard alongside those of the dominant western discourses that value certainty, action and decisiveness. All of these notions have contributed to a greater recognition of the importance of the relationship between the storyteller and the listener, and between the knower and what is known, and what each brings with them into the research relationship to create meaning and understanding of the topics under exploration.

Back in 1994, John McLeod had forecast much of this development in his first edition of *Doing Counselling Research*, one of the first UK books concerned solely with counselling and psychotherapy research. He wrote that 'research findings would make more sense to readers if they were truly *reflexive*' (p.185, original emphasis). He ended that book by reflecting on six emerging strands in counselling research: a greater awareness of the relationship between research and practice, permission to be reflexive, openness to new methods of inquiry, the researcher being oriented to discovery rather than verification, appreciation of the power relationship between researcher and researched, and displacement of an over-psychological concept of the person (pp.189–190).

Since he wrote those words a great deal of those ideas have been put into practice in the world of counselling and psychotherapy research although this shift was already occurring in other disciplines, such as anthropology. I believe these changes have deepened the experience of research for qualitative researchers as well as for our participants (Etherington 2001c; Hart and Crawford-Wright 1999; Wosket 1999).

This book, therefore, is based on a study of researchers who value the use of reflexivity. When I began I was aware that reflexivity means different things to different people, so I clarified each participant's personal meaning of the word in the early part of our conversation. Because I was curious about how people become researchers, and in particular researchers who value using reflexivity, I found myself listening to some very interesting stories of education and learning, devel-

opment of personal philosophies, understandings of ethics, research experiences –
many-layered stories of what had shaped each person's thinking and practice as a
researcher, and the (sometimes) profound personal development and transformation that they have experienced, and go on experiencing, while undertaking research. As I listened to the stories contained within these conversations I was very
aware of the impact of gender, culture, history, and the socio-political context of an
individual's experiences of their journey, and how all of this influenced the way
people ascribed meaning to their experiences.

I have attempted to capture some of this and represent it in a variety of ways
that will engage and interest the reader. Some of you might be thinking about
whether or not you want to become a researcher; some may have made that
decision and just started out on the pathway towards becoming a reflexive
researcher; some of you may already be immersed in that process; others may
recognize some of their own journey in other people's stories and feel inspired to
continue. There will no doubt be some readers who have a very different philosophy about research and feel puzzled about, or resistant to, these ideas.

My hope is that this book will be read at several levels: as a piece of reflexive
research which is an example of a 'bricolage' of narrative, heuristic, autoethnographic, and feminist methodologies; as a way of using stories to open us up to
creative and new ways of thinking; as a contribution to learning and teaching
about reflexive research; and as a demonstration of a human-world understanding
of the journey towards becoming a reflexive researcher. If this book resonates with
your experience, affects you emotionally and intellectually, if it raises new
questions in your mind and/or moves you to write or take any other action, if it
challenges assumptions and sustains interest – then, in my terms, it will have
succeeded. This, of course, depends as much on you, as reader, as on myself, as
author.

As the researcher, I believe I need to be transparent so that you can inform
yourself about my part in the co-construction of these stories. In his article on the
place of the unconscious in reflexive research Walsh (1996, p.383) stated:

> If human knowledge is co-constructed, then any research project must involve
> some degree of mutual exploration and discovery. The unmet challenge for quali-
> tative researchers is to document this process in an open and honest way.

By including my own story with the others in this book, and my personal
responses to other people's stories, I may have found a way. But, more than that,
being transparent and including myself also seems like a moral and ethical
approach to this kind of work. Being open is also an attempt to balance the power
relations between myself and those whose stories I have used in this book. As Ruth
Behar (1996, p.273) says: 'We ask for revelations from others but we reveal little or
nothing about ourselves; we make others vulnerable but we ourselves remain invul-
nerable'.

However, I can only tell what I know about my story at any given time. As the reader you might notice some of what may remain unknown to me about my stories through the language I use, just as the language used by other participants may reveal them to the reader in ways they do not know. Language is just one of many aspects of our lives that shapes and reveals our experience (Walsh 1996). But we are more than a product of our language or our individual psychology: we are also embodied beings and a product of history and culture.

Clandinin and Connelly (2000, p.70) tell us: 'Narrative threads coalesce out of a past and emerge in the specific three-dimensional space we call our inquiry field'. The three-dimensional inquiry field they refer to is created by viewing participants' stories as evolving over time, within their contexts, and in relationship with the researcher. They describe the focus of narrative inquiry as

> *inward* and *outward*, *backward* and *forward*. By inward, we mean toward the internal conditions such as feelings, hopes, aesthetic reactions, and moral dispositions. By outward, we mean toward the existential conditions, that is, the environment. By backward and forward, we refer to temporality – past, present and future. (*ibid.*, p.50 – authors' italics)

## How this book is arranged

Trying to arrange this book has been like trying to dress an over-active baby in a Babygro! No sooner had I pushed one leg in, than the other came out; as soon as I tucked that leg back in, an arm was free, and so on. Postmodern texts are notoriously messy to handle, and as a person who likes some degree of order and clarity, this has caused me more than a few problems.

This is the part of the introduction when I am supposed to make some erudite comments on the contents of each chapter – the part I usually skip when reading other people's work, wanting instead to get on with finding out for myself what it is all about. So I am not going to do that here.

Suffice it to say that I have attempted to create some order by dividing the book into four parts. Part 1 provides a contextualizing chapter on how theories and ideas about reflexivity have emerged over time, and this is followed by two chapters that show the type of conversations I have had with participants in this study. The last chapter in Part 1 explains the methodologies I have used.

Part 2 focuses on the Masters stage of the journey, providing a glimpse of my own journey through the pages of a diary I wrote when I was at that stage. Further chapters in Part 2 focus on the role of the supervisor in reflexive research; how this kind of research impacts on the researcher's personal and professional growth; and the use of a reflexive journal in research. The final chapters in Part 2 focus on autoethnography.

Part 3 takes us a step further along the researcher pathway – the doctoral stage. I begin this part by focusing on doctoral candidates' relationship with their supervisor, and use my own experiences as a PhD student to show some of the problems that occurred for me when the supervisor I was allocated did not suit my needs – problems that might occur for others, too, when they are deprived of choice in forming hierarchical relationships. That is followed by a conversation that involves contracting the relationship between a doctoral candidate I supervise and myself. Other chapters in Part 3 focus on the delights and dilemmas created by researching topics that are connected with our own life stories, whether we are consciously aware of those connections or not.

Part 4 tells some of the stories of postdoctoral researchers: several full-time academics, one full-time social researcher, a practitioner–researcher and myself. In this, the last stage (for now) in the journey, some of the stories are concerned with the links between reflexivity and gender, academics' lives, creativity, and life-stages. The book ends with a community of voices, taken from snatches of conversations 'overheard' throughout the book.

There are limitations to this study in that the focus is on the lived experiences of participants who are predominantly from western cultures, although several are from mixed heritages. Sadly this reflects the reality of the culture in which I am immersed because currently there are only a few research students attending from overseas. This is, however, slowly changing.

However there *are* many different voices heard throughout the pages of this book. My own voice takes many forms: my personal voice, my professional voice, my academic voice, my voice as a woman of a 'certain age', as mother, grandmother, and wife – and overall, as storyteller. You hear the voices of those I have known as participants, friends, colleagues, teachers, students, supervisees and fellow researchers. Maybe you will also hear your own voice echoing through these pages. Perhaps I should encourage you to open this book slowly and carefully lest the cacophony of voices is too sudden and too loud!

*Chapter 2*

# Reflexivity
## Meanings and Other Matters

Why do research for which you must deny responsibility for what *you* have 'found'?

(Steier 1991, p.10)

Academic research has traditionally been seen as an impersonal activity: researchers have been expected to approach their studies objectively, and were taught that rigour demanded they adopt a stance of distance and non-involvement and that subjectivity was a contaminant. This 'God's eye view' of the world can seem unchallengeable, expert, hard to connect with, and sometimes, for me, uninteresting to read. Without sight of the person at the heart of the work I feel no relationship with the writer, even if I am interested in the topic. But this is a very personal view. Personal views and beliefs do, however, guide our choices between paradigms and methods, as well as our topic of research and what we intend as our purpose (Crotty 1998).

When I set out to write this book I wanted to explore how practitioners become researchers and what happens to them in that process. But as my thinking developed I realized that I was not interested in just *any* kind of researcher but those, like me, who have risked using themselves transparently in their research and in their writing. By allowing ourselves to be known and seen by others, we open up the possibility of learning more about our topic and ourselves, and in greater depth. This then becomes a personal journey, and it was the stories of those journeys that I hoped to capture – my own and those of others.

As I tell you my own stories and those of other people, I am also telling them to myself and I am changed by them; as I listened to and wrote these stories down I had a chance to make sense of my own and other people's experiences in new and different ways (Frank 1995). As you read them, perhaps you too will be changed and find new meanings in your own life as you resonate with participants' stories of lived experience (Bruner 1990; Frank 1995), both through the content of those stories and the ways in which they are told.

However, there are some areas of research that are best served by using more traditional methodologies and methods – especially evaluative and efficacy studies, where quantitative facts are useful in their own right or as an overarching 'narrative' against which qualitative data can be supported. Surveys can provide important information about statistical incidences of phenomena that would not be possible to gain through using reflexive and narrative small-scale research. Such surveys raise our awareness of the need for social action and policy changes and serve as a background context against which researchers can explore phenomena and individuals' experiences in depth and detail. But as a practitioner and researcher in the human sciences, who is interested in exploring human experience and relationships, these methodologies would not suit my purposes. I am interested in researching the richness and complexity of being human and do not seek to reduce that in any way.

## Societal changes

Research methodologies in general have been greatly influenced by the changing traditions and trends in society as a whole, and to understand reflexivity we need to locate it within those changes. The world of psychological therapies has been similarly influenced and has developed its own grand narratives in line with these trends. John McLeod (1997) gives an interesting overview of how these shifts have impacted on each other in *Narrative and Psychotherapy*, and Peter Cushman links the changing views on concepts of self, which are at the heart of psychological therapies, with a range of cultural factors, such as the move away from religion and the Church, and the growing influence of science (Cushman 1992, 1995).

With the development of science, which sought to release society from the dogma and superstition of religion, people thought they could create a better and more predictable world. Certainty, and a belief in a measurable reality that existed independently from subjectivity, provided a sense of power and progression. However, in spite of the success of these ideas, questioning voices emerged from those who challenged objectivity and the idea that the creation of knowledge *could* be non-subjective and value free. There was a growing recognition that even the most objective observers or interpreters brought themselves, and their prior knowledge and personal and cultural histories, into the equation.

During the 1970s and 1980s women's voices became louder, both in society and in research as the Women's Movement challenged the dominant discourses of patriarchy, recognizing that *women's* views of women's lives needed to be placed alongside the views of men. And often women's ways of knowing and relating were different from those of many men (Alcoff and Potter 1993). Researchers began to address power issues, not just in relation to women's issues, but also issues of concern to other oppressed minority groups, espousing greater equality and transparency that required different ways of collecting data and representing it. Equality required that researchers came from behind the safe barriers they had erected from where they had made their 'expert' interpretations, unchallenged because unseen and unknown, and therefore a source of mystery that could be oppressive.

Knowledge is intimately connected with power and can sometimes be used to oppress (Foucault 1980), especially when knowledge is withheld. Feminist research approaches (and there are many), and their emphasis on equality, challenged researchers to make transparent the values and beliefs that lay behind their interpretations, lower the barrier between researcher and researched, and allow both sides to be seen and understood for who they were and what influenced them. This meant that researchers had to take responsibility for their views, using the first person pronoun, 'I', thus losing the security of the anonymous third person – 'the researcher', or 'the passive voice that distances subject from object' (Crotty 1998, p.169).

These changes in research practice raised new issues about research ethics, validity and representation, and the purposes of undertaking research (Josselson 1996). Researchers began to encourage voices that had previously been marginalized and oppressed and provided platforms for the stories of minority group members, such as gay men and women, abuse survivors and people of colour. Research was used to effect changes in society and reveal the sources and symptoms of powerlessness as well as promoting the idea that people could work together to change oppressive and unhealthy practices within society (Freire 1972, 1985).

More recently, during the postmodern era, we have been encouraged to view all that has gone before as important 'stories' that were constructions of their time. All of those stories have served a purpose and are part of where we are today – and this too is changing: nothing is fixed; knowledge can only be partial and built upon the culturally defined stocks of knowledge available to us at any given time in history; reality is socially and personally constructed; there is no fixed and unchanging 'Truth'. This is the thinking that underpins my own beliefs, and I know that what I write today on these matters may be different from what I might have written yesterday or will write tomorrow. Mine too is a story of its time.

Traditionally, knowledge was passed from generation to generation through storytelling, myths and legends. And now we have returned to valuing local stories and lived experience. By positioning ourselves within the text, by deconstructing dominant discourses and taken-for-granted assumptions about the world (Derrida 1981), by refusing to privilege one story over another, and by allowing new stories to emerge, we have come to a 'narrative turn' in the world. As well as gathering local stories, narrative research encourage the inclusion of the researcher's story, thus making transparent the values and beliefs that are held, which almost certainly influence the research process and its outcomes. This is what I am calling researcher reflexivity, and others call 'critical reflexivity' or 'critical subjectivity', and it is by this means that we co-create multifaceted and many-layered stories that honour the messiness and complexity of human life (Geertz 1973, 1983; Speedy 2001) and enable us to create meaning out of experience (Bruner 1986, 1990).

The topic and concept of reflexivity has been written about across many social science disciplines. One of my tasks in researching for this book has been to discover meanings ascribed to the term 'reflexivity' by the social science research-ers I have spoken with (mainly in the counselling and psychotherapy field) and to place those meanings alongside those found in other social science discourses. My own understanding of reflexivity has developed over time and expanded greatly while undertaking this study. When I first heard the word reflexivity, I thought it meant the same as reflection, as indeed did many of the people I conversed with. So it may be safe to assume that some of you, as readers, are also confused about that distinction (there are some who say there is no or little distinction and describe the meaning of one in terms of the other) and that addressing the differences and simi-larities might be a good place to start.

## Reflection and reflective practice

As counsellors we are familiar with the word 'reflection' and strive to become reflective practitioners. We reflect upon our practice in training and continue to do so when we are qualified, and afterwards in supervision, perhaps eventually devel-oping an 'internal supervisor' to help us reflect upon the process while still in it.

The *internal* process of reflection can be aided by writing notes after sessions and thinking over what clients have said. We may reflect on our life and work by writing a daily journal or diary, poetry or prose, and these are usually solitary endeavours that are kept private. These reflections usually stay at a conscious level, using what we already know about ourselves, while at the same time opening up the possibility of knowing ourselves better as we create new meanings and gain new understandings through the process of writing and reflection. I see reflection as a mainly cognitive process, although not limited to thinking alone: we can think about our feelings and capture images as part of this process of reflection.

But reflection is not only the preserve of therapists or clinical practitioners; reflective practice is advocated across many and diverse occupations. Schon (1983) in his study of the 'reflective practitioner' suggests that we form theories as we reflect on practices that are based upon the knowledge we bring from earlier actions or experiences. But first we have to understand the internal and external forces that propel us towards the actions we take, and how we make sense of our experiences. In his later work (1987) Schon proposed that our need to reflect upon our practice came from a crisis of confidence that arose as a result of postmodernism when people no longer necessarily believed in 'objective' facts and a scientific model of rationality that had hitherto served to resolve differences of opinion and disagreements. There was a growing recognition around this time that our subjective, 'tacit' knowing, and intuition, which did not conform to rationality or rules, made an equally important contribution to the interpretations and decisions we made about our practices. And not only did practitioners need to understand themselves at this deeper level, they also needed to make their understandings explicit in order to go beyond and learn from them.

When we are able to communicate explicit knowledge of our total experiences, 'we can allow our perspectives to be transformed by discussion', being open to including others' views that might extend, challenge or validate our own (Winter, Buck and Sobiechowska 1996). In discussion with others, we can co-construct new meanings in response to their critical reflections and our own. This critical, *external* reflecting allows us to check for distortions in our interpretations that might be based on past experiences held outside our full awareness, or based on indoctrination within our personal or social cultures that we may have accepted without question since early childhood.

When another person mirrors, reflects or paraphrases our words we can notice (sometimes for the first time) what we are *really* thinking or feeling. When they summarize what we have been telling them we might begin to create links between ideas, stories, experiences, and relationships of which we had been hitherto unaware. When others ask us curious questions as they listen to our stories and notice our physical presence, our body language, our inconsistent behaviours (such as laughing when talking of painful issues) this can lead us to reflect more deeply and become more aware of lesser known aspects of our selves. Another person can reflect back to us what *they* can see, which is often more than *we* can see ourselves, thus opening us up to less conscious aspects of our selves.

Gillie Bolton, in her book *Reflective Practice* (2001, p.3), takes the idea of reflection further by stating that an examination of our personal practice

> needs to be undertaken alongside open discussions with peers on the issues raised, an examination of texts from the larger field of work and politics, and discussions with colleagues from outside the practitioners' own milieu.

She sees this way of reflecting 'becoming politically, socially, as well as psychologically useful, rather than a mere quietist navel-gazing exercise' (*ibid.*).

## Reflexivity in counselling practice

In the literature there are different uses of reflection and reflexivity which typically draw attention to the complex relationships between *how* knowledge is created, the part that context plays in its creation, and what the individual brings to the process.

Reflexivity in counselling practice involves operating on at least two levels. First, we need to be able 'to reflect on our selves, which in turn requires an awareness of our selves as active agents in our process' (Wosket 1999). Second, we also need to know what we feel, think, imagine and what is happening in our heart, mind and body; we need to know the inner story that we tell ourselves as we listen to our clients' stories (Rennie 1998). So we move in and out of several levels of awareness as we listen to a client and to our selves. This helps us to understand the decisions we make about what we might say next, what we pick up on, what we ignore and how our own life experiences and contexts might be impacting on our listening and responding.

But there are many different models of counselling and psychotherapy practice, some of which are more reflexive than others. Self-awareness in the therapist is a shared goal in most trainings but how we use that self-awareness is a highly contentious issue.

Reflexivity is not necessarily the same as self-awareness. Tim, one of my participants for this study, pointed out how he saw similarities and differences between self-awareness and reflexivity:

> I don't know that it is so different, except that for me self-awareness is a term that tends to be used by people who think of themselves as a constant, in some way, or who will talk about getting to the 'real me'. Whereas for me, another dimension of reflexivity implies a reciprocity between what you experience out there and changing yourself in response to it.

So reflexivity implies a difference in how we view the 'self': as a 'real' entity to be 'discovered' and 'actualized' or as a constantly changing sense of our selves within the context of our changing world.

Irvin Yalom recognizes and uses the power of reflexivity in his existential approach, responding to clients from his conscious awareness of his relationship with himself and his context (Yalom 1989, 2001). Feminist approaches encourage therapists to be transparent in their relationships 'letting slip the cloak of authority' with clients as a way of addressing the imbalance of power in therapeutic relationships. David Rennie (1998) sees reflexivity as a major feature of consciousness and integral to action, and in his description of his experiential person-centred approach he shows how the counselling relationship is impacted by reflexive meta-communication. He proposes that reflexive communication between the client and counsellor enhances the quality of the working alliance, enables the client to think intentionally and follow through with action, and helps the client choose whether or not his intention will be directly communicated to the counsellor, and if so, how.

Each of these approaches views reflexivity as enabling clients to become agents in their own lives.

## Reflexivity in research

Reflexivity has become an increasingly significant theme in contemporary social research, and there is an ongoing debate about its meaning and value that runs across discipline boundaries in social science (Berg and Smith 1988; Braud and Anderson 1998; Crossley 2000; Ely *et al.* 1997; Hertz 1997; King 1996; May 1999; McLeod 2001; Parker 1994; Pels 2000; Steier 1991), with some social researchers wholly embracing this principle (as in the journal, *Qualitative Inquiry*) while others reject or question its value.

For some researchers, reflexive awareness may involve little more than a means of checking against possible sources of subjective bias creeping into an experiment or survey (Stiles 1993). For others, reflexivity may become the primary method-ological vehicle for their inquiry, as in research using autoethnography, autobiog-raphy, heuristic methodologies, narrative inquiry or 'social poetics' (Ellis 1995; Ellis and Bochner 1996; Ellis and Flaherty 1992; Katz and Shotter 1996; Moustakas 1990; Riessman 2002). For yet others, reflexivity may represent a means of constructing a bridge between research and practice (Etherington 2000; Heron 1996; Reason 1994). With such a variety of meanings it is clear that the concept might more appropriately be referred to as 'reflexivities' (Lynch 2000).

Gergen and Gergen (1991, p.79) explain how a constructivist approach to reflexivity alone provides 'no exit from personal subjectivity' which might lead to 'an infinite regress of cognitive dispositions'. They go on to say: 'In contrast, a social constructionist view invites the investigator outward – into the fuller realm of shared language'. A balance between both positions can help us avoid accusa-tions of solipsism, self-indulgence, navel gazing or narcissism. Including our selves in our work needs to be intentional, in terms of the research outcome: a means to an end and not an end in itself. It does not mean 'anything personal goes'.

> The exposure of self, who is also a spectator, has to take us somewhere we couldn't otherwise get to. It has to be essential to the argument, not a decorative flourish, not exposure for its own sake. (Behar 1996, p.14)

My adoption and valuing of researcher reflexivity has its roots in a complex mix of cultural and social changes (Giddens 1991) and philosophical critique (Gadamer 1975; Heidegger 1962). I have been strongly influenced by feminist thinking, reflexivity being at the heart of feminist methodologies and increasingly other methodologies too.

> It permeates every aspect of the research process, challenging us to be more fully conscious of the ideology, culture, and politics of those we study and those we select as our audience. (Hertz 1997, p.viii)

This book is a contribution to the debate based on my own belief that it is necessary and important for all researchers in the field of counselling and psycho-therapy to adopt an informed position regarding the role of reflexivity in their work. The reader will have understood by now that I have come to value reflexivity myself while also understanding that there are others who challenge my views.

## What does it mean?
I understand researcher reflexivity as the capacity of the researcher to acknowledge how their own experiences and contexts (which might be fluid and changing)

inform the process and outcomes of inquiry. If we can be aware of how our own thoughts, feelings, culture, environment and social and personal history inform us as we dialogue with participants, transcribe their conversations with us and write our representations of the work, then perhaps we can come close to the rigour that is required of good qualitative research.

By using reflexivity in research we close the illusory gap between researcher and researched and between the knower and what is known. By viewing our relationship with participants as one of consultancy and collaboration we encourage a sense of power, involvement and agency. When we enable other people (and ourselves) to give voice to our experience, those voices create a sense of power and authority (Hertz 1997; McLeod 1997). One of my participants, Jane, picks up this point when she describes reflexivity as

> a kind of circulating energy between context of researcher and researched…so we've both got agency in this.

Reflexive feminist research encourages us to display in our writing the full interaction between our selves and our participants so that our work can be understood, not only in terms of *what* we have discovered, but *how* we have discovered it. For myself and other like-minded individuals this is both a moral *and* a methodological issue (Frank 1995; Josselson 1996; McLeod 2001).

John McLeod addresses the point about morality when he states: 'The adoption of a critically reflexive approach to research involves developing an awareness of [these] moral dilemmas, and sharing them with readers' (2001, p.199). I would add that the use of reflexivity exposes and makes explicit many of the moral dilemmas that are there but go unnoticed in non-reflexive research. This point is particularly well illustrated by Josselson (1996) and Riessman (2002).

One of the methodological issues for me is that our interpretations can be better understood and validated by readers who are informed about the position we adopt in relation to the study and by our explicit questioning of our own involvement. This means 'interpreting one's own interpretations, looking at one's own perspectives, and turning a self-critical eye onto one's own authority as interpreter and author' (Alvesson and Skoldberg 2000, p.vii). In my view this enhances the trustworthiness of the findings and outcomes of research.

For some people, greater transparency of personal involvement as a researcher, and acknowledgement of prejudices towards, or personal connections with, the topic of study may feel too great a challenge to a sense of certainty and security that may be based on well-established and familiar practices. Giddens, a sociologist, observed that doubts and uncertainties created by challenging familiar practices are 'not only troubling to philosophers but [is] *existentially troubling* for ordinary individuals' (1991, p.20).

Lynch (2000, p.26) in his challenge to those who view reflexivity as an academic virtue states:

Reflexivity is a central and yet confusing topic. In some social theories it is an essential human capacity, in others it is a system property, and in still others it is a critical, or self-critical, act. Reflexivity, or *being* reflexive, is often claimed as a methodological virtue and source of superior insight, perspicacity or awareness, but it can be difficult to establish just what is being claimed.

As I talked with my research participants I became aware that reflexivity did indeed seem to them to be an 'essential human capacity' and they questioned how it was possible NOT to be reflexive. This is unsurprising in a group of people who were invited to talk about their process of becoming 'reflexive researchers'. However, many of my participants had been trained in positivist paradigms which they now viewed as 'deeply, deeply flawed'. One participant, John, told me:

> I thought: that's wrong, that's not the way to go, you'll end up with a sterile meaningless [piece of work]... For me there's never been a separation between that kind of work and who I am.

During a conversation with another participant, Jane, we spoke about how we inevitably influence the kind of data that are collected, and assist in co-creating and shaping meanings when reflexively responding to our participants. She pointed out that this happens anyway, whether or not it is acknowledged:

> I don't believe people when they say that they don't do that [influence the data]! It seems to me – that even with the most objective and positivist of chaps with his numbers (and I'm saying 'him' already), at his computer screen with his multi-modal modelling or whatever – there is reflexivity going on. So it's more about 'When did I become a person who acknowledged that they were reflexive?' So [maybe the question should be] is this a person who either denies it or hasn't noticed it, or is aware of it but is choosing to do nothing with it? It's about being a reflexive researcher who acknowledges that and thinks: Right! This is going to be in there.

She went on:

> There seems to be a war between the reflexive and the non-reflexive, which is to me..., that some people are picking up these pieces and other people are leaving them on the floor...! I can't quite see what the war's about, if you see what I mean.

It seems to me that 'war' is perhaps a good word to describe the feelings of outrage that are sometimes expressed on both side of the arguments for and against the use of our selves in research. However, reflexivity too must be open to deconstruction (Bridges 2003) if we are to avoid falling into the trap of it becoming just another dominant discourse that disallows the possibility of any other way. John McLeod reminds us:

> On the one hand, qualitative research is indeed personal, and the promotion and communications of the reflexive awareness of the expectations and experiences of

the researcher contribute to the meaningfulness of a research report. On the other hand, the subjectivity of the researcher does not command a privileged position. Personal statements made by researchers are themselves positioned within discourses. (McLeod 2001, p.199)

## Reflexivity in research writing

There are some researchers who, even though they would agree that critical and purposeful reflexivity is an essential ingredient of rigorous qualitative research, do not include reflexivity in their representations of their research – or maybe they do so in a very limited way. Some recognize this as part of their 'crisis of representation' that they face as they 'struggle with how to locate themselves and their subjects in reflexive texts' (Denzin and Lincoln 2000, p.3).

Reflexive texts are complex and multilayered and therefore difficult to manage: the line between text and context is blurred. Such texts might include a wide range of data, including interviews, field notes, conversations, photographs, drawings, dreams, poems and diaries. If we are able and willing to know and relate to the data differently we might open ourselves up to creative and transformative opportunities for personal growth and new learning. Laurel Richardson (2000, p.931) states:

> We find ourselves attending to feelings, ambiguities, temporal sequences, blurred experiences, and so on; we struggle to find a textual place for ourselves and our doubts and uncertainties.

Others are constrained by injunctions about subjectivity being a contaminant of research that stem from their previous research trainings in positivist paradigms. Within academia the dominant stories of positivism still hold enormous influence that can be hard to challenge as simply *one* of the ways of doing research. There can be a lot to lose if we try to introduce new ideas and they are then rejected. Eric Mykhalovskiy (1997, p.234), a sociologist, wrote about how his first attempt to apply for doctoral studies was rejected because one of the papers he submitted for consideration with his application was judged as 'self-indulgent, informal biography…lacking in accountability to its subject matter' (p.232). In his appeal against this decision he argued that naming his work in this way 'is an ad hominem criticism without scholarly merit'. He suggests that someone making such an evaluation is unfamiliar with the wealth of work by 'women of colour' and other feminists who adopt autobiographical forms to explore issues of sociological relevance, such as Ellis (1995) and hooks (1989, 1994).

In an email communication with a sociologist I heard speaking at a narrative-based medicine conference, and who had subsequently lent me his PhD to read, I asked him why there was no evidence in his dissertation of his own interest in the topic he was exploring – no reflexivity – especially as I knew he valued reflexivity in research. His email response was:

> Re. reflexivity – I take your point wholeheartedly – but try explaining that to the PhD examiners! My first submission had stuff about how I got interested, lots on the process (including stuff of pen and ink vs. the word processor), why I like stories, etc. But it wasn't academically appropriate! So it went out.

His external examiners did not understand or approve of his methodology, which he had described as 'narrative analysis'. The choice of external examiners who have an understanding of reflexive methodologies is still limited, even though there is a growing interest in some disciplines. However, neither of the aforementioned men were working within the fields of counselling or psychotherapy where, hopefully, there is a greater valuing and understanding of the importance of our selves and what we bring to our work, whether as practitioner, trainer or researcher.

Others may not use reflexivity because they lack the necessary level of self-awareness and so are unable to recognize *what* they are thinking and feeling. Yet others are constrained by lack of self-confidence, anxiety about exposure, fear of judgement, shame, or a wish to retain their personal privacy. During my research for this book two participants spoke to me separately in terms that indicated that they questioned my wisdom in 'exposing' myself in previous writing. I asked one of the men, Jim, what he thought about that.

Jim:    Well, I thought 'extremely self-exposing and risky' because you were in effect or indirectly…I can't remember precisely how you put it…but referring to your own experience of abuse. And that was the striking thing. It's what I remember most of all about your paper…but that's *all* I remember about you (inaudible), at least with the distance of time. But even as we were sitting at lunch today, somehow that came into my mind, I just remembered that, and…

Kim:    I'm getting a sense that you think it's not a particularly wise thing to have done.

Jim:    Well I don't know. I think it's…, it will have an impact on people seeing it in a certain way, because that might be the main thing they remember out of everything else, which I think is my experience… On the other hand I think it is important now for people to be putting themselves there at the centre of what they're writing about, in an open and professional and responsible way and perhaps in our profession, more so than in any other profession. And I think that's what I want to do as well, so from that point of view…

Kim:    I suppose in the end it's about…somebody writing from the position of being a survivor, writing about working with survivors…that seems to me to add something to the topic I'm writing about… But I think you're touching on something that lots of people worry about, and it is one of the dilemmas of reflexivity. I don't think it requires us to over-expose but I think it requires a judicious use of self and self-disclosure.

Jim:    Yes, it's knowing how to get the balance right.

Kim:    That's the art really, isn't it.

Jim:     Absolutely. And I'm just very aware while speaking…the sense I have is like being on a pontoon…we're right there, and it's an exciting place to be, it's tremendously exciting. And the sort of rapport I feel in talking to you about this. It's so relevant to the work that we're doing… And that's also very exciting. And the fact that it's like breaking new ground – frightening – it's frightening as well.

Clandinin and Connelly (1994, p.423) comment on the risks that come with using a personal voice in research writing or presentation:

> The researcher is always speaking partially naked and is genuinely open to legitimate criticism from participants and from audience. Some researchers are silenced by the invitation to criticism contained in the expression of voice.

But reflexivity is not simply subjectivity – a point I picked up with Tim, at a later date when I asked him how he saw the difference. He told me:

> I think one of the reasons why reflexivity has become more accepted within the social sciences is the recognition of the power of subjectivity as a countervening voice to objectivity, but for me subjectivity and reflexivity are not one and the same. I really want to escape that sort of objectivity/subjectivity binary divide. Similarly, the rational/emotional binary divide. So reflexivity seems to me to challenge those dualisms and to allow and create a conceptual and lived space in which we can be more open to the rather more blurred genre of our experience.

★     ★     ★     ★

In this chapter I have located reflexivity within the traditions and trends in society as a whole and within the literature, in order to understand some of the theories, meanings and related issues; its history; uses in counselling and research; the dilemmas it might create; and arguments for and against including our selves in our writing as researchers.

To summarize what reflexivity means to me at this stage in my understanding:

- There are many ways of understanding and using reflexivity.

- Reflexivity requires self-awareness but is more than self-awareness in that it creates a dynamic process of interaction within *and* between our selves and our participants, *and* the data that inform decisions, actions and interpretations at all stages of research.

- Reflexivity recognizes a 'circulating energy between context of researcher and researched' and that both of us have agency.

- Reflexivity challenges us to be more fully conscious of our own ideology, culture, and politics and that of our participants and our audience.

- Reflexivity in research conversations and writing creates transparency and addresses the ethical issues and power relations between researcher and researched.

- Reflexivity enables us to provide information on *what* is known as well as *how* it is known.

- Reflexivity is not the same as subjectivity but rather it opens up a space between subjectivity and objectivity that allows for an exploration and representation of the more blurred genres of our experiences.

- The judicious use of our selves in research needs to be essential to the argument, not just a 'decorative flourish' for it to be described as reflexivity.

- Reflexivity adds validity and rigour in research by providing information about the contexts in which data are located.

I am aware that my understanding is still incomplete and ever-changing and that by the time this book is published I will probably have reached another stage upon my journey. So this chapter needs to be read as simply one way of telling a 'story of reflexivity'. I have tried to tell it in a range of ways using my academic, personal and researcher's voices and by showing my participants' voices.

One of the best tips I learned from a creative writing course some years ago was 'show – don't tell' and because I imagine that many of you, as readers, might, like me, learn best by being shown, I have arranged the next two chapters to show reflexivity in action, using two conversations I engaged with for this study. In Chapter 3 I show an edited version of a first conversation with a participant, including my reflexivity and reflections layered between our spoken words. In Chapter 4 I show our second conversation and the new stories that the participant had brought with her, as well as those that emerged as she told me them to me. I have attempted to capture and re-present those stories in stanza form to show how new meanings were created and new selves were being formed in the process. In later chapters you will see other conversations and stories, as well as different methods of representing data and ways of creating a multilayered narrative that, I hope, shows how this research was designed, undertaken, represented and where it led me on my own journey.

# Chapter 3

# Everything but the Kitchen Sink

> Interviewers can show their human side and answer questions and express feelings. Methodologically, this new approach provides a greater spectrum of responses and greater insights into the lives of respondents…
>
> (Fontana and Frey 2000, p.658)

This is a multilayered story of how two women who are experienced counsellors, supervisors and counselling trainers are in the process of becoming reflexive researchers. It is built around a conversation between Sue Webb, the co-ordinator of counselling training at Massey University, New Zealand and myself. My own story is interwoven with hers, using my reflexive voice to show my own responses in an effort to address what Speedy refers to as 'political responsibilities' (2001, p.44) and dispel the 'myth of silent authorship' (Charmaz and Mitchell 1997, pp.193–216).

I have tried to embrace reflexivity in all aspects: during the conversation itself, as I ask curious questions related to gender, culture, and the era in which our stories are contextualized, and as I present the conversation in this chapter, showing both voices. Our conversation is set in a different font from the main text. As I write this chapter I use my reflexive researcher/storyteller's voice. At the same time, I reflect upon what I had been thinking and feeling during our conversation that had been unspoken or out of awareness at that time – a process that is akin to interpersonal process recall described by Kagan (1986), thereby thickening the stories. I use my personal voice (which, of course, includes my academic voice) reflexively to include relevant parts of my own history to allow the reader to judge how I might have influenced the stories.

As I re-read this work I noticed that my own story seemed to dominate the first part of the chapter and with the words of Lincoln and Denzin (1994, p.578) echoing in my head, when they warned us about 'putting the personal self so deeply back into the text that it completely dominates', I have tried to balance both voices and stories as the chapter progresses. Clandinin and Connelly (1994) also warned about the researcher's 'signature' being written too strongly, resulting in over-subjectivity, while also drawing attention to the consequences of our signature being written too thinly, when other texts and theories 'sign the work', or we give away our researcher role to participants and *their* texts.

My intention in this chapter is to provide an example of how reflexivity can be used in research conversations and how explicitly co-constructed conversations can evoke stories that create meaning as they are told. This kind of 'interviewing' is experienced by both parties as more of a conversation between equals than as a hierarchical interview in which the interviewer holds all the power. Ellis and Berger (2003, p.162) suggest that the interviewer 'tries to tune into the interactively produced meanings and emotional dynamics' that emerge as the conversation unfolds.

Sue's current story of becoming a reflexive researcher is contextualized against a remembered past and leads to an anticipated future. Her memories evoked my own stories and new stories began to emerge.

★   ★   ★   ★

I met Sue for the first time in May 2002 at the British Association for Counselling and Psychotherapy Research Conference where she gave a paper based on the work she was beginning for a PhD on *Women Counselling Women*. As I listened to her presentation I felt curious about the journey she had so far made towards becoming a reflexive researcher. I learned that she was visiting Bristol the following week, so I invited her to visit me at home and tell me something of her story.

Sue had begun her working life as a French teacher, having been awarded a French Degree and postgraduate Certificate in Education from Bristol University in 1974. When she first went to New Zealand she discovered that she was expected to teach English as well as French and quickly realized that teaching English was much more fun because people talked and wrote about themselves: this was what fascinated her most of all. The school where she was employed had a very strong guidance network, a pastoral care system where counselling was highly valued. The school employed two counsellors and there was a strong focus on the emotional and holistic development of the students. All of this influenced her decision to train as a counsellor, and seven years after becoming a teacher she sought out information about counsellor training. Sue began:

> When I was picking courses I looked for the one that would enable me to look most at myself. I didn't really realize I'd done that until afterwards but when I look at my motivation now, it was as much the personal development and self-awareness as the skills and the theoretical knowledge that I was after. And I certainly got that out of the training!

My mind went back to my own decision to train as a counsellor when I was 47 years old. Like Sue my decision had also been made partly in response to my need to pay attention to my neglected selves – although I did not know that at the time. I had been well trained as a little girl, with seven brothers and Irish parents, to see the female role as one of service to others, especially males. Catholic indoctrination within my family, church and convent school, taught me that it was selfish to think about my own needs, and upheld self-sacrifice and self-denial as a value to which I should aspire. Stories of martyrdom and sainthood were my bedtime reading.

I had been working as an occupational therapist (OT) in various contexts since qualifying at the age of 21 after three years of full-time training. I worked in a full-time capacity for only 18 months after qualifying, and thereafter my working life was fitted around rearing our three sons and supporting my scientist husband in his research career. For the first year after qualifying I worked in a child guidance clinic until the funding for my post expired. The children I worked with at the clinic were referred to as 'maladjusted' back then in 1961. Those children would nowadays be recognized as having been emotionally, physically and sexually abused and/or neglected, an important and subtly different story allowed by our current recognition and the naming of abuse that was not possible before feminism provided a language in which women and children could describe their experiences. A month after I left the child guidance clinic I married and obtained a full-time post in an NHS psychiatric day hospital where I worked until just before the birth of our first child 11 months into our marriage. Since then I have always worked part-time and for a while, during a period when our eldest son became disabled, I did not work outside the home at all. Subsequently I have worked with people diagnosed as autistic, with the elderly, disabled and chronically ill, and in community, further and higher education.

Sue's emphatic words 'And I certainly got that out of the training!' (personal development and self-awareness) made me smile, recognizing that I had certainly got more than I bargained for too! After all, I saw myself as 'the helper', not the one in need of help or personal development. It had been a bit of a shock to discover that I needed to talk about my *own* distress, and it was at this point that I sought therapy and began one of the most important journeys of my life: a journey that is still ongoing and has led me along the path towards becoming a reflexive researcher.

How did you make the transition between being a counsellor and being a researcher?

Well, part of the counselling course I did in England required writing a dissertation. By that time I was back in New Zealand and I had the possibility of this job at the University. I decided to write the dissertation about the development of guidance and counselling in New Zealand because I thought it was the best way for me to find out about and get the culture straight in my mind so that I could function within it. So that turned into a much bigger piece of work than I think the University needed it to be. I got a really good grade for it, which gave me more confidence than I'd had. When I did my French degree I got a 2:2 and I lost all confidence in my academic ability. I became the sort of 'fodder' of middle level graduates: part of the bunch. At secondary school I'd been in a small country grammar school where I stood out as one of the brains and so it was very, very hard to be just nobody much. Yes, I think I probably got quite depressed by that. Looking back now they taught us abominably badly and it's not surprising that I didn't learn to write good essays, but there was a huge hurdle to overcome to actually conceive of myself as academically capable.

I sensed the pain of that experience was still quite close.

> So that must have been quite healing then to get a really good mark for your dissertation…

That remark came from a resonance with my own earlier experiences of learning. My training as a professional counsellor had helped me heal, not so much from the effects of harsh criticism, but like Sue, from a lack of confidence in my own ability that stemmed from a combination of poor teaching and my emotional and cognitive unavailability as a learner while I was at school. Although my teachers at preparatory school recognized that I was bright and intelligent, during my adolescence at grammar school I lost any sense of myself as a curious learner. I was grappling instead with my sense of self in the social world, feelings of inferiority, dissociation and unresolved childhood trauma resulting in anxiety and depression. I did go on to obtain O levels and A levels but always with a sense of fooling everybody by wearing the masks of the joker, the performer, the sportswoman, while struggling internally to overcome a sense of disconnection and dis-ability.

I caught up with Sue's story again:

> So you graduated as a counsellor – well not quite graduated yet, because you hadn't finished your dissertation. And you went straight from there to being a school counsellor?

> Yes, I was a school counsellor to start with in South Auckland, which is a racially mixed, and a low socio-economic area. I started the dissertation then and very quickly, embarrassingly quickly, I got this job at Massey University. I got the job because I had some overseas training and I'd done lots of experiential stuff which was really highly valued, but the down side of that was that when I got to the University they immediately said: 'Professionally qualified as you are, academically you're way behind. You've got a lot of catching up to do.' So first of all I had to finish the dissertation for the course in England and then I launched into doing a Masters.

I asked Sue if her Diploma dissertation had involved doing research and she explained:

> It was literature research. I think what you said before was really nice (about it being a healing experience). I was using it to situate myself, so if you'd asked me at the time, I would have said I was just doing a huge review of literature, but I probably read just about everything that had ever been written about guidance and counselling in New Zealand by that stage. What I was really doing was trying to dig myself in. And it did that really well.

Sue went on to talk about her research at Masters level:

I think I started out with wanting to know which was the best approach for working with anorexia. I had this niggling idea that family therapy would probably turn out to be best. Nothing as conclusive as that came out of that study, but again I think I was trying to sort out if I had ever been anorexic and what was the difference between what had happened to me and what happens to anorexics. But more profoundly, I was trying to sort out where I stood in relation to the various theoretical perspectives because my training had been pretty psychodynamic, Kleinian. I had this growing interest in family therapy, partly from being in South Auckland where, working with the individual student in the school who was Samoan and suffering from some obvious problems in school, I could see it was the tip of the iceberg in terms of what the family was coping with. I ended up working quite a lot by going to people's homes and talking to the families overall and so on. So that was how I got interested in family therapy.

For anorexia, the major treatment at the time in NZ was behavioural interventions, dreadful hospital regimes which horrified me. I'd never had any soul connection with behaviourism at *all* and still don't have. But because it was the primary method of treatment at the time, I chose to examine it alongside family therapy and psychodynamic theory.

I noticed Sue's comment about her interest in anorexia being rooted in her own experience and a need to make sense of that. It seems to be generally accepted now that the topics we choose to research often have some personal significance for the researcher, whether conscious or unconscious. Indeed, methodologies such as Heuristic Inquiry, *require* that we have a personal connection with the topic.

Sue told me she had used a grounded theory methodology for her anorexia study. She had interviewed seven people who had been diagnosed with anorexia, and some family members, doctors and teachers who had been mentioned by participants: about 12 people in total.

I was quite impressed that Sue seemed to have had a better sense of methodology than I had had at that stage. Sue had been guided through her research by a supervisor, a psychologist who was very firm about ensuring that Sue removed her subjectivity from the study except when she referred to herself as 'the researcher'.

It was a very good supervision. Looking back now I think the boundaries were very unreal but it was a good discipline from my point of view. At the time ethnography was only newly being considered in relation to psychology – anthropology and sociology were the areas where it was developing – so my big struggle was to take it from those disciplines and apply it in a way that would suit examiners within the psychological arena. So I don't think at the time I was particularly aware of my impact upon the environment: I was the naïve enquirer, struggling to forget everything I had read before and anxious about being found out that I knew too much. I enjoyed it far more than I expected to enjoy research.

When I asked Sue if she had stated *anywhere* in her work why she was interested in the topic she replied vehemently:

> No, no. My supervisor would have had a fit if I'd done that. I think I might have started that way. I think I wrote the beginning of the first chapter somewhere very early in the process and I was still writing from a sort of arts/creative writing/this-is-my-response position, and it got absolutely lambasted. I went home and cried buckets and wondered if it was worth carrying on, and I think it took me a week to write a paragraph after that, to start again, to get the voice right. And eventually I did get it right, and I don't think anything else would have been possible at that time.
>
> I don't hold that against the supervisor at all and I don't regret it because it was important to learn to write that way in order to be able to move back to a sense of self. I think reflexivity in research comes really easily to counsellors because they're there in their work so readily, and I think that's why it's caught on so fully within the counselling field. And I probably was a little self-obsessed anyway and therefore making me remove myself was quite a good thing at that point.

This was the first time Sue had used the word 'reflexivity' so it seemed a good opportunity to clarify what it meant to her and if that was the same or different to my meaning. I checked with her what she meant by reflexivity:

> I think it's about…increasingly I'm aware of the way in which research is a co-creation, that the postmodern notion of multiple selves and the influences of selves upon each other, makes very good sense to me. It speaks to something that a part of me might have known for a very long time but wasn't able to put into words.
>
> I am convinced that what I say to you now is very much influenced by who I think you are at this moment in time, and what you might want to hear from me. I'm not trying to please you hugely, but I'm making sure that my conversation will reach you, and I'm a good teacher, always have been, and I think that's because I'm good at knowing what will reach the other person. And sometimes I get worried that I do try and please people too much. I've got that female conditioning and I've got the sensitivity to know whether I'm succeeding or not. But I'm sure that when the participant talks to the researcher, that the researcher's expectations have a huge impact on what the participant says. And the researcher doesn't have to have been very clear about what those expectations are. I think a lot of that happens unconsciously, and that's where I guess I'm interested in Lacan and I'm not just sticking with Foucault because I suspect a lot of the negotiating around co-construction happens out of people's awareness.

As Sue was talking I marvelled at how, in spite of her earlier conditioning in more traditional research methods, she seemed so much in tune with my thinking. Not having had traditional research training, I didn't know what it might be like to move from that position to where she now seemed to be.

Kim:       When I heard you speaking at the conference the other day I experienced
           you as being in a very different place from that. Could you say something
           about how that transition happened?

Sue:       I think feminism has done that. I think the notion of the personal as political,
           that sense that one is embedded in systems that impact upon one and one
           impacts upon, that nothing is simply a product of you and me...

Although I had lived through the 1960s, 1970s and 1980s as an adult, I had little
sense of feminism in my personal world, being still bogged down in my own life
experiences and the strains of bringing up three children. Feminism was
something that existed on the fringes of my consciousness but something I only
really learned about *after* I became a counsellor. It seemed astonishing to me, when
I eventually looked up and out into the wider world, that all these changes that
affected my own life so profoundly had been happening out there – and I had
hardly noticed. When I hear my colleague talking now of the time she spent at
Greenham Common I wonder where I was. And then I realize that she is 15 years
younger than myself and had been childless at that time.

Sue went on to talk about how feminism had impacted on her thinking:

> I think feminist research right back from the late 1980s/early 1990s has been a
> progression from 'the personal is political' through to 'I am personally present
> in all my political acts,' through to 'I'm present in the research.' And I think
> people using grounded theory in the 1980s have tended to move... The
> stance of neutrality was always suspect and now, rather than our presence
> being a flaw to be covered up and not talked about because it makes life too
> difficult, as it has been, the spotlight has been put on it and that's enabled
> people to say: 'That's actually how it is: that's not a flaw, that's the world, that's
> how things work, yes.'
>
> I'm not sure beyond that. It's just a sense I have. I guess it's also...I don't
> know whether this is being a bit erm...flighty or not but it seems to me that
> reflexivity is something that will come more naturally to women. It fits with
> women's culture more easily than objectivity: the notion of the existence of
> objectivity is something that belongs within patriarchal traditions. The notion
> of the Judge who is completely removed from the sides of the case and
> *therefore* can see clearly what is truth and what is not – I think that's a very patri-
> archal notion. I think it's obviously been important along the way and I'm not
> denying its right to exist, but I think it's not a particularly female way of
> approaching the world.

I noticed a rise in energy as we engaged with these ideas. *This* was the sense of
kinship I felt when I had met Sue at the conference, our connection as women, who
were born within seven years of each other, in a patriarchal world.

Kim:       Absolutely! Yes! When you were talking about feminism I was thinking: it's
           something about women claiming their voices, actually learning to say 'I' and
           to tell their stories and to come out of the closet, stand up and be counted.

Sue:     And women have had their 'I's before, but not in the research arena and not in the academic world. The 'I' has existed across the back fence…

(I laugh and say 'I really like that image')

     …and in the Women's Institutes and those sorts of places.

As she spoke I had an image of myself as a ten-year-old girl, listening from the living room to conversations in the adjoining kitchen between my mother and her friend who lived around the corner. I knew that my mother's backside would be perched against the sink, teacup in hand and her friend would be leaning against the opposite wall. I loved to eavesdrop on their conversations, aware that if they knew of my presence their talk of men, childbirth and women's ways would cease.

Kim:     Yes. They've had their place, but the place wasn't in academia and research, in intellectual discourse.

Sue:     Yes. And the 'I' that comes easily to women is the 'I' that doesn't necessarily have a very clear notion of product at the end of it – its 'process'. And sometimes…I'm thinking of those sorts of conversations that women can have together which don't go anywhere, that I personally now find very frustrating, which are just like all-women committee meetings that won't stick to the agenda and will discuss everything under the sun and nobody notices what the time is and nobody cares if no decisions are made. I *hate* that too. But it's like the 'I' has existed in those places and it's now being allowed to emerge in an arena that has traditionally been male.

Kim:     And it was the feminists who said 'actually research so far has been written by men about women and it's time women started…'

Sue:     And Jane Austen said that too! It's a quote in my PhD! I'm collecting quotes for the chapters in my PhD and one of them is from *Persuasion*. It's at the very end when Anne is talking to Captain Harville about notions of constancy, and whether women or men are more constant in relationships. And he says that everything in literature would suggest that it's women who are inconstant; that all the poetry is about women's inconstancy. And she says, 'Ah yes, but *we* haven't had a chance to write it.' She goes on to make this lovely statement which is absolutely postmodern because what she says is: 'And anyway, each of us will say what we think is out there in the world on the basis of our own personal experience without disclosing what our personal experience is to the other one, and we'll each be influenced by that without letting on!' So it's the most lovely quote.

She laughs delightedly.

Kim:     Very postmodern! I didn't know about that, yes.

Sue:     I've paraphrased it. You mightn't read it the same way but it's a really good example of women's understanding of the way in which facts and truth are constructed, first of all by who has the pen and secondly, constructed on the basis of our own personal experience and personal feelings rather than something out there that can be accessed.

Kim:    And for me the notion of reflexivity is about having awareness in the moment of my thoughts and feelings, my bodily responses and reactions to what I'm hearing, and in some way using that as part of a dynamic process in research as research data.

Sue:    I think that's how I work naturally. If we take the keynote speech at the conference the other day: while I was listening, all I knew was that there was something horribly wrong. And I was so busy trying to follow the ideas and make sense of the tables and that sort of stuff, while also being aware of my irritation about the fact that he hadn't got clean, final versions of the overheads (they were clearly adapted from some other presentation). So I was distracted from the core issues but I knew they were there, and what happened was that I went away and thought about it. It's my discomfort that leads me to do the thinking.

Kim:    What happens to me is that I hear it and immediately recognize what I hate about it and then I can't listen to it any more. I just spent the rest of the time writing my feedback to the conference organizers. I can't listen to it because I just hate it so much.

But going back to your progression as a researcher (that sounds like some sort of stately progression) – you're now in this place where you're obviously using reflexivity. What's that been like for you?

Sue:    Well I guess I'm not far enough along in the process to know what it would be like to be sharing it with others. A very interesting thing happened when I was writing my paper for the conference. I'd clearly written 'I' into it and I gave it to my partner to have a look at it before I left (which is something we both do for each other and which always causes both of us enormous angst). We don't like being told by the other one what's wrong with it but it's also such valuable feedback that you couldn't get anywhere else.

I had only recently begun to feel comfortable about asking my husband to give me feedback on my writing. His positivist position had caused frequent debates about whether or not my approach was 'proper research'. For many years I knew he did not believe it was.

Sue:    His first comment was, 'You've got far too many "I" statements in this piece,' and part of me bristled around thinking: these ideas are really old-fashioned and I'm not going to take any notice of this. And then thinking: it *is* possible that, in terms of elegance of language, I have got 'I' in here too much. So I went back to it again and one of the last things I did before I decided it was finished was to rework some of the sentences so there were fewer 'I's! So it's like, go from no 'I's to virtually every main clause and subordinate clause has got an 'I' or a 'me' in it – which is not good. It doesn't read well then. So I did actually reduce the number of 'I's.

This is exactly my experience! I have come to value how my husband's approach can improve my writing and I know he has moved in his own thinking to appreciate the way I work.

Sue:     So yes, how is it now? I think my sense is that there are so many other people who are also excitedly on the same path that it's not too difficult. I also think the first person whose writing I read that really impressed me with the way she'd used 'I' was Celia Kitzinger. She's a lesbian and a feminist and she writes a lot in *Feminist Psychology* (I think that's what it's called). I read an introduction to a paper that she was writing which was all about ideas, which said: 'First I shall do this and then I shall do such and such…' and it was so sort of, 'Here I am!' – right there in the introduction, and I thought: Oh I want to write like that, I want to be able to say 'I'm in charge'. She seemed to be saying: 'I know what I'm doing and I'm not scared to say so and I'm owning it.' I really liked that.

Kim:     It's powerful, isn't it?

As I say this, I realize that I have been risking writing more confidently since I gained a PhD. I felt able to state my views more strongly without apologiszing for them once I had the credibility afforded me by having a doctorate. In my PhD dissertation I had 'bracketed off' myself – including myself just enough for the reader to have sight of my values and beliefs so that they could see more clearly where I was coming from and how this position might have influenced my analysis of the data. At that stage I could have done no more in the public arena; to be more reflexive and included myself any more than that would have felt too risky and not 'proper research'. I had, however, used the personal pronoun 'I' throughout rather than 'the researcher'.

Sue:     Yes. I think the other key event for me, when I think back, was a piece of research that I mentioned briefly in the presentation the other day, about one of our students who wanted to research her own experiences after her baby was born. When she first suggested that (this would have been in the mid-1990s probably), a variety of people said she couldn't do it, and I thought: there must be a way she can do this.

Kim:     She wasn't allowed to do it as part of…?

Sue:     Yes, this was not 'proper' research, yes. The person we first looked at to supervise her research was somebody in the early childhood education field who is much into evaluation of early childhood education centres and prides herself on being able to mix and mingle qualitative and quantitative methods, and she just took one look at Julie's initial idea for her proposal and said, 'Well she can't possibly do that. I'm not having anything to do with that.' And then she developed this tidy little plan for what Julie should do instead – something Julie didn't want to do at all.
         The whole reason Julie wanted to do this was because she was trying to make her life fit together in a way that will work for her, and if she researches what happens to her after the baby's born (she proposed this when she was still pregnant), she sees a way in which she might manage to keep all these

different bits of herself on the go. I talked to my partner about it and he wasn't very enthusiastic either and I thought: Damn it. This has to be possible. I feel so excited about this idea. We have to make it work.

Julie and I went away and delved into the literature and I think that was when I first came across the term reflexivity. I didn't even know it existed. And when we found it, it was like 'Yes!' and then we also found a PhD thesis in the library of somebody in the nursing studies department who'd done a study of breastfeeding and had, in a minor way, included her own experience of breast-feeding. It was more like an ethnographic approach but she was much more present in the research in a minor role, and we used some of the references to build a rationale for what she wanted to do.

Kim:    Am I right in thinking that what you were saying is that you haven't been tested in the wider world in terms of your reflexivity because you haven't published in that way, using yourself?

Sue:    Not yet.

Kim:    Do you think about what that might be like?

Sue:    I've been around long enough to know that you pick your journals and I'll do that, yes.

Kim:    What about yourself? You're thinking about that in terms of where it will be acceptable, but I was thinking about the impact on us when we…

Sue:    …put ourselves out there, yes. Oh I've got a long history of doing that! Yes. I use myself an enormous amount in my teaching. I make a joke that if I use myself as a case example then I don't have to worry about confidentiality and informed consent. And I think it's very good modelling in training. I can talk about the therapy I had in London and I very *rarely* experience a sense of people misunderstanding me. I think it happens sometimes, but I very rarely feel at all shaken by that.

I think I've probably been putting myself out there for so many years that, unless it comes from an unexpected quarter, or is the sort of negative response that I am not at all expecting or haven't had before…

Kim:    Why do you think – well I am assuming that you think – that reflexivity is important? Why do you think we should be reflexive in research?

Sue:    Because if you don't have the model of the world of 'the Judge', establishing Truth with a capital T, then everything that happens is constructed by those involved in it, and therefore *not* to be reflexive, not to self-examine and not to put that process and the results of that out there, is to withhold some of the information that exists about the context which you're examining.

Kim:    Mmm. So is it something about validity or credibility?

Sue:    Yes, yes, absolutely. And by putting myself out there, I enable the reader to form a better picture of what it is that I'm then saying.

Kim:    They can make up their own minds then. They're better informed?

Sue:     Yes, they're better informed about the process, they're better informed about the particular light that I might have chosen to shine on that particular topic. And I also think that it's more likely that the reader or the listener will access *their* personal response if I've done that. They have a personal response, inevitably, which then impacts on…and now I've lost my thread (laughter). What I think I was saying is: If I have said as author, 'This is who I am in relation to this topic,' then the reader/listener is freer to decide who *they* are in relation to the topic and to declare that to themselves or others, as the case may be. So it makes for a more human interaction; it makes for a more dynamic energy around the research and its ongoing life.

Kim:     So thinking back over your 'stately progress' (shared laughter) to becoming a reflexive counselling researcher, what's that been like for you? Do you have an image or a metaphor?

There's a long pause as Sue tries to find an image. I love asking this question because it often brings some real surprises, both for me and for the other person. Occasionally it backfires because imagery is not always easily accessible to everybody.

Sue:     I didn't have – but I'm working on one right this minute! Yes… I think I have a sense of having walked into a room that was previously locked but well known to me, and it's full of all the best things about the way in which I work in conjunction with the world. It frees me to make use of various pieces of me that didn't look like they could belong in the research context. I have a sense of a fairy story where there's a room full of lots of different things, which is very rich…and warm and familiar that I can now access. I can use Jane Austen: I can use lots of different literature. I use literature a lot in my work with clients. I think it was Carol Gilligan who introduced me to the idea that I could write chapters about books as well as about people. I think it was *In a Different Voice* she did an analysis of Margaret Drabble's book and George Elliot's *The Mill on the Floss*. I was really drawn to all that and the idea that all these pieces of me that might have been able to enter the research room are accessible and usable in this new way.

I was thinking about how John McLeod did that in his book *Narrative and Psychotherapy*: writing about David Lodge's work.

Kim:     What teases me about this whole business about becoming a reflexive counsellor-researcher (and I suppose it's because I see myself primarily as a practitioner who also does research and writing) …and I'm very excited about research as you know, and I'm very excited about encouraging and teaching our students to become researchers, and most of them are also primarily practitioners: that's mainly who our students are. They're not academics and they don't work in universities (some of them do as teachers), but my own journey has been… Every piece of research I've done has come from curiosity born out of my practice, in some way, and not because I wanted to get papers published or meet any requirements of any external body.

And here I am now at this stage in my career and my life where I am a researcher and I can't get any grant money because I don't have a big name and because I don't have status and because I'm applying for studies that are steeped in narrative and reflexivity, which is not rated highly among the people who hold the purse strings. And my anxiety is that maybe we're setting up an awful lot of people who follow on behind, to have the same kind of frustrations. Our students do Masters and a few of them are doing PhDs because, like me, they're interested in something enough to want to find out about it in depth, and they're not being paid by anybody to do that, they're not getting funding, very rarely do they get grants, very rarely, and I sometimes wonder about the ethics of that. It's like training people for jobs that aren't there. It's like setting people up to be disappointed and frustrated in the way that I've been disappointed and frustrated. And I just wondered if you'd thought about that at all.

You're in a university where there's an expectation of you doing research and presumably you have a remit within your paid time to do research?

Sue:    Supposedly – yes!

It's a frequent complaint among academics that, although they are supposed to have time for research, there is always so much else to do that they usually end up doing their research in their own time.

I was slightly surprised by my statement about research funding and if we were ethically wrong to train counsellors for jobs that are not there. I wondered where it came from: it did not seem connected to what we had been talking about at the time. My frustrations all seemed to be pouring out! But now as I write this I remember that just a few weeks prior to my conversation with Sue I had been turned down by the University for a Teaching and Learning bid for funding, and two months before that, a bid I had made to the Economic and Social Research Council jointly with John McLeod had also been turned down. That joint bid was for research into the use of reflexivity in research. I had spent too much precious time on funding bids that had been turned down and I was feeling angry and frustrated. In response to that disappointment I had decided to embark on this study, unfunded as usual (although I was later awarded a very small grant to assist in this process). In thinking about John's work just a few minutes before, I now realize that I had unconsciously connected with some of those unresolved feelings.

Kim:    And you have expectations to be paid for time to go to conferences? You don't lose any income when you go to conferences as a practitioner does, or to be asked to sit on an examinations committee and all those things that go with being an academic? I suppose I struggle with some of these ideas: we're educating people to be researchers in the field of counselling. What do you think about all of that?

Sue:    Yes, and I don't think the type of research really makes any difference to that problem. There's no money for quantitative research in counselling either in my experience, not that I've tried much but I just know…so in that sense it's not like 'Oh dear, if we do qualitative research we won't get money but if we do something a bit more traditional and mainstream we will.' There isn't money regardless. I think (this might be a bit like Pollyanna), but students choose to do their research around things that they're passionate about, whether it's because it has some deep personal meaning for them or because it's a crucial issue in their work with clients, or in their existence within an organization. They always choose something that is bugging them, something they want to know more about, and I do believe in people learning more about things because they want to, not because it's going to lead to anything. I come from a generation where education was for its own sake, for quality of life rather than for earning power. So I think that still applies. And I also think that counselling *has* to do this. Politically it's a requirement of the profession that this happens and the profession needs it to happen. I think the area that I'm not comfortable with is that I don't think we do enough to get students to disseminate their work. We tend to say 'oh that's nice' and put it on the library shelf. And we don't take that extra step towards getting it published, finding the arenas or creating the arenas for it to be published so that it reaches others. I think the other thing is that once you've done a piece of research, you look at other people's research with a different eye and you're a much more discerning consumer of research and that's really important too.

Kim:     So it sounds like you're saying it's enough to train our students for those reasons and not to have any expectations that they will go on to become researchers, but to leave it where it is in terms of it being an extension of the practitioner self.

Sue is right of course, and it feels good to be reminded of that. My dilemma is also compounded in the University's attitude to PhD research training. The decision to make training in positivist methodologies, that are not of interest to many counsellors, compulsory seems to be based on the idea that people who study for a PhD are training to become academics and should therefore be competent in the whole range of approaches. This may be true for some people, but mature counsellors who want to do a PhD because they are interested in studying in depth something that is of interest and relevant to them in their work and lives should not be constrained by these rules.

This decision also seemed to be biased in favour of the dominant paradigms of positivism. PhD students are expected to study further statistics but in-depth training in non-traditional postmodern methodologies that are frequently more useful and relevant to counsellors are *not* compulsory to all PhD students. I believe there should be more choice and that decisions should be based on relevance and individual need.

I think so, yes. What I want is a profession that's *comfortable* with research, that can pick it up and read it and not think 'Oh I don't know what this is on about,' or 'I don't quite know where I stand in relation to this.' Somebody who can say, 'There's this really good book on working with males who've been sexually abused and she's done it in such a way that I can relate it easily to my own practice and I can learn a lot about how to work with my clients by what I read in this book, but I also know that because she's done it this way that I won't find out such and such.' I think counselling for many years has seen research as something that somebody else did, that they might or might not understand – sort of coat-tailing on the knowledge rather than owning it.

Nice plug for my *Narrative Approaches* book there!

Kim: So is there anything else you'd like to say before we wind up? What's it been like talking about becoming a reflexive researcher?

Sue: I'm aware of my anxiety about wondering: am I really a researcher?

Kim: All the students say that!

Sue: Is that right? There you go then, I'm just another student! One of the reasons I want to do this PhD is that I want to show that I am a 'real academic', that I have academic value, which is not how I felt when I left university after my first degree.

Kim: So it's a kind of healing journey?

Sue: Yes.

Kim: What would make you feel like a 'real researcher'? What would you have to be, to do?

Sue: Well I wouldn't want to be one because when I think about those people who I think of as 'real researchers'... I pick the extreme – colleagues whose holidays, whose every breathing moment is spent in writing, who are increasingly cut off, not just from students but from colleagues. Another colleague of mine...he's got this lovely statement about universities being 'sheltered environments for the intellectually...'

She fumbles for a word and my wicked humour interjects:

Kim: Crippled?

Sue: Crippled! I know people like that. I would hate to be them. Their wives have brought up the children, they haven't. They're like another child in the house...

Kim: But what would *you* need to do to feel like you were the kind of researcher *you* might want to be?

Sue: I'd have to get a PhD. Various people have said to me, 'Oh why bother at your age?' which really pisses me off, and I bother because I've always wanted to do one and not just in order to be Dr Webb, but because I want the experience: it's an experience I haven't had. But also it feels like I can't work in a university for decades and *not* do a PhD, it's ridiculous. But will I be a 'proper' researcher when I've finished?

Maybe this is just part of being a woman in the world of research, which often seems very masculine. Having been awarded a PhD, at the age of 55, I really understood what she meant about doing it for the experience.

Kim:      So have you published already?

Sue:      Yes, a variety of things: a couple of chapters in books. Just like the students, I tend to write about the things that I have some other reason for being interested in. I did a lot of writing about infertility at one stage because I had a horrible time being infertile. It's a bit like the anorexia. I did wonder if I was going mad, and then when I started to read, realized that, wondering if one was going mad was a very common experience with infertility. And then I've written about boundaries. I had a couple of things in *British Journal of Guidance and Counselling*. Recently I've done a lot of writing about the profession because I've been president of the New Zealand Association of Counsellors for three years, which I finished in 2000, and I did a lot of writing then about the profession in New Zealand. We started on a process of re-examining the Association's objectives and that led me into a whole lot of philosophy about what the professional association was for and what its dilemmas were. And I also did quite a lot of policy writing at that stage and submissions to government. I got a lot of pleasure out of that. I'm a person that likes something *new*, so that was a *new* challenge; I hadn't done anything like that before.

Kim:      And she says she's not a researcher! She just likes doing something new!

As our conversation ended I thought that maybe I should have explored our meaning of the word 'researcher' earlier in the same way I had explored 'reflexivity'. It seemed to me that Sue had been researching most of her life and that she fulfilled most of my own criteria for being a 'researcher' – yet she was anxious about applying that word to herself. I too had struggled for a long time to apply that word to myself, recognizing that I did not fit with many people's use of it. Nowadays I feel quite sure I *am* a researcher and work hard to enable our Masters students to become more at home in those roles too.

Sue and I had another cup of tea and fell into talking of other parts of our lives. I had made a new friend. Two women living at opposite ends of the globe, both white, middle-class, middle-aged lecturers, discovering that, although there were many differences between us, we also had much in common. Sitting comfortably in my conservatory overlooking a spring garden – not propped up against the kitchen sink like my mother and her friend – over 50 years later and still talking of fertility, children, men, and other women's issues but now, too, having the kind of conversations my mother and her friend would never have dreamed of – our rightful place in the world of academia and research.

*Chapter 4*

# Re-telling Stories of 'Everything but the Kitchen Sink'

[The] dailiness of women's lives structures a different way of knowing and a different way of thinking. The process that comes from this way of knowing has to be at the centre...of a woman's scholarship...the point is to integrate ideas about love and healing, about balance and connection, about beauty and growing, into our everyday ways of being. WE have to believe in the value of our own experiences and in the value of our ways of knowing, our ways of doing things.

(Aptheker 1989)

The previous chapter presents the first conversation between myself and Sue Webb and my responses as I listened to her, as I transcribed the tape and as I reflected upon that conversation in the writing. I sent Sue a copy of Chapter 3 about one month before our second meeting, which took place almost a year after the first, in the same setting. In our second conversation I was seeking her responses to what I had written and particularly her response to my use and reporting of my reflexivity in the first conversation. I needed to know if she was happy for her full identity to be known, if she needed any changes to be made for her own or other people's sake and how reading it might have moved her own story on in any way.

## How and what

In their recent book, *Postmodern Interviewing*, Gubrium and Holstein (2003, p.3) note how the present era of interviewing has taken on board 'postmodern sensibilities' and describe processes that reflect those I have used in this study: '*Reflexivity, poetics,* and *power* are the watchwords as the interview process is refracted through the lenses of language, knowledge, culture, and difference' (original italics). Reflexive approaches to interviewing have been developing over the last decade as more and more researchers have come to recognize the research interview as a social encounter (Dingwall 1997; Gubrium and Holstein 1998;

Silverman 1993). Although my conversations with Sue were indeed social encounters, they were also more than that: they were a means for gathering data concerned with the topic under exploration and, as researchers, we need to keep this purpose in mind.

Ruth Behar (1996) reminds us that we need to ask ourselves where we locate ourselves as researchers in the field, how much we reveal of ourselves, and how we reconcile our different roles and positions. She invites us to see the researcher, writer, participant and interview, not as separate entities but intertwined in a deeply problematic way. In doing so we allow our biases and taken-for-granted assumptions to be seen, and provide the reader with the opportunity to make different interpretations of the data we have gathered.

Madan Sarup (1996), encourages researchers to examine these kinds of story-telling interviews on two levels:

> Each narrative has two parts: a story (*histoire*) and a discourse (*discourse*). The story is the content, or chain of events. The story is the 'what' in a narrative, the discourse is the 'how'. The discourse is rather like a plot, how the reader becomes aware of what happened, the order of appearance of events.

So as well as gathering the story about becoming a reflexive researcher (the content), I wanted to examine 'the how' of the discourse. And in doing so I wanted to make explicit not only what I had learned from the content of the stories but also how that knowledge was created – what Rosanna Hertz (1997) calls 'reflexive knowledge'.

## Re-telling stories

As human beings we learn a great deal from re-telling stories, creating new meanings and deepening existing ones. Jane Speedy (2001, p.122) observes how, when people re-tell stories of their life and work, quite different stories might emerge, or previous ones may be elaborated upon. She reminds us that 'telling and re-telling and listening again to other tellings has become central to the practices of the narrative therapies' and, although Sue and I were not engaged in a therapy, there was nevertheless something helpful and maybe even therapeutic occurring during our research conversations. There is a growing literature in the counselling world that recognizes the therapeutic value of research and the value of blurring the boundaries between research interviews and therapy (Etherington 2001c; Gale 1992; Hart and Crawford-Wright 1999; Rosenthal 2003; Skinner 1998; West 1998; Wosket 1999). It is often at such interfaces that creative experiences occur. This has also been observed by Denzin (1989, p.15), a distinguished writer in the field of communications and a sociologist, who describes 'those interactional moments that leave marks on peoples lives [and] have the potential for creating transformational experiences for the person'. These moments might occur when the 'topic of inquiry becomes dramatized by the focus on existential moments in people's lives, hopefully producing richer and more meaningful data' (Denzin and Lincoln 2000, p.657).

## The new stories

During my second conversation with Sue I asked her what it was that struck her most powerfully as she read the previous chapter. She had clearly thought about this before our second meeting and had highlighted three main stories that she wanted to take further.

Her first story was about her reaction to seeing on paper what she had said, and the apparently confident manner in which she had spoken. This story is called: *god, I sound so big and bold compared with how I feel.* I was reminded of Ruthellen Josselson's (1996) warning about the power of the written word and the impact on our participants of seeing their own words in print. I felt pleased that I had sent the chapter to Sue and given her an opportunity to tell me of her reactions.

Her second story was a reflection on the use of researcher self-disclosure in research conversations and how that produces data that might be more true to lived experience. This story is called: *Kim, you shared a lot with me.*

The third story was related to her question about whether or not she was a 'real researcher' and how she had learned as a child from her mother about women's ways of relating to different kinds of knowledge. This story is called: *mothers and knowledge.*

## Representing the stories

I wanted to find a way of capturing our conversations as they had happened and to make as transparent as possible how I had influenced and shaped the way the stories were told by their discursive nature. Research interviewers have been criticized for producing 'silently orchestrated' conversations (Speedy 2001) and disallowing any view of the power relations within research (Kvale 1996, 1999; Mishler 1986, 1991).

I have arranged these three stories in stanza form, with Sue's words arranged on the left of the page and my own on the right. This breaks up what might seem a dense format that might otherwise be less accessible and allows for the disjointed natural breaks and hesitations, more normal in speech, to be maintained without it being too difficult to read, as advocated by Gee (1991), Leftwich (1998) and Speedy (2001).

Sue began by saying she had been feeling miserable about the fact that since we last met she had done nothing further on her PhD. The pressure of other work left no time for her own research. She went on to comment on her reaction to seeing herself 'in print' when she received Chapter 3 from me.

## god, I sound so big and bold compared with how I feel

I was aware of that thing I've read
in the methodology books
about people's experience
of what they've said in writing
being different to what they experienced
when they said it,
at the time.

I felt quite anxious about how
'out there' I was, really.

And then I thought:
Well, there's a couple of places
Where there's a need to soften
or generalize
a little bit,

...and I thought about how to do that,
so it wasn't that that bothered me,
but it was this sense of,
god,
I do sound like I know what I'm on about.

And I thought:
do I?
Is that really me?

And then I thought:
well,
why shouldn't it be me?

                    It *was* you, it was nobody else.

No, quite!

                    And it comes back to that thing you said:
                    'Am I a real researcher'?

Yes, do I have the right to speak on this?
So yes I...

So that was my first response.

Sue's second story was about the process of gathering research data and my part in that. She raised points about how researcher self-disclosure might produce more in-depth data that might therefore be more valid, contrary to traditional thinking. This fitted with my own view that researcher reflexivity in interview conversations allows a closer relationship to develop between interviewer and participant. Methodologically this provides greater opportunities for open-ended responses and a more intimate exploration of a person's lived experience and therefore, perhaps, greater potential for understanding.

Sue also commented on how her perception of our similarities (particularly our shared gender and age) allowed, in this instance, greater risks to be taken, especially in terms of her self-doubt. Fontana and Frey (2000, p.658) also comment on the influence of gender on interviewing:

> The sex of the interviewer and that of the respondent do make a difference, as the interview takes place within the cultural boundaries of a paternalistic social system in which masculine identities are differentiated from feminine ones.

Much of my conversation with Sue had centred around our relationship and meeting as two women, both in content and in process.

### Kim, you shared a lot with me

Each time you shared things
I was aware that it made it that much easier for me.

I actually told you far more revealing stuff
about myself
because of the extent to which
I had a sense of
the reciprocity of the conversation,
and when I read what you had then written
[afterwards]
there was a lot more of you in there
and I felt,

…I almost felt disappointed
that you hadn't told me that at the time.

Now I can see that that wouldn't work
…in terms of a research interview
but it was that sense of…

the more of *you* that you put out there,
the more confident I felt
about what *I* could share.
…and I thought that was a really…

…I thought that was really fascinating
   in terms of all that traditional stuff about,
   you know,
   the researcher needs to keep themselves,
   either neutrally absent, or scarcely present
   but you know
   just enough to be…
   to be real
but my sense as the participant was
that
the more of you that was in there,
the more of *me* that could be in there.

What was it about my sharing myself that made that
possible?

I think it was the sense of shared experiences, or,
    not necessarily shared,
    but parallel experiences,
it's that way in which…
(and I think this fits with the back fence stuff)
'that's what women do',
that's what…

I think it was either Gilligan
    or some of Gilligan's colleagues,
worked out that when little girls
talk to each other
…and when women talk to each other,
they parallel experiences,
whereas boys set about problem-solving.

So if I tell you I've got difficulties
with my…
    that I'm worried about my stepfather,
as well as showing an interest in that,
it's quite likely
that somewhere in the conversation
you'll share something about *your* family background
that enables me to feel comfortable
with what I'm sharing about mine.

But if I was a boy
I'd be trying to sort out
how you could make it better?

Yes, what I *ought* to do,
    including things like:
    'you ought not to take it so seriously'
    or:
    'you ought not to be bothered at all'.

So I thought that was really revealing
and thought-provoking around
…around this type of research.
about a research conversation.

Yes.
That kind of interactive dialogue in some way thickens
the story or deepens the story; invites more stories to
be told?

Yes. And invited more layers
of the story,
that it didn't stay with…,

I mean I was impressed
by what you got out of me really.
(laughter)

Except that's not the right language really is it?

Ve haf ways of making you talk!!!

(laughter)

...but I thought it didn't come across
as a set piece
    if you know what I mean,
and it wasn't
no...,

but why didn't it?

I think the answer is partly the *way*
in which you share yourself as well,
and I thought:
that's not something that's hugely valued
in research interviews.

Yes, and each of those times when that happened, it
was in response to something that you said. It was that
dialogical thing wasn't it, that...

Yes, yes...

I mean,
    you know,
we've heard for years
that our self-disclosure
invites further self-disclosure.

We take that for granted,
    in a way, in the counselling world,
but in research,
    as you say,
the positivist idea that
to invite yourself into the conversation is to...,
kind of,
contaminate the data.

Yes,
whereas my experience was
that it enriched the data considerably,
and made the data,
not just richer
but more true.

It was like...

I lost all sense of needing to construct carefully
so that what was visible

was an acceptable person.

> Yes, you could be more genuinely yourself?

Yes.

> Gosh, that really does make a difference doesn't it,
> when you think about that
> in terms of validity,
> about learning from research.
> That's really important isn't it?

> After all, what we're trying to get
> is a kind of
> 'near experience',
> not some sort of fabricated story
> that looks good.

Yes, and it also struck me that,
    somewhere in there…
I said something about
counsellors being good at this sort of research,

and it fits with that idea
that the reflecting,
and the encouragement
that one does in counselling,
is matched in this sort of interview
with the same sorts of skills,
plus the…

…as I've said
the opportunity to self-disclose for the researcher,
leading to greater self-disclosure.

So I guess it's a question then
of how…, to what extent
the researcher self-discloses usefully?
At what point does self-disclosure become,
'well I'd better not tell her about that then
because that won't fit with her',

and in that sense
the fact that you and I had such a lot in common…

> But in a way,
> because this is a narrative inquiry,
> it doesn't matter about differences,
> it doesn't have to fit,
> that's part of what we're finding out
> isn't it?
> Because actually,
> you have this experience
> but mine,

actually,
was very different from that,
or whatever.

Yes, but I'm thinking
that,
had you been some wonderfully academic
young woman
who walked straight into
a PhD at 22…

(laughter)

…I'm not sure if you'd have got
out of me some of what's in there.

Yes, I probably wouldn't have said,
'Will I ever be a researcher?'
and
'I'm not sure I know
what the word "research" means.'

I was really interested in
*your* notion of research as well,
that it was like…

I think at the end
where you said that perhaps you should have asked me
what I thought research was…

Or what a researcher was.

Because you said…,
you ended up saying
that your concern was,
'Am I really a researcher?'
And I was amazed at that because,
you know,
there you were telling me of all the things that you'd
done
and that you loved to find out new things.

Some of the above points were raised by Oakley over twenty years ago (1981, p.49) when she pointed out that researchers who were attempting to minimize status differences by being more transparent and including themselves in interview conversations were creating a climate that allowed for deeper connection: 'there is no intimacy without reciprocity'.

The third story came back to the doubt that Sue expressed about being a 'real' researcher. She had been trying to make sense of where that uncertainty came from in her own life, and she had come to an understanding that it was related in some way to what she had learned implicitly from her mother's attitude to knowledge as she was growing up.

## mothers and knowledge

I talked about women
gossiping across the back fence
and what you put in my mind
with what you've written,
    which I really like,
is the notion that there's
a progression here,
and the progression for me is
actually,
that I *haven't* come from
a mother who gossiped over the back fence.

I've come from a mother
who was absolutely committed
to education herself, but who…
I think that what's happened is that
    if I go back two generations
my grandmother,
    my mother's mother
didn't have an education
and she was married to a farmer
who would have loved an education
but also didn't have one.
    He wasn't a very good farmer.

He died when my mother was quite young
and my grandmother
was absolutely insistent
that my mother got an education
    and she was one of the first six girls
    to go to a grammar school
    that had previously been a boys' grammar school.
They were incredibly poor
and my grandmother sewed
in order to keep them
and
to keep my mother at school
and
then to put her through university.

But the difference,
    the thing that's moved on
    between my mother and me,
is that I think she was very convinced
of the importance of knowledge,
    *other* people's knowledge.

Her generation would not have thought
of their capacity
to *make* knowledge,

they would have only seen it as their right,
their privilege,
to *access* knowledge.

And the progression to me,
which is probably why I'm still struggling with
   'Am I a researcher?',
is the movement from a person
who is really good at absorbing
other people's knowledge
and who loves the newness of other people's knowledge,
to becoming a person who has the right to,
   if I say *make* knowledge
   that sounds a bit simplistic,
but to generate new ideas.

                  I know what you mean, yes.

And that's the difference.
My mother was terrified of gossip
over the back fence and she…,

we didn't ever live next to the sorts of people
that she wanted to gossip over the back fence with,
and she's a bit…,
she's easily bullied
and therefore gossip was always
something that worried her,

but she did love sharing conversations.

                  Well my mother didn't gossip.
                  That standing in the kitchen,
                  that was all women's talk,
                  that was sharing women's lives
                  together.

I think what I'm saying is that
when I was a child
I don't think my mother
had very close relationships with women
whom she talked with easily,
the way I think I probably do.

And I'm not sure what that's about
but it may have been a sort of dislocation,
a midway position between
   being a woman who liked talking about
   whether the baker was coming
   at the right time or not
   and what the washing was up to these days,
and being able to talk about
the ideas in her head.

She had, she has,
    a classics degree,
classics and theology
and she was horribly miserable at home
when I was a child:
went back to work when I was about 14.

We were disgusted,
    my sister and me,
we thought it was a dreadful betrayal.

Well you see,
my mother didn't have an education,
she grew up in Ireland,
in the country.
    I mean,
she went to the local school.

I think she was quite shrewd
and I think she wasn't unintelligent
but she was uneducated.

But my father had been educated
by the Christian Brothers in Dublin
and he, he was,
he was the person in our house
who really valued education.

He made sure all my brothers,
    my older brothers,
went to boarding school.
We didn't have any money,
but he got them places
by hook or by crook,
in an army boarding school
because he'd been in the army.

I went to a prep school at seven,
among girls who were all being paid for,
    but I wasn't.
My father had found some way of me getting some
sort of scholarship
to get in there.

And he highly valued education.
He was looked up to
by the men in the pub as educated,
and he,
    what he did,
was actually to advocate,
for them in the courts.

He had no legal training
but he used to go and fight
their causes for them,
write letters for them,
and things like this.

But he thought education
was one of the most important things
in the world.

But education for me,
   as a woman,
   as a girl,
   as a little girl,
was only in order to make sure
that I could meet an educated man.

So the convent school education,
which would teach me
to behave like a lady
and speak properly,
was what he saw as important,
whereas for my brothers,
an education meant something different.

But my mother
she read.
I think she lived in her fantasy world,
   you know,
she would read.

I would go to the library
and I would have to bring back
six books for my mother
and they were all romantic novels.

She never went to the library herself.
I don't think she'd even know how
to choose a book in the library,

but I'd go to the librarian
as a little girl
and I'd say
'I want some books for my mum'
and the librarian knew who I was
and she'd give me the books
that I hadn't had before,
and then
I'd go into the children's section
and spend the whole morning
sitting on the floor
choosing books
for myself.

And I was reading books
at the age of 11 and 12
    like Mazo de la Roche
    and North and South (Mrs Gaskell)
    and things like that
you know,
adult books, family sagas.

And my mother taught me that.

It was her that introduced me,
to valuing reading books.
My father never sat down
and read a book.

That's *women's* stuff.

I think if I had been able
to ask my mother why she was so keen
on me getting an education,
she would have talked about
'financial security'
because that was the *key* lesson
from her family background,
after her father had died.

But she would also probably have
said something about
'in order not to be bored'.

Oh right,
Oh that wouldn't have occurred...

Financial security, yes, of course
marrying an educated man was part of financial
security,
that would be part of that,
but it wouldn't be about
having stimulating conversations.

but because of her background in,
    I guess,
both the classics and the theology,
her love of that was 'story'
    and they did a lot of textual analysis
    you know.
When fundamentalists went on about
'the bible says such and such',
she'd say
'Yes, but that's such and such a translation,
if you actually go back to the original...'

And when people came knocking on our door,
when we were kids,
    trying to convert us
    to something extraordinary,
she would invite them in and
have a discussion with them.

So I think probably my love of stories
    and the way in which stories could be told,
    that the same story could be told in many different ways,
I would owe to her.

                Yes it's a very different background
                    in that respect
              that you came from.
              I'm in the generation of your mother.

Yes, well it's almost like
you've done in one generation
what my family's done in two generations.
I enjoyed thinking about the difference
About where I'd come to from
where my mother was,
what was the difference between
her approach to knowledge
and mine,
I thought that was really…

The progression that the women
in my family have made,
is something
I'm very proud of,
and something that's very precious to me,
and the sacrifices that they've made along the way,
and
    I guess,
understanding the way in which
those dilemmas fitted within their own times as well.

My mother's dilemma
    as a wife and mother
was: how could she meet her own needs,
    her own intellectual needs,
when she had this prescribed role?
The continuing acquisition
and imparting of knowledge to others
that she had acquired,
    whether it be us as children or
    eventually back in a classroom.

That was where the stimulus was.

And my comment,
my contribution to that is,

despite the fact that my mother
sat at the front of a classroom
rather than leaning on a kitchen sink,
she would also not have had this conversation.

I'm still puzzling as to…,
haven't quite got my head around
all of the difference to that.

So it's not really to do with education?

No, it's about…

Is it something to do with research?

It's the extent to which you can,
the world will let you,
live the things that you've dreamed about.

I think we live in a time when,
    OK, we've had to battle
    and women still haven't got it sorted,
but it's possible to envisage
doing things that it wasn't possible
to envisage for my mother.

When I think about that,
because of the war,
my mother,
    as I said,
did classics and usually her class,
whatever,
would have gone to Greece
and done some archaeology
and they couldn't go because of the war,
and in a way
that says it all.

I mean that would have been research
but they never got to go,
    because of the war,
    but also,
    I mean,
that's just a metaphor for it really,
it was out there but it wasn't,
it wasn't,
easy to grasp.
To go and make,
to generate ideas,
to find things out for yourself,
rather than just read other people's books,

it was something that was just beyond your grasp.

The world wasn't a safe place
to go out into
to find things out.

No, no, that's right.

And women went into work
that was sufficiently close
to what they'd done at home
to be acceptable,
and also safe.
I mean teaching and nursing, social work,
were all the things that were close to women's caring roles.

As we located our mother's stories within history we could see that although we were only seven years apart in age, our mothers' education (or lack of it in my case) had impacted hugely on our lives. Sue's mother went to university in 1939 (a year before I was born – my mother's sixth child), and had been studying for her degree throughout the period of World War II. She trained as a teacher and, when she later married another teacher, she gave up work. She returned to work in 1961 when Sue was 14 years old – the same year I was finishing my training as an occupational therapist and taking on my first job in a child guidance clinic. It is easy to see from our conversation how, as we look back, we find ourselves remembering our lives in terms of our experience of others (Schwartz 1999). Biographical memory can then be understood as a social process.

Our conversation continued as we checked over the manuscript of the previous chapter and amendments were made for the sake of clarity and other people's anonymity. Further stories emerged, conversations that highlighted once again the difference between being a practitioner-researcher (as I am) and an academic researcher (like Sue). Sue does not currently practise as a counsellor or supervisor (except to supervise one person) and is mainly concerned with teaching and supporting students' research. These themes later became the focus of Part 4 of this book.

In the following chapter I will explore further the methodology I have used to create this book and ideas about data collection using narrative approaches.

*Chapter 5*

# Methodologies and Methods

Narrative research is an umbrella term that covers a large and diverse range of approaches, the result of a rapid expansion of this area of inquiry over the past dozen years.

(Mishler 1999, p.xv)

During the past few years of being involved in learning about and practising narrative research I have frequently been surprised and confused to discover that the term has so many different meanings: so when I read Mishler's work (1999) I felt reassured that my confusion was perhaps understandable in the face of so much diversity. The lack of unity within these approaches reflects one of the basic tenets of postmodernity: that there is no one 'right way' – an exciting and (perhaps) troubling idea! What does seem important is that I describe what it means to *me* (at this point in time) and the assumptions upon which my ideas and practices are based. In previous chapters I have introduced my understandings of what I mean by reflexivity and its uses, and I have provided examples of reflexive conversations for this study. In this chapter I want to introduce the reader to my philosophies, and the methodologies and methods I have used.

## Philosophy

When setting out on any research journey I need to find ways of working that fit with who I am: my underlying values, my philosophies on life, my views of reality and my beliefs about how knowledge is known and created. My view of reality or the nature of being or what is (ontology), and my understanding of what it means to know (epistemology) are intertwined. I do believe that the world exists out there independently of our being conscious of its existence. I also believe that 'it becomes a world of meaning only when meaning-making beings make sense of it' (Crotty 1998, p.10). My understanding of, and connection with, these concepts guide the decisions I make about my choice of methodologies and methods, and the ways I make sense of the data and represent it. Because I believe reality is socially constructed and subjectively determined, the means I use need to be suited to the purpose of discovering something of *how* those constructions came about and the meanings that people give them.

Choosing how to do research is therefore a personal decision about what I need to do to discover what I want to know. One or more of the existing methodologies might suit my needs or I might create a new one for the specific purposes of the project I want to undertake.

## Background

The beginning of this project was much less clear and more 'messy' than is usually the case for me. It began when a colleague, John McLeod, and I had a conversation about using reflexivity in research. In conjunction with the British Association for Counselling and Psychotherapy (BACP) John had set up a new research journal, *Counselling and Psychotherapy Research* (along with Maggie Pettifer as Managing Editor) which encouraged reflexive, contextualized and engaging writing that was practitioner-oriented. I was a member of the Editorial Board for the journal and later appointed as Assistant Editor. We noticed that there were relatively few papers being submitted that could be described as reflexive, contextualized and engaging. We wondered if this might be because reflexivity was a concept that was not fully understood (or valued) and/or that it was not included in research training. This conversation took place in January 2002, when one of the major funding bodies, the Economic and Social Research Council (ESRC) was inviting bids on their research methods programme that focused on the teaching of methodologies. So John and I decided to put in a bid for funding to explore the concept and meanings of reflexivity across the social sciences, nationally and internationally, to find out if and how the concept was being taught, and to create learning resources. It was an ambitious project and the bid was unsuccessful. However, while planning and writing the bid my interest in, and knowledge about, these ideas had grown.

A while later I submitted a similarly focused application for funding to support new learning and teaching initiatives within my own university's Teaching and Learning Group. This too was turned down. Both these bids had taken a great deal of time and energy and had led me into new areas of reading and discussion with colleagues. In the meantime a group of us had begun to meet regularly to talk about the relationships between reflexivity and our own learning. These discussions fed my growing interest and led me once again to try and find some funds to support a pilot study of these ideas. I was awarded a small grant within my own department – so at last I was off.

The money allowed me to meet with people who were interested in telling me their stories about how they saw themselves becoming reflexive researchers, and paid also for the transcribing of some of those conversations (although I did many of them myself), as well as the purchase of a few books and some recording equipment.

This was the very first time I had ever been funded for research. Everything I had done hitherto had come out of my freelance time. As a practitioner-researcher who has a very part-time post at a university (one day to teach the MSc and, latterly, a half day for my own research and the supervision of doctoral candidates) I am in a very different position from full-time academics. Most of my week is taken up with freelance counselling, supervision, training or consultancy and so time I give to research or writing limits my time for earning a living. Attending conferences, giving papers or performing any of the usual roles expected of an academic researcher (outside of my allocated contract time) means my income is reduced or lost. I am not complaining about this – I would not want to be employed as a full-time academic – I am merely pointing out something of what it means to be a practitioner-researcher. This is part of *my* story that might be relevant to the overall story.

At this stage I realized that my project would need to be less ambitious if I was to manage it within my time constraints, so I abandoned the idea of collecting stories from reflexive researchers globally across the social sciences and decided to focus mainly on the stories of counsellors and psychotherapists. However, by then I had already interviewed/conversed with a sociologist, a social work educator and a medic. These conversations had become part of my internal narrative and growing understanding, and were therefore available to inform the later conversations. I have drawn upon those conversations as part of the data for this book.

## Participants

Preliminary exploration had also informed me that explicit teaching of reflexivity rarely formed part of a person's research training. However, I knew that research methodology taught by my colleagues and myself at my own university *was* informed by reflexivity and therefore this seemed like a very good place to begin. Past students on a course I was not involved in, and those from one I taught and supervised, were contacted and invited to tell me about how they were becoming/had become reflexive researchers. Invitations were also passed through academic colleagues at two other universities and one independent training organization in the UK for whom I provide doctoral supervision. Some conversations for this study were spontaneously arranged upon meeting people who were interested – an example is Sue Webb, who I had met at a conference, and also doctoral candidates who began spontaneously to tell me their stories and agreed for me to tape them with a view to deciding later if they were to be included in this study.

I had more offers to participate than I could use from past students at my own university but fewer from other places. As well as the three conversations with people from other social science disciplines (two of whom were men from other institutions and one of whom was a woman from a different social science department at my own university) I ended up with taped conversations from eight people connected to my own university and six people from other institutions. From my own university there were three female past MSc students whom I taught and supervised, two past female MSc students whom I had neither taught nor supervised, two colleagues (both postdoctoral, one male and one female), and one of my female full-time MPhil/PhD students. From other institutions I met with two male academics, a female PhD student, a male postdoctoral researcher in the NHS, another male who was undertaking a doctorate, and a female academic from New Zealand who was doing a PhD. Including the three people from other social sciences that made ten females and seven males.

It seemed important to talk with people who were at different stages of 'becoming' researchers as well as having a mixture of genders. Five of the women and two of the men would probably call themselves primarily 'practitioners'; three of the men and two of the women are academics who also see some clients and supervisees. One woman was a part-time doctoral candidate (and a counsellor trainer) and one a full-time PhD student.

However, because narrative inquiry permits the gathering of a wide range of different kinds of data, I invited interested parties including *and* outside of those mentioned above to submit anything else that would add to our understanding of what it meant to become a reflexive researcher. These offerings included parts of reflexive research journals, group conversations with doctoral candidates, written stories and poems and one transcribed tape recording made by a past student who asked for it to be played as a farewell to her fellow students as she went off around the world after submitting her dissertation.

## Narrative knowing

Over the last decade I have been moving more and more towards valuing narrative ways of knowing, working collaboratively with research participants, seeking 'local' stories that would offer me opportunities to share in the 'lived experiences' of others that I could place alongside my own life in ways that would inform myself and others.

My interest in these methodologies led me to write a book with two of my ex-clients about their experiences of childhood trauma, their recovery and my therapeutic relationship with them (Etherington 2000). That book also gave me an opportunity to explore my developing philosophy and role as a researcher and to experiment with reflexive, heuristic and narrative ways of knowing. Through undertaking that project I realized that the knowledge gained from my clients' stories was profoundly rich and multilayered. Others, on reading the book, told me that they gained more from the personal, subjective, reflexive approach I used to represent those stories than from studies based on traditional research methodologies that they found hard to remember or link with practice.

Around this time I became more aware of ideas from the field of narrative therapy where therapists were assisting people to co-construct stories of their lives by asking curious questions, inviting them to thicken their stories and noticing emerging, half-told tales (Freedman and Combs 1996; White and Epston 1990). I became interested in using some of these ideas as ways of helping people tell (or write) their stories for research and I edited three further books using some of these methods (Etherington 2001b, 2002a, 2003). The stories I gathered were edited and collected together, along with my own stories, to create books that informed us about topics such as *Counsellors in Health Settings, Rehabilitation Counselling in Physical and Mental Health* and *Trauma, the Body and Transformation.* So it was with those experiences that I came to this study and chose narrative inquiry, underpinned by a heuristic process, as my preferred methodology. I will explain what I mean by 'a heuristic process' in Chapter 8.

## Narrative inquiry

One way of describing narrative inquiry (and as I said before, there are many) can be described as a methodology based upon collecting, analysing, and re-presenting people's stories as told by them. The kind of narrative inquiry I am using is based on a worldview (ontology) that:

- we live storied lives and our world is a storied world (Gergen and Gergen 1986; Howard 1991; Mair 1989; Sarbin 1986);

- narrative represents, constitutes and shapes social reality (Bruner 1987, 1990, 1991; Frank 1995; Ochberg 1994; Spence 1982);

- competing narratives represent different realities not simply different perspectives on the same reality (Freeman 1993; Gergen 1994);

- and telling and re-telling one's story helps a person create a sense of self (Burr 1995; Cushman 1995; Frank 1995) and meaning (Bruner 1990).

These approaches are based upon epistemologies that view reality and knowledge as socially constructed, and on the idea that knowledge is situated within contexts and embedded within historical, cultural stories, beliefs and practices (Burr 1995; Crossley 2000; Gergen 1985, 1994). They challenge the accepted nature of modernist certainties, and question how we know what we know and who tells us what we know (McLeod 1997; Polkinghorne 1988).

Because there is a complex interaction between the world in which a person lives and their understanding of that world, narratives are particularly suitable for portraying how people experience their position in relation to a culture: whether on the margins, in the centre, or on becoming part of a new culture. Embedded in people's stories we hear their feelings, thoughts and attitudes, and the richness of the narrative helps us to understand how they understand themselves, their strategies for living and how they make theoretical sense of their lives.

Listening to people's stories meant that I could gain an 'insider's' view of the cultures in which the stories are embedded (Polkinghorne 1995), going further than obtaining historical accounts (although the historical backdrop against which the story is lived is also important), by showing how individuals create meaning *within* a culture.

The structure of a story depends on a remembered past that leads to anticipated futures, showing how changes occur over time, and how cultural patterns evolve and link with an individual's life (Carr 1986; McAdams 1993; Widdershoven 1993).

Stories allow the reader to enter into the narrator's experience and invite questions and hypotheses that might lead to further inquiry. They depict actions and perspectives across social groups that might be used for comparative studies, perhaps with other professions or work settings. Narrative methods highlight the value of a person's individual story while also providing pieces in a mosaic that depict a certain era or group (Marshall and Rossman 1999).

So I believe narrative inquiry is a useful methodology for helping me understand how our socialization and life choices have impacted on the creation of our identities as reflexive researchers. Identity researchers generally recognize the importance of locating individuals within the local features of family and work settings, while also recognizing that these, in turn, are situated within, and influenced by, wider historical and sociocultural contexts (Mishler 1999). These perspectives enable us to move away from the view of identity as 'fixed' or entirely intrapersonal and towards the view of identity as something that is constantly being reconstructed and constituted through interpersonal processes and 'performed' through the stories that we tell: 'Our identities are defined and expressed through the ways we position ourselves vis-à-vis others along the several dimensions that constitute our networks of relationships' (Mishler 1999, p.16).

## Research questions

I was curious about where people would begin when I asked them to tell me their story of 'becoming a reflexive researcher'. I was also curious about the *way* they would tell their stories.

In advance of our meeting I sent a letter explaining my research interest and providing a working description of reflexivity – although this did not happen with those I spoke with more spontaneously. Once meetings were arranged I sent a note with a few suggestions of topics that I might like to include in our conversation:

1. What do *you* mean by reflexivity?

2. How did you/are you become/ing a reflexive researcher?

3. Why do you use reflexivity?

4. What was/is the impact of doing reflexive research on you personally/professionally?

5. What happens in the process of using reflexivity?

6. Is there anything else you might want to say? Possibly about the use of supervision, any stuckness, dilemmas, or anything else at all.

When I sat down with my participants I always began with the broad invitation: 'Where does your story begin?' The above topics were often included as part of the conversation but if they did not come up spontaneously I introduced them into the conversation. Each conversation was very different, and the examples I show in Chapters 3 and 4 indicate how those stories were co-constructed between us. You will see from those chapters that very few of the questions above formed part of our conversation but they were answered within the conversation nevertheless. Inevitably my curious questions shaped the stories to some extent, while also enabling them to unfold.

## Methods

Postmodern times have opened up new freedoms in methodologies and also in methods of data collection. In their chapter on interviewing, Fontana and Frey (2000, p.657) describe a view of collecting data that matches my own: 'Interviewing and interviewers must necessarily be creative, forget how-to rules, and adapt themselves to the ever-changing situations they face.' However, Wengraf (2001, p.3) who describes research interviews that are designed for the purpose of improving knowledge as a 'special kind of conversational interaction' has written a kind of 'rulebook' for those who like to follow rules, while also maintaining that:

> ...what is planned is a deliberate half-scripted or quarter-scripted interview: its questions are only partially prepared in advance (semi-structured) and will therefore be largely improvised by you as interviewer. But only largely: the interview as a whole is a joint process, a co-production, by you and your interviewee.

Reflexive interviewing can follow the usual format of the researcher asking questions that the participant answers: where it is different is that the interviewer also notices and/or shares personal experience of the topic and comments on the unfolding communication between both parties. Ellis and Berger (2003, p.162) see the researcher's disclosures as

> more than tactics to encourage the respondent to open up; rather, the researcher often feels a reciprocal desire to disclose, given the intimacy of the details being shared by the interviewee.

As noted by Sue Webb in previous chapters, this style of interviewing created an opportunity for her to reach more deeply into her lived experience than might have been the case had I not shared some of myself in the conversation. In the dialogue that ensued, new meanings are created and new selves are constituted.

My meeting with each participant is like a snapshot in time: each of us is uniquely embedded in whatever is happening in our lives at that time. As we talk we are 'becoming' and new selves are forming (Frank 1995). Therefore I need to be free to meet them wherever they are at that point in their lives, and to recognize that stories are constantly being reconstructed. As you come to read these stories they will probably have changed. Each story is told for a purpose, and how it is told, and how it is heard, will depend on the listener as much as the narrator. How you, as reader, make sense of the stories will depend on what you bring to the reading from your own life and experiences.

Another of my intentions in gathering data in this way is that, in telling their stories, participants (and researchers) may also gain something for themselves. It seems to me that the very best possible outcome of research is that it provides an opportunity for growth and learning for both researcher and researched as well as for the wider community (Etherington 2001a, 2001c; Gale 1992; Hart and Crawford-Wright 1999; Rosenthal 2003; Skinner 1998; West 1998; Wosket 1999).

## Transcribing

Audiotaping and transcription is rarely acknowledged in research reports (Lapadat and Lindsay 1999), although both are frequently used in qualitative research. If we are explicit about this part of the process in our reporting we are less likely to mis-represent our data. As we listen to and transcribe audiotapes of interviews/conver-sations, we will almost certainly be analysing the data and making choices based upon the theories that we hold. Each individual researcher will make a decision about whether or not to tape all of the conversations, whether or not to transcribe, what to transcribe, and how to represent the transcription in their re-presentation, but without explicit knowledge the reader will end up with 'an impoverished basis for interpretation' (Kvale 1996, p.167) and be denied an opportunity to under-stand our use of the data.

In a previous work (Etherington 2000, p.292) I proposed that *only* by tran-scribing tapes personally could we remain close enough to the speakers' meanings:

> A researcher who does not undertake this part of the work loses the opportunity that transcribing presents us with.

> When we listen to the tapes and transcribe them personally we have an opportu-nity to pick up on nuances, hesitations, pauses, emphasis and the many other ways that people add meaning to their words. It is a difficult and time-consuming task but I believe that the outcome is more than worth the extra effort. Not only does it help us to listen and hear more of what we might have missed in the moment but it also gives us a chance to check that we have been ethical.

In this study I began by transcribing the tapes myself and, on gaining some research funding, I handed the task over to a professional transcriber once I had listened to the tapes myself. On receiving the typed transcription as an email attachment from the transcriber, I listened carefully to the tape again while going through the typed text to ensure that it was correct. So freed of the need to actually transcribe, I was available to pick up and note nuances, hesitations, pauses and emphasis, or anything additional that seemed important (e.g. 'that was the second time she said that and with the same giggle').

Having recognized that I was no longer practising what I had previously been preaching, I asked myself if I had changed my beliefs. From my current position I would still encourage an apprentice researcher to grapple with transcriptions themselves, as part of their learning about how that keeps us intimately connected to the data. However, having experienced that part of the process for ourselves, I think we can remain sufficiently close to the data, even when we do not ourselves transcribe, providing we listen repeatedly to the tapes.

For the first few conversations of this study I had used an inadequate micro-phone. The quality of the recording was so poor that the task of transcribing was laborious and time-consuming, and I did not think I could ask someone else to do it. Having been part of the recorded conversation I believed I had a better chance of hearing what was said than a transcriber. Sometimes just one word can change the meaning.

The grant money allowed me to purchase a better microphone and, on hearing the resulting difference, I realized how important it was to invest in good equipment. Having learned by past mistakes (when I found that I had picked up a local football match instead of the research conversation – Etherington 2000, p.284), this time I ran a test before we began the conversation. But even testing does not guarantee that the batteries will not run out. For this reason some people use two tape recorders simultaneously.

After checking the transcripts myself I returned them to participants and asked them to censor anything they were not happy to have included (perhaps for the sake of anonymity) and to verify that *their* meanings had remained intact. These have been referred to as 'member checks'. However, some researchers, who see their purpose as allowing participants to comment on the whether the researcher's interpretation of the stories is correct, dispute the value of member checks. This thinking is based on the view of narratives as representing reality, or providing access through a window onto a reality, and not on the view of narratives as consti-tuting reality. However, as one of my doctoral students, Nell, commented, partici-pants 'would know when they [the interpretations] were *inaccurate* – when they were being *mis*represented' (Bridges: personal communication). And for me that is a good enough reason. But more than that, my experience of allowing participants to read what I have written has enriched the stories in ways that would not otherwise be possible. The conversations or written feedback that ensue from members checking what I have written frequently add further knowledge and new layers to stories – and even new stories. This can be seen in Chapter 4.

However, returning what they have written to participants for their comments can create anxiety for some researchers, who worry about losing control of the research. Sometimes participants do not want us to include them beyond the actual interview, and when asked if they would like to receive copies of transcripts, they refuse the offer.

Some participants worry about how they come across in the transcripts of conversations with researchers, especially people who are normally very correct and particular in their speech (see Etherington 2000, p.293). Until we see the transcripts we are rarely aware how much of the spoken language is made up of incomplete sentences and incorrect use of grammar or language generally. I have agreed with participants in this study that I would make minor alterations, removing some 'erms' and 'ums' and 'you knows', etc., and any other small adjustments that would contribute to the flow of the reading without changing the sense or meaning. Of course, these changes do make a difference to the data and require a further check by participants to ensure that the meaning remains intact.

Because I wanted to represent 'lived experiences' I used participants' original words wherever possible (sometimes in stanza form), with some editing as stated above. In some places, for the sake of brevity, I have reported parts of the conversations – which I acknowledge as 'my stories'.

The time spent with tape recordings and transcriptions is an important part of the immersion phase of heuristic research: noting our feelings and responses can enhance the depth and quality of the research process. At the end of the day, however, it is important to acknowledge that transcripts are social constructions; they are re-tellings and re-creations of stories that have already happened and not a faithful copy of a static world (Lapadat and Lindsay 1999).

However, data for narrative inquiry are not confined to interviews and conversations. Email communication, research journals, diaries, poems, drawings, paintings, photographs and official records are just a few of the various 'stories' that can add to the richness of the overall narrative.

## Analysis

For many counsellors and psychotherapists the gathering of the stories through conversations (or other means) is familiar and comparatively easy. The problem usually arises at the stage of analysis – so much useful data but how on earth do we make sense of it and represent it?

Polkinghorne (1995) helpfully makes a clear distinction between two methods of analysis when using narratives: the analysis of narratives and narrative analysis.

*The analysis of narratives* uses narratives as data through which it is possible to access the world of the storyteller, seeking 'to locate common themes or conceptual manifestations among the stories collected as data' (Polkinghorne 1995, p.13).

He suggests that analysis can be based on:

1.  Concepts derived from previously known theories which are applied to the data

2.  Concepts derived from the data

Four possible approaches to analysing narratives are: content analysis, conversational analysis, grounded theory and thematic analysis, any of which could be used to analyse stories.

In all of these approaches the narratives are the starting point rather than the end point of the analysis – the data rather than the product (*ibid.*). The stories provide us with a representation of an individual's reality, based on the idea that stories hold the raw material of inquiry. These analyses can be simply seen as descriptive accounts of 'what happened', accounts that may be reported as anecdote or case history, or be applied as theoretical models that may be used to explain similar stories. Methods of analysis that can be applied to produce this kind of understanding can be found in work on content analysis by Holsti (1969) and Polkinghorne (1995); discourse or conversational analysis by Cortazzi (1993), McLeod and Balamoutsou (1996) and McLeod (2001); grounded theory by Glaser and Strauss (1967); and thematic analysis by Boyatzis (1998), Kleinman (1988), Prosser (1992) and Schneider and Conrad (1983).

*Narrative analysis*, on the other hand, starts from an opposite position. Rather than treating narratives as representing reality, or providing access through a window onto reality, narrative analysis treats stories as actually *constituting* the social reality of the narrator(s) (Bruner 1991; Frank 1995; Ochberg 1994; Riessman 1993). Narrative analysis views life as constructed and experienced through the telling and re-telling of the story (Bruner 1987, 1990, 1991; MacIntyre 1981), and the analysis is the creation of a coherent and resonant story. The analysis does not seek to find similarities across stories, and is not interested in conceptual themes, but instead values the messiness, depth and texture of lived experience.

So narratives can be analysed for the knowledge they contain (the analysis of narratives), or can be treated as knowledge in themselves (narrative analysis) (Baron 1991). In producing this book I have attempted to bring together these two different approaches. In some chapters I represent the stories as knowledge in themselves and requiring no interpretation by me (see Chapters 11 and 14 in particular). In other chapters I have allowed themes to emerge from the stories heuristically (see especially Chapters 8 and 18).

## Validity criteria

My main aim has been to gain insiders' views on the process of becoming a reflexive researcher so that others can learn from those who have gone before. The stories are intended to inform practitioners, researchers, academics and teachers about process, philosophies, methodologies and methods.

Polkinghorne (1995) suggests six criteria for narrative analysis in order to achieve insider information. We need:

1. knowledge and information about the cultural context;
2. to know who the author is and how they are involved in the context;

3.  to know the significance of others within the context to allow us to understand events and meanings as described by the author and to allow this to create resonance with the reader;

4.  to be told something of the choices that are made and the actions taken by the main protagonists – this will bring the story alive and provide sufficient depth to understand why particular choices were made, by particular people, in particular contexts;

5.  to have a sense of continuity and history of the characters involved – by this means we can understand the characters as individuals who are influenced by their histories, but not necessarily determined by them.

6.  to have a beginning, middle and an end, which will provide structure, without which, the story might seem chaotic. The telling of stories may bring some coherence to episodes that may otherwise remain fragmented.

When these criteria are met, the narratives are said to come over as 'good stories', which engage the reader and capture the storytellers' experiences. As the reader you will know if my aims have been achieved.

However, when measuring validity in qualitative research we need to heed the words of Lincoln (1995, p.280) when she reminds us that texts:

> ...are always partial and incomplete; socially, culturally, historically, racially, and sexually located; and can therefore never represent any truth except those truths that exhibit the same characteristics.

Validity therefore rests on questions about: whether researcher reflexivity has provided enough information about the social, cultural, historical, racial, sexual context in which all the stories are located; if multiple voices give broad enough perspectives to take in different views; if the style of representation offers enough openings to creative expression; and finally, if the work contributes to our understanding and new learning about the subject of inquiry.

## Ethics

Ethical issues abound in the practice and representation of reflexive research, perhaps no more so than in other kinds of research, but the greater transparency allows us to have a greater awareness of them. One example of an ethical dilemma is in knowing how to protect the confidentiality of people who have not given their informed consent to be included in the research when storytellers' or narrators' stories are closely bound up with theirs. Because reflexive research is collaborative, dilemmas like this can be discussed with participants so that mutually agreed and morally satisfactory decisions might be reached (Ellis 2001; Etherington 2000; Josselson 1996). Working from ethical principles and guidelines, rather than a rulebook, leaves greater responsibility for negotiation, as well as greater flexibility, within the grasp of the research partners.

Other ethical concerns are raised by questioning. How do I balance out fairly so that I am received as genuinely open while also taking care of myself, and at the same time, trying to take care of my participants? Even though I was well aware of the value of my internal process in research, a more difficult task for me was how much of what I think and feel personally should I disclose in my research writing? How much of my life, context, culture or class do I disclose? But, as I wrote, I was encouraged by Ely *et al.* (1997, p.331) who observe: 'Qualitative writing by its nature involves the Self too intimately to ignore wounds, scars, and hard-won understandings that are to some degree part of our baggage.'

## Representation

Reflexive research that overtly acknowledges the life and presence of the researcher as part of the research, and deals with issues such as gender, culture, race and class, has contributed to what has been called a 'crisis of representation' (Denzin and Lincoln 2000). This crisis has been created in response to the falling away of traditional notions of truth, reality and knowledge that previously provided us with familiar structures for presenting our 'findings'. If there is no objective truth to be found, then there can be no 'findings'. What we have are the voices and experiences of our participants and ourselves, and a need to find new ways of re-presenting them.

As well as transparency about the impact of the researcher (and researched) on the process and outcomes of the study, reflexive research also requires transparency about the process of data collection. So although the content and process of the research might become seamlessly interwoven stories, affecting each other, it is important that the voices of researchers and researched are not merged and reported as one story – which is actually the researcher's interpretation. By reporting each part and showing how the different roles and voices are separate, differences and problems in encounters are discussed rather than ignored.

How we represent the voices of research participants (ourselves as co-researcher and others) will have consequences for us, personally and professionally. My hope is that by writing this book my professional life will be enhanced by increasing my knowledge and competence as a teacher of research and by influencing others to become engaged in research that is meaningful to them, and from which I can learn. The publication of this book will also enhance my professional reputation (or not!) and might contribute to further promotions and career progression (although realistically, at my age that doesn't leave a lot of time!). Personally, I hope to create new meanings through my writing, to progress my own journey as a reflexive researcher, and to document another aspect of my life story to satisfy a generative urge to pass something on to others as I approach the latter years of my professional life.

Research writing is a social construction, and there have always been structures that we can use as a form or template for our representations. New paradigm research methodologies have invited us to deconstruct these forms and find different ways to write about and represent data. In recognizing that people perform multilayered stories, linear representations become problematic, in that they create a false impression of order in what might be 'messy' and complex layered accounts. Patti Lather and Chris Smithies (1997) have created one of the few examples of a multilayered account that captures something of this complexity in their book *Troubling the Angels*. However, although they work collaboratively with their participants, and try to negotiate the final text, their 'split text', representing the stories of the participants at the top of the page and their own commentaries at the bottom, does not meet with approval from many of their participants. I too found this representation difficult at first, until I found a way of reading it that suited me. So I think familiar tried and tested structures may be difficult for us to abandon, even while experiencing them as constraints. In a previous work I tried new ways of representing the different voices of my participants, by using participants' diaries (rearranged in stanza form or fleshed out with their letters), poems, metaphors, drawings, interview reconstructions, analogies and prose to provide richly layered, complex accounts of their experiences of child abuse and their therapeutic journeys. In this book I have also used a variety of ways to represent the complexity of the different kinds of data I have gathered.

Although prose is the conventional way of reporting research, Laurel Richardson reminds us that 'nobody talks in prose' (2003, p.188). Conversations normally consist of pauses *and* speech but it is usually reported only as speech. Poetry 'writes in the pauses through the conventions of line breaks, spaces between lines breaks, spaces between lines and between stanzas and sections, and for sounds of silence' (*ibid.*, p.189). However, representing research data in what has been referred to as a 'nonscience' way (Danforth 1997, p.105) means that we run the risk of being marginalized by the dominant institutions of academia, although there is a growing recognition of the effectiveness and validity of writing that engages the reader and offers social researchers opportunities to honour speech styles, rhythms and syntax (Richardson 2003, p.190).

In this book I have included other people as co-authors, inviting them to provide pieces of writing or to be involved in conversations, and become part of an adventure that includes experimenting with different ways of representing the many voices that add to the richness and layers of our stories. By including my own stories alongside those of others I offer the reader an opportunity to judge the validity of the overall narrative and how my personal stories might impact on my opinions and analysis that are undoubtedly influenced by my history and culture.

Drafts of texts have been passed around for comments, alterations and permissions. Others have added words that have been lost from audiotapes or slight alterations to clarify meanings. I have experimented with different kinds of representations, such as stanzas; layered accounts that include aspects of experience not usually included, such as our 'hidden' voices; memories that have been stimulated; interviews that include both (all) voices; entries from diaries and research journals (including my own); and a variety of fonts for different kinds of data.

I have struggled with the presence and balance of my personal voice. Bruner (1993, p.2) asks about 'the extent to which the personal self should have place in the scholarly text', a question that perhaps rests upon the false assumption that there can be any text that does not show the presence of the author – in *some* form.

Sometimes I juggle with old 'programmes' that I have carried as a woman, that maybe I do not have anything really important to say, and other (more recently heard) stories that I have a right to speak, and that what I say is of value and interest. Many people whose stories are included in this book also have this struggle: students tell me of *their* lack of confidence in using their own voices, sometimes for similar reasons but sometimes because they have been programmed into believing that 'good' research only speaks in graphs, figures, and numbers – the language of the dominant discourse in mainstream research that does not necessarily fit with the world of therapy.

There are some voices that have been only partially heard. In my re-presentation of the research data I have chosen which stories to tell and which to leave out. Sometimes I have been very conscious of doing this, and I am sure that there may also be times when I have been unaware of ignoring or avoiding stories that may be in some way too difficult or not sufficiently interesting to tell.

Smith and Deemer (2000, p.891) provide a reassuring reminder:

> We are finite human beings who must learn to accept, for example, that anything we write must always and inevitably leave silences, that to speak at all must always and inevitably be to speak for the someone else, and that we cannot make judgements and at the same time have a 'constantly moving speaking position that fixes neither subject nor object' (Lather 1993, p.685). To lament and search for solutions to these 'problems' is actually to lament and search for a solution to our human finitude. But that we are finite is something we can do nothing about.

# Beware

Now that I am older
and a woman
I am reflexive
in research
and cock a snook at those
expecting me
to leave me out of it.

I converse with you,
not simply 'interview',
use everything you give to me:
diaries, paintings, poems too.
I write in wobbly stanzas
and different fonts
to show your life as well as mine.

I say 'I' as well as 'you'
and let you see my part
in what's been said
even when they worry I will spoil
the precious data
by being up too close
and *personal*.

I tell stories at conferences
without overheads
and walk about the room,
write journal papers
of more than 4000 words,
and use funny titles
that make you laugh.

Sometimes I even dress
in purple,
no shoulder-pads at all.
And maybe soon,
when speaking from a platform
I'll wear a hat that's red
that really doesn't go.

(with apologies to Jenny Joseph's 'Warning: When I am an old woman I shall wear purple')

Part 2

# The Masters Stage of the Journey

In this part of the book I focus on the experience of those at the Masters level, some of whom were in the process of writing, or had finished, their dissertation and obtained their degree. I had been closely involved with a few participants as their course tutor and dissertation supervisor. I had been less involved with others who, although they had been taught by me, were supervised by my colleagues, and there were some participants who had studied at other institutions and with whom I had had no previous contact.

All of the participants in this study who were at the Masters stage of the journey were women. It is fair to say that most of our Masters students are women, reflecting the gender balance within the counselling profession generally. It is also true to say that very few of the men I have met at this stage would describe themselves as 'reflexive' researchers. The men I conversed with who valued reflexive research were all postdoctoral researchers, and their stories will be presented in Part 3 of this book.

Chapter 6 tells my own story during the Masters stage of my journey, using an edited version of my diary from that time to show how, as a naïve researcher, my heuristic process was operating even though I did not have such words to describe it at the time.

In Chapter 7 I reflect on how Masters students use supervision to support reflexive research, and illustrate this by using a conversation with an ex-student who describes how her relationship with me (her dissertation supervisor) raised issues that became the central focus of her research.

Chapter 8 illustrates the need to have a supervisor who understands how the process can impact on the researcher and who can provide a 'safe anchorage' as the researcher steps into the unknown. This chapter shows how heuristic research can be experienced as a vehicle for profound personal and professional development and change, using my conversations with two women who both dared to let go of their usual need for structure.

A research journal is an important tool in reflexive research, and in Chapter 9 I show how a journal vividly captures one woman's heuristic process as she moved through her research journey. This chapter also includes a conversation between doctoral candidates and myself as we talked about the different ways we keep and use journals as researchers.

Chapter 10 describes what is meant by autoethnography and how, by using our selves as 'subject', we can produce research that profoundly affects our own growth and learning, as well as that of our readers. In this chapter I use a variety of communications with participants: a transcribed tape provided by a woman as she reached the stage of submitting her dissertation; email correspondence with participants and from a reader, both of which tell of the impact on them of writing and reading autoethnography.

The final chapter in Part 2 (Chapter 11) focuses on creating and using creative research data and includes a personal story of a woman's experience of using painting and poetry as a means of depicting her journey through recovery from addiction.

The endnote to this section of the book is a poetic representation of part of a research conversation that captures the essence of one woman's experience of how reflexive research led her to want to explore the world and learn to play.

*Chapter 6*

# A Personal Journey

## My Masters Stage

As I begin to think how I might tell my own story of this stage of my becoming a reflexive researcher I dig out the diaries I had written around that time. Piecing them together 10 years later is helping me to make sense of how that period of my life contributed to my becoming the person/researcher I am today. As I read them I am analysing them as data and selecting portions to use for this chapter. I am noticing the parts I leave out and the parts I include. I leave out some of the judgements I made about colleagues and tutors, not wanting to upset people, while simultaneously trying to include enough about what seems important as part of this overarching narrative. I also leave out entries that are not relevant to the topic of this study.

In telling my own story I am inevitably telling other people's stories and they have not given permission for me to do that. So I tread a careful line between telling it as it seemed to me at the time, and reporting my experiences as truthfully as I can, while also being aware of other people's right to privacy. It's a dilemma that most of us have to deal with in doing this kind of research.

(Journal notes)

Diaries can be used in many ways, for a range of purposes, and are different from research journals in that they do not necessarily focus on the research itself but rather are a record of a person's life written at a time that is pertinent to the area of research. Two participants in a previous study who had been my clients gave me their diaries (written at the time they were in therapy with me) to use as a contribution to a book on working with adult male survivors of childhood sexual abuse: many readers told me they found those diaries the most interesting parts of the book (Etherington 2000).

In this case I am both researcher and participant in my own study, and the diary entries below are used as data about my process of becoming a reflexive researcher when I was at the Masters stage. In other chapters I will be using excerpts from participants' research journals.

This diary focuses on my progress during the time I was studying for an MSc (as well as other areas of my life). At that time I did not know words like reflexive, heuristic, phenomenology, narrative, or autoethnography but my diary does reveal that I had an awareness of how my personal story and the research journey were inextricably linked. I was studying father–daughter relationships (Etherington 1992), and it was not until writing this chapter that I realized how much I had been immersing myself in that concept during this whole period – not only intention-ally by interviewing people and reading the literature, but also in my therapy, in my dreams and by noticing our friend's relationships with his daughters during our visit to France.

From my current position I can see, even then, glimpses of the researcher I am today: I notice as I read my diary that, unlike most of my peer group on the Diploma, I began to publish very soon after completing the course because I had a strong desire to share my learning with the wider community. Those early attempts to be published (and the process of receiving peer review feedback) served my learning well.

The reader will notice how, in telling the story of being at the Masters stage of the journey, I contextualize it within an earlier stage of studying for a Diploma in Counselling. At the time I began the Masters (1990) there were very few courses available: indeed the Diploma in Counselling I had attended was the first ever post-graduate counselling diploma at the University of Bristol. Nowadays the depart-ment offers Certificate courses, postgraduate Diplomas, Masters and doctoral programmes, all of which have grown from that first course. For a year or so after completing the Diploma I had been hearing rumours about the possibility of a Masters course being developed but whenever I asked about it I was told it was 'only in the planning stages'.

Also embedded in this story is a glimpse of the stage of my journey that followed – doing a PhD. It was while I was attending the Masters course that I first began to enquire about doing a doctorate so this diary goes backwards to the Diploma and forwards to my PhD, although at the time I began the Masters stage a PhD was not even a twinkle in my eye.

So the diary I use below, in true narrative structure, tells of a 'present' that rests upon a remembered past and leads to an anticipated future. It is a story about one period of my life that contains absent but implicit stories that have gone before that shaped my life up to the point at which we join the diary – on the day I attended for an interview for the MSc in Counselling (Training and Supervision) at the University of Bristol.

*23 July 1990*

Went for my interview today for the new Masters course at the Uni. I've been hassling them for ages to find out when it was going to happen. I've been trying to find some way of developing my learning further but there are so few courses available. A group of us from the Diploma did start going to some training days in Bath last year but the model was so different from ours that we didn't find it helpful really.

Anyway, I have a real sense that what I'm wanting is to stretch my academic ability as well as my practice, and a Masters seems the logical next step. Until I did the Diploma I didn't even think I was capable of doing work at that level but I enjoyed the opening up of my mind so much (painful though it was!) that I want to go on doing that.

I don't know how I survived the Diploma really! I was quite ill most of the time and missed quite a few sessions. It was like being on an emotional roller-coaster. It triggered me into my own therapy and I discovered all sorts of bits of myself that been hidden from me – including my brain!

The interview today was quite a painful reminder of all that. Going back into the same room, meeting up with staff from the Diploma who probably had mixed feelings about seeing me turn up like a bad penny. I'd not been an easy student – being in such turmoil most of the time. It was a bit embarrassing really because Sally, one of the interviewers, had been my therapist for a while after the Diploma ended and she had really let me down by not informing me that she was going to be away on holiday. But I'd worked through all that stuff about being let down by the 'mother' in my life in subsequent therapies and I just saw her as a flawed human being like the rest of us.

The MSc runs over two years, one day a week, and it's for experienced and qualified counsellors who are ready to become trainers, supervisors, and researchers. I told them at the interview that I was really excited about the research aspect but I was told research wouldn't be a major part of the course, which was a bit disappointing. But it does say in the brochure that we will be expected to complete a dissertation. I did a small dissertation on the Diploma and I enjoyed that so I'm really up for doing something like that again.

Anyway, now I'll have to wait to hear if I've got a place.

*29 August 1990*

I got my letter today and I've been accepted. The tutor had put a little note in with the formal letter saying 'It feels fine! Hope it does for you.' That was a bit of a relief really because I didn't want to spend two years being taught by people who didn't really want me on the course.

I rang Mary to find out if she'd been offered a place too – she has. That's really good. We did the Diploma together and now we can do this together too.

*24 September 1990*

Received my copy of the *British Journal of Occupational Therapy* in which my second academic paper was published! It's called 'The Disabled Persons' Act 1986: the need for counselling' – based on my Diploma dissertation. My first paper was published in May this year in *Counselling* – on the same topic but from a counselling perspective. One thing I learned from submitting papers to different journals is that they need to have different titles even when they are taking a new focus on the same study. It seems obvious now but I didn't know that before.

I realize also now that it is very rare for papers to be accepted without suggestions being made for changing/re-writing – at least some parts. I felt very deflated
and angry when I first received the referees' remarks and nearly gave up altogether,
but after a couple of days I read the feedback again and realized it wasn't such a lot
they were suggesting when I took one comment at a time. I did rework the paper
with their remarks in mind and it was accepted. I feel quite chuffed really because I
don't think any of my peers from the Diploma have done anything with their dissertations. It does seem a shame to do all that work and not share the knowledge
gained. I sent my dissertation to the Director of Social Services because I wanted
him to see what people were saying about their need for counselling. I met with
him and he agreed that there *was* a need and that OTs were probably the best people
to offer the service BUT there was a long waiting list for our services, etc...

It's hard to keep on working in the same old way, like running on a treadmill,
putting on sticking plasters when I know there is something I could be offering
that people would value. I'm not sure how long I can go on doing this as it makes
me feel very dissatisfied with the service I am offering. However, I have been given
permission (and some funding) to set up a group for disabled women as a pilot.
Let's see what happens there.

### 4 October 1990

Started the MSc today! It's a big group – with quite lot of men. I noticed the men
are quite a lot younger than the women. It appears that men seem to get into more
senior positions at a younger age than women. I suppose most of us women have
come into counselling once our children are off our hands a bit. Quite a few men on
the course are managers of counselling services; one already has a PhD, one is a GP.
One of the women has been in quite senior positions in education. One bloke looks
just like my dad – so I warned him there might be some trouble ahead.

Mary and I had a good old gossip about everybody on the way home in the car.
Quite like old times really.

### 23 November 1990

Received my copy of the November OT journal in which I have published a paper
that was based on an essay I wrote for the Diploma called: 'The Occupational
Therapist as a Counsellor Towards Attitude Change in Disability'. It feels good to
bring the two worlds of OT and counselling together.

### 18 February 1991

It's nearly three months since I've filled in this journal. We've been learning about
adult learners this term. I'm a bit fed up with the course. It seems like a
do-it-yourself job. There's not a lot of organization – we seem to be expected to
provide most of the input. They call it self-directed learning! Seems a bit of a
cop-out really. One of the women who did a self-directed Diploma seems quite at
home with it and tries to encourage us to organize ourselves.

I am enjoying it though. It makes me have to rely more on myself. Even though
I'd like to be fed a bit more maybe it's going to help me in the long run.

### 12 May 1991

Got my second essay back with peer and tutor feedback. This one was a case study
of client work. I did mine about one of my clients who was sexually abused in
childhood.

I suppose a case study is a kind of research. I'm doing quite a bit of training on
this topic these days so the essay helped me with that too.

*27 June 1991*

End of term. It will be good to have a break, although we have an essay to do on our developing model of supervision.

*11 August 1991*

Today I handed in my notice at Social Services. This is the end of an era. I am giving up being an OT. I've been qualified and working as an OT since 1961. Thirty years! It's a big decision, not least because Dave is currently a full-time student at UWE doing an MSc in Information Technology and earning £10 per week on a government training allowance.

*3 October 1991*

Start of the second year. The bloke like my dad (who has been causing me hassle because he turned out to be *very* like my dad, pompous, self-opinionated, and domineering!) has left. Tutor rang me before term to let me know because she had a suspicion that I might think I drove him away! She's right of course. But I'm actually really pleased he's left.

This term we are focusing on groupwork. We keep asking about when we are going to have some research training. We should be starting our research soon and haven't been taught anything yet! This self-directed learning lark is OK but if none of us know anything about research how are we going to find out?

I'm trying to decide what topic to study. I've got three ideas and don't know which one to go for. I'll have to decide soon.

*24 November 1991*

Had an article published in the *Observer* today! I wrote it under a pseudonym and as part of my journey towards recovery from my childhood experiences. It was quite scary to see it in print. I had one in the *Guardian* in January 1990 which was about my relationship with my father. I received a lot of very positive letters that were sent to the newspaper which they then forwarded on to me. I wonder if that will happen this time.

*9 January 1992*

New term begins. Maybe we'll do some research training this term. Handed in my essay on setting up a group for women with disabilities based on the learning from the group I ran during my last six months as an OT. The group was a fantastic experience and the women really valued it but when it ended, just prior to my leaving, there was no further funding (and of course nobody to run it).

*23 January 1992*

Had a tutorial to discuss my research topic. I've decided to do a study of 'The Father–Daughter Relationship and Its Impact on Women's Adult Lives'. I've been doing all this work in therapy about my father and I'm a bit concerned in case my negative feelings about him might be interfering with my work with women – by expecting those relationships always to be negative. But more than that, I really want to know if some women have had a *good* experience of fathering and what that would look like if they have.

I'm going to interview 12 women about their relationships with their fathers. We are going to have a supervisor for the research bit. I'm not really sure yet how it's going to work. I don't think anybody does. I have to keep reminding myself that this is the first time this course has run and we are all on a steep learning curve, including the tutors.

## 31 January 1992

Today I ran a training day at the University about 'Working with the aftermath of abuse' and there were about 24 people. During the round I asked them to say why they were attending. One woman said she was doing a PhD to study what kind of resources were available for survivors of sexual abuse. I pricked up my ears.

During coffee break I asked her a bit more about it. I realized I had no idea how one went about signing up for a PhD. Nobody in the counselling unit has done one and there doesn't seem to be much interest in things like that. This woman told me she was doing it in Social Policy and suggested if I wanted to know more that I should contact them.

Well, I've still got six months to go on the Masters but it might be worth thinking about.

## 19 February 1992

Rang up Social Policy today and asked about doing a PhD. They seemed encouraging and suggested I wrote a proposal saying what I wanted to study and why.

## 14 March 1992

Dave's degree day! He received a Masters degree at Bristol Cathedral. Lovely day. Its nearly 30 years since he got his PhD, but having been made redundant he decided to try something new. I really admire him for it. He was the oldest swinger on the campus and he's worked really hard. This time next year maybe I'll be getting a Masters degree!

## 26 March 1992

Term ended last week so I'm using the Thursdays to do my research interviews: first ones today. I did four (each one was one hour) with women who are my peers on the MSc. They went well I think – very interesting. I taped them. I had a list of areas I was interested in and had a kind of checklist that I used at the end to see if we'd covered everything. But mainly they just talked. They seemed to find it really easy once they got going. An hour wasn't really long enough, and four in one day was definitely too many. I'll make sure I space the others out more.

## 13–25 April 1992

Dave and I went to Bordeaux. We stayed with Jacques and his two daughters. I was really noticing the father–daughter relationships. He seems very possessive of them. They are early to mid-teens: one seems to sleep most of the time and the other is very studious. They both look sad. He does all the cooking, shopping, etc. and they have a lovely home. One of them said it was like a 'gilded cage'. I think she is worried about when the times comes to leave home and how her father will cope.

## 30 April 1992

I did another interview today at lunchtime. I'm finding it really interesting. It's not all that different from counselling really except that I've formed some questions to ask each of them about how they experienced their father during childhood, adolescence and adulthood – trying to get a sense of how their relationships might have changed over time. Because my dad died when I was 15 I didn't have a chance to form an adult relationship with him and can't imagine ever doing so.

I've been thinking quite a bit about myself as I've been doing it. How did Pop affect those aspects of *my* life? I've found a really good book called *The Wounded Woman* recommended by Jane, my Jungian therapist. I've been dreaming a lot about Pop recently and remembering some good things about him.

### 16 May 1992

Did an interview with a client, and I think it might have been a mistake. She'd been talking a lot about her father recently so I asked her if she'd be interested to contribute. She said she would like to but now I have my doubts. Not sure why yet though. Maybe it's blurring the boundaries of our relationship too much.

### 21 May 1992

Went for my appointment to talk about doing a PhD. I don't believe I'm doing this. At some stage very soon someone's going to tell me it's all been a joke.

She seemed very interested in my idea of studying male survivors of sexual abuse. I know there hasn't been much done in the UK. It all seems a bit muddled though. There don't seem to be any clear guidelines so I'll just keep moving forward and thinking about it. I'll have to pay for it somehow.

### 4 June 1992

We actually did a written exam at the University today!

I'm planning my input on the course as a trainer. I'm going to run a session about working with the elderly. Since I've been working as a counsellor in a nursing home I've become quite interested in this age group. Of course, I've been working with them as an OT for years, but not as a counsellor. It seems that most people don't consider older people's needs for counselling.

I've been doing training for the University for a while now (in my new fully freelance capacity) but I've never had someone assess what I'm doing. Scary!

### 11 June 1992

I got really good feedback about the training session I ran today on the course. That was a relief. We all have to do it as part of our assessment.

### 1 July 1992

Had an aromatherapy massage for the first time in my life. Amazing! Could it be that I am getting more in touch with my body at long last??

### 2 July 1992

Last day of the MSc course. I had my ears pierced! Frogmarched into Dingles by three of my friends who wanted to make sure I'd done it by the end of the course. I have been saying I wanted to do it but haven't plucked up the courage so they gave me no option. Ears a bit sore this evening.

Although the course has ended we will continue to do our research, and the dissertation will be due for submission at the end of October. We can have tutorials during the summer and meet with our research supervisor.

### 1 August 1992

Went all the way to South Wales to see my research supervisor. I've talked to her on the phone a couple of times. She seems quite good. I think we are allowed to see them two or three times. I feel very muddled about how I'm going to use all the data. How am I going to put it all together?

*14 August 1992*

Had a really powerful dream last night. It must be something to do with my research.

I dreamed that I had arrived at my wedding on the back of an awesome elephant. I arrived at the church (which was actually the Taj Mahal) to meet my bridegroom, an Indian prince. I wore a long flowing satin gown and I felt beautiful. The Indian prince and I were united while Dave and other supporters from my past watched and celebrated the union. When I woke this morning I felt strong and whole and sensed immediately that the dream was about an integration of my feminine and masculine aspects.

*28 September 1992*

Handed in my dissertation. Felt like I'd given a baby up for adoption!

*29 September 1992*

Registration for PhD at Senate House. Informal meeting at Social Sciences Faculty.

*28 November 1992*

Ran a workshop on Fathers and Daughters today. There were about 14 women and we met in a very nice room at Emmaus House. It felt like a safe place. We did some very powerful gestalt exercises. I asked them all to introduce themselves as if they were their fathers introducing their daughter to the rest of us. I did it first. I was really surprised at what I found myself saying about me from my father's position.

One young woman was at a university in another town but had come home for the weekend especially to do the workshop. She was talking about how her father intrudes into her space all the time and how she feels as if he won't let her go. The group were listening and being very supportive of her. Just then there was a knock at the door – which was really surprising because usually we are left alone when using this training room. I went to the door and a man stood there with a packet in his hands. He said 'Here are my daughter's sandwiches for her lunch'. I took the package and closed the door and came back and sat down. The young woman was weeping copiously. She said 'That was my dad'. We had all been shown what she had been talking about. Even at the workshop she wasn't safe from his intrusion.

I used so much of what I had been learning from my research for this workshop. The women seemed to want to form a group that would continue to meet. I felt a bit wobbly when I came home. It had been a very powerful day and a lot of my own material had been evoked.

*17 February 1993*

Degree Day! It was a great day. I'd never worn a gown before (OT training wasn't a degree when I did it – I had received a Diploma). Hazel held a little party in her room and we all toasted our successes. It was very interesting to see other members of the families!

*Chapter 7*

# The Supervisor's Role in Reflexive Research at the Masters Stage

The interviewers might reflect deeply on the personal experience that brought them to the topic, what they learned about and from themselves and their emotional responses in the course of the interview, and/or how they used knowledge of the self or the topic at hand to understand what the interviewee was saying.

(Ellis and Berger 2003, p.162)

In cases where the research being conducted is for a Masters degree the research supervisor might also be the student's tutor, and in this chapter I will describe how these roles develop over time.

The supervisor's role is particularly important for researchers engaged in reflexive research. Reflexivity, as has been stated earlier, requires the researcher to include their own experiences of being in the field and of their relationship with their participants. Topics chosen by researchers are usually related to issues with which they have some relationship, whether they are fully aware of that or not (Devereux 1967; Ellis and Berger 2003), and in heuristic inquiry the researcher is *required* to have some personal connection with the topic through which they 'filter' their participants' experiences.

Students use their supervisory relationship to 'tell the story' of their research in order to process their learning and experiences. These layers of experience can best be reached through dialogue between the researcher and a supervisor or advisor. Latterly, in academic circles, the word 'advisor' has replaced 'supervisor', to imply a more supportive and less hierarchical role. I prefer to use 'supervisor' because I am familiar with being a counsellor/counselling supervisor, where the word has been applied to a role that provides support, education where needed, and focus on professional responsibility concerns, such as ethics and boundaries – a relationship that is less to do with control and more to do with being at a slight distance, giving the possibility of a wider and different perspective while 'hovering' over the scene (Inskipp and Procter 1993).

Several of my participants in this study spoke of their relationship with their supervisors and, as I am aware that there has been very little attention paid to this aspect of research in the literature, I will focus on what I have learned from those stories.

My own experience of research supervision was very limited during the earlier stages of my journey as a researcher. I did not receive supervision for the research I had undertaken at Diploma level back in the late 1980s. I believe this was not unusual for that era; indeed the value of supervision for counsellors was also less understood at that time.

In the previous chapter I have mentioned the limited contact I had with my supervisor for my Masters research and, in reading my diary now with greater knowledge of reflexivity than I had at the time, I realize there had been several opportunities for greater focus on my reflexive process had I or my supervisor recognized it. In conversation with my participants for this study I could hear how their experience and quality of data had been enriched through good reflexive supervision.

I have explored the role of the supervisor for this study alongside experiencing myself as supervisor for both Masters and doctoral students (and interviewing both). I have become aware of the differences between them, and I will address these in Part 3.

## The Masters stage

Masters students often come into research training believing they are going to have to abandon the familiar practices, beliefs and values that underpin their work as reflective and reflexive practitioners. As newcomers to research much of their initial experience consists of learning what seems like a new language and struggling with uncomfortable feelings of confusion and ignorance. Students frequently complain that words like ontology, epistemology, phenomenology, heuristic and so on, are disabling and excluding. So initially tutors/supervisors create a space in tutorials for students to come to terms with the feelings of anxiety and incompetence evoked in these new circumstances and encourage them to recognize that, although they may need to learn new words and new skills, it does not mean they need to abandon previously held competencies and valued ways of being and working.

Another message delivered early in the training is that their chosen topic may have some personal meaning for them, and that they might need to think about this before their first tutorial, at which the tutor/supervisor helps them to explore any possible connections. This preliminary stage of exploration might create an opportunity to open the student up to aspects of themselves of which they have been only partly aware or even unaware. In terms of personal and professional development this can be profound and useful learning and can only be of benefit in the research process.

Catherine, one of my own students, came for her first tutorial knowing that she was interested in exploring aspects of child abuse and knowing that this emanated from her personal experience of being a mother of two boys who had been abused. At first she thought she wanted to research the question of why abusers offend. But on further reflection she realized that she was really much more interested in exploring the lived experience of mothers whose children have been abused. She realized that as well as this being an under-researched topic that would enhance her learning and contribute to the field, it might also become a healing journey for herself and maybe even for her family. However, it would also entail the risk of opening up painful areas of her life that could surprise her and reverberate within the family.

Having reached this point of understanding about her interest in the topic, ethical and methodological issues could then be addressed: one of my concerns about this particular study was that in telling her own story, Catherine would also risk exposing her sons, who might not want their stories told, thus creating potential for further invasion of their personal boundaries. I was also concerned for Catherine's well-being. Through careful teasing out of these issues she was able to negotiate with her sons and use a pseudonym. In response to my concerns for her welfare, Catherine eventually agreed with my suggestion to find herself a therapist for the duration of the study.

Once students have decided on their topic and understood something about their relationship with it, they begin to think about what kind of methodology is best suited to their purpose and move into a different stage of dissertation supervision. At this point they connect with the supervisor who will work with them until they submit their dissertation (and maybe beyond if they need to resubmit). The focus at this stage is on doing the research and on supporting them through data collection, analysis and writing up. In qualitative research, reflexivity is an inherent part of the process. As stated previously, while interviewing, analysing and writing, awareness of our own presence in the research can enhance the process and the outcomes.

There are times when students who have set out believing they knew where they were heading are surprised to find they have lost their way. Maybe the interviews do not reveal what they hoped for or, with new learning, they discover they have not chosen the most satisfactory methodology for their developing purpose.

Students who value narrative ways of knowing, tacit knowing and/or creative organic ways of undertaking research (Braud and Anderson 1998) may decide to focus on their own lives as the topic of their research (see Mel's story in Chapter 10 and Sue Law's story in Chapter 11). These methodologies are of course particularly relevant in counselling, psychotherapy and other helping professions, where it is important for practitioners to understand their motivations, and the influences of their history on the work they do and the people with whom they work.

Liz's story (reported below) shows something of how her relationship with me as her supervisor, although difficult at one time, took her into new parts of herself that eventually led to her changing the focus of her research. Initially she had set out to undertake a study entitled: *A reflection on the process of integration of the learning from personal therapy and post-graduate counselling training into the role and practice of a Human Resource Manager.* After conducting four interviews with human resource managers (who had subsequently trained as counsellors – as she had) she realized that they did not satisfy her curiosity and need for further knowledge. She realized at that point that she had really wanted to focus on her own story as part of her self-development. This realization occurred shortly after she had been for a tutorial during which she had experienced me as a 'critical parent' – something she had experienced from her father throughout her life – and something she often experienced in relationships with people she perceived as authority figures. My frustration and impatience with her during a tutorial had sparked off a powerful response that seemed to have been a catalyst that led her to reconsider what she really wanted to achieve from her MSc.

I met with Liz on degree day and she asked if we could meet two weeks later: she had some unfinished business with me. This was just one of many conversations I had had over the years with students who had experienced a sense of profound growth through undertaking their research, although this was the first time I had an opportunity to tape what was said and use it for research purposes. This had been agreed with Liz before she came. I have edited our conversation to remove anything not directly related to the focus of this chapter, viz. the supervisor's role in relation to reflexive research with Masters students.

Liz turned up carrying a huge bouquet of flowers for me – to my surprise. I made a cup of tea and we sat together in my conservatory and settled down to talk.

Kim:    So here you are, having been awarded your MSc and you wanted us to meet and have a chance to reflect on the process. Is that right?

Liz:    Yes I did. I just felt that there was a loose end for me, because, I suppose reflecting on it, the relationship that *we* had was really important to me in terms of how I did the dissertation, where I ended up, and how it all came together really. And because that was the most significant part for me, I wanted to find a way to draw to a close, or at least for me to recognize, that part of the study. Because it was interesting, Kim, the day in December when everyone did their presentations, and coming to the graduation, I didn't feel *connected* to others and I'm not sure if that's just generally about me or my study, or the nature of the course. It just felt that actually the person I felt connected to was my tutor or my supervisor.

Kim:    So what d'you think it was that made our relationship important?

Liz:    I think I found you very challenging. Just reflecting back in my journal I remember that one day when I got quite upset, and…but in another way I found you very understanding and accepting of me. I know that sounds quite contradictory but once you tried to understand how I was, and how I worked, and then worked *with* that, you know, that was really important.

Kim: Well, that's what we say about a counselling relationship isn't it, that there's challenge *and* there's support; it's not either–or, it's both. What was very important for me when you got upset was that you told me about it. Yes, so I had to stand back and think, 'Well, you know, I got something wrong there, to create *that* degree of upsetness', and, 'or did I?' I really wanted to open that up, but I couldn't have done that unless you communicated your upsetness to me. And it might be worth capturing what that was about, from this position, would that be OK?

Liz: Yes.

Kim: Remind me, because actually I've forgotten the details.

Liz: Not surprised (laughing). I've just found it in my journal. At first I couldn't find it and I thought, 'Is it one of those things that I was so upset about that I didn't note it?' And I *had* written a little bit about it, but not a lot. And what I remember is coming for a tutorial and feeling unprepared, so I didn't come with my usual list of things I wanted to explore, and we agreed to look at an essay I gave you.

Kim: Oh yes.

Liz: I think it was possibly the second one [essay] we did, and I can't remember what it was on now. Was it on the…(pause)

Kim: Was it the methodology one?

Liz: Yes, and you took the opportunity to re-read it in my presence and then to give me some feedback and all I heard was the negative. It felt like you were tearing me…that's how it felt, like you were tearing me apart. I'd struggled so much with the essay and had this overwhelming feeling of failure. So that's what was happening and I just… I know I stopped it, I think I said…(pause)

Kim: You said: 'I can't deal with this.'

Liz: Yes, I can't deal with it in this way, and it took me a few days to sort of…, I suppose I went away and then I think I emailed you.

Kim: Yes you did, that's right…it's coming back to me. My memory of it (and you can correct me if this isn't how it was), but my memory of it was that, in your first essay, I'd started noticing and picking up on (and you'd started noticing it too) that you didn't put yourself into what you were writing. You would write 'you' rather than 'I', and 'it seems like' rather than 'I think', and I'd been showing that to you and saying it'd be really good for you to find your voice and to be able to say 'I' more clearly… And then in the second essay, there it was again. You were doing the same thing again, and I was thinking that I hadn't managed to get the message across and wondered how was I going to get it across this time so that you would really be able to change that.

   And I probably…maybe I was also a bit irritated, because I think I do get irritated when people don't say 'I', when they keep on saying 'you'. There's something about me wanting people to be able to put themselves in the centre of what they write, and it feels like it's a really difficult shift sometimes. For some people it seems harder than for others. And I suppose…maybe I was also aware – because that was what your dissertation ended up *being* about – maybe I was also aware of your frustration with *yourself* for not doing that, at some level, and yes – maybe wanting to shake you (laughter).

Liz:     Absolutely!

Kim:     And that really was not OK, doing it in that way – at that time.

Liz:     I don't know, because part of me thinks that I was hearing an authoritative voice, which was probably overwhelming me. Because the message *was* clear, I think I *had* heard the message before. But I didn't know how to translate it in terms of how I wrote. I understood at one level but not another. It wasn't actually connecting with me at the time. Although at some level I could hear it, it wasn't affecting how I wrote; or how I thought and therefore expressed myself. So I think when you *did* give the message – I noted in my journal what the overarching message was – but I heard the authority voice before I heard the… I was able then to ask myself 'What's she really saying?'

Kim:     Yes, and what was I saying?

Liz:     About me bringing myself into the centre of my own life and me expressing myself as I *want* to be expressed and not relying on others really.

Kim:     Yes.

Liz:     Saying what I want in a way that's centred to me.

Kim:     So by hearing the authority voice before the message, it had been frightening or confusing or…

Liz:     Yes, it just overwhelmed me. It's like in some ways it took away the 'I' message again.

Kim:     Right, yes, yes…

Liz:     …because here it was again, somebody telling me that I'd got it wrong…

Kim:     Yes, yes…

Liz:     …rather than somebody *encouraging* me to actually believe in myself.

Kim:     So how did you move from that position? You went away then feeling upset and then you emailed me. What happened between leaving here and the email?

Liz:     I think I got very upset. I did get very upset and it stayed with me for a while.

Kim:     When you say upset, what kind of feeling was that?

Liz:     Just complete failure. It's like an overwhelming sense of crying and hurt and shame and humiliation. And that overwhelms me and it did overwhelm me for probably two or three days, but then there was something… I don't know, there's something about the…this *core* bit of me that comes back up and says 'Actually Liz, it is all right' – the anchor I think.

Kim:    *You're* all right.

Liz:    Yes, I think the anchor's there saying 'Yes, it's OK'.

Kim:    And it's OK to be angry.

Liz:    Yes.

Kim:    But were you angry? Because you didn't say angry, you said hurt and sad and upset and ashamed.

Liz:    Yes, I think I was angry, but again it's the sort of second emotion that comes through, all the other things have to work through first.

Kim:    So maybe when you were able to get hold of your anger that helped to bring you out of it, to stand up and say I'm going to deal with this.

Liz:    But my way of dealing with it was to actually try the sort of straight approach which was just to say; 'Kim can I have another tutorial?' I wasn't sure what I was going to do with it. That was my way of making contact. It wasn't to say 'Kim I'm really angry with you.' I couldn't do that at that time.

Kim:    So then we had another tutorial and what d'you remember about that?

Liz:    Not very much really. I suppose what I remember is us talking about what happened, and me recognizing what I was putting onto you as well, which is this 'authority figure'. With the relationship I have now with my father and others, sometimes that's all I hear. Sometimes I'm better now at recognizing it, but it's not always instant.

Kim:    You react to what you call the authority voice and that closes your ears to the supportive message that might be in there as well?

Liz:    Yes, and I have to, somehow I've got to, yes I've given myself permission to allow the emotions to be there, because I can't do anything about it, but know that that solid part of me will come back and I'll be able to deal with it. That just takes some time.

Kim:    In some way, I can hear that what happened between us was both helpful and hindering, …(pause). I don't know. On the one hand, I can accept and own that the way I gave you feedback probably was not sufficiently sensitive for where you were at that time, but the moment when I became aware that you were in that sensitive place, I think that was useful, because then I was able to take that on board. But there's almost like another layer of message in there which I suppose maybe I'm just *trying* to hear (laughter) rather than just hear how destructive that might have been, that in some way, it was a point at which you were able to climb back by getting angry with me. Does that…

Liz:    Mmm. Yes, because I kept thinking if you'd said it in a very softly, softly way, you know, very gentle, and I *hadn't* got upset, would it have had such an impact? And I suppose I don't know. No.

Kim:    Because I think I'd already said it that way last time round.

Liz:    And maybe by working through the emotions and tapping into that anger (because there is a bit, I write in my journal 'I feel like I'm going to give up the course'), but there was something in me which also happened when I was writing (I used to call them my little crises… I'd have my daily or weekly crises). But I can remember saying quite a few times, 'I'm going to give up, I cannot do this, I am going to give it up.'

Kim:    I remember you saying that.

Liz:    But there was something in me that says 'No you're not'. I don't know, I wonder if I hadn't tapped into that whether I would have grown so much, or so quickly. Maybe I'd have got there, but just a different pace. You just don't know do you?

Kim:    And it was around that time, or just after that, in my memory, that you began to change your dissertation. Do you want to say something about that?

Liz:    Mmm. Mmm. I think there was something growing, and re-reading my journal, there's something in there about wanting to put the different parts of me together and see myself as a whole, rather than as separate parts. But also about this growing need of self-discovery: to find out more, not quite sure what.

        And the third thing was that when I taped my research interviews and then analysed my tapes, I found them so boring. I felt awful about it, because it felt that I was saying something about the individuals rather than myself, and I think just having your encouragement to actually just *go* with that, and allowing myself to *go* with it, rather than struggling with the…

Kim:    Well, yes, just to follow and see where it goes: not judging yourself for feeling bored, but 'maybe there's a message in this boringness'.

Liz:    Yes, and I suppose at first that felt quite…working without that structure…because if I had the research participants' data, I had something to work with, but if I was just going to work with something different to that, where would that take me? I like structure.

Kim:    That's right, yes.

Liz:    And here I was, potentially working without structure.

Kim:    Throwing it away almost. But how you used those tapes more and more was to start noticing what your selves were saying to you, and your bored self turned into your angry self, is that right?

Liz:    Yes, there was a lot of anger there. Yes, anger which was tapping into old anger as well. I suppose I felt some frustration with participants, which was also reflecting something about me. But I can remember that August bank holiday, when I'd been struggling with the tapes, but then feeling very freed up once I'd decided to work with them in a different way. I spent the whole weekend struggling with the structure and finding it tedious, but then feeling freer and just working with the emotions that the tapes were raising for me. I can remember spending what seems like days, just sitting there thinking, and not doing anything, you know? As *I* would say, I wasn't *actively* doing anything. And that felt all wrong.

Kim: Yes, that's not you (laughter)…

Liz: No, unless I'm producing something… And that felt so alien. My partner, Jez, would say to me, 'Well, what have you done?' I'd say, 'I don't know really.'

Kim: So what d'you think was happening in those times?

Liz: I think it was just allowing myself to be, and just allowing things to settle in me really.

Kim: That sort of process of incubation that Moustakas talks about?

Liz: Yes, because I wasn't writing long journal notes (because that would have been OK – I would have been producing something). It was just like *being*. I'd go for long walks; I wouldn't want anybody around me; I couldn't bear to have music or TV on. I was quite happy to sit in the garden or sit looking out the window and just sort of…allowing it to grow inside me. Allowing it to settle, I wasn't necessarily thinking about anything specifically. I think it was really important for me. I suppose what was going on was maybe just getting in touch with 'me', just allowing me to be. Whatever that was.

Kim: And why was that important in terms of this research process?

Liz: I think it was important in two ways. One, heuristic inquiry is about filtering things through yourself, and I think I had to create space and time to do that, because each time, it seemed to be going down a level. Even though I've finished the MSc, it feels like *that* hasn't stopped. And the second part for me was, it [the dissertation] was *about* discovering self, so unless I'd allowed that process to happen, I'm not sure I'd have found out as much about myself.

Kim: Yes, that's what you really needed to do, what you wanted to know.

Liz: Yes, and I wonder if I'd gone for some other methodology what would have happened.

Kim: Because I remember us talking about one of the reasons why it seemed as though you weren't getting what you wanted from your interviews was that you had a kind of structure of questions that you had asked. You weren't just having a conversation about something and not knowing where it was going to end up – a bit like we're doing now. You were dealing with it more as a phenomenological study, weren't you, and so what you got back wasn't hitting the spot in some way. So it's something about using the tools that

> belong to a different methodology and then being stuck with it until you started thinking about your own responses to what you had done.

Liz: Mmm, and staying with that. Because I didn't know where it was going to take me. And I suppose that was…it felt quite… I don't know what it felt. How did it feel? It felt quite frightening in one way.

Kim: Frightening, yes.

*Liz:* Yes, and it was frightening because actually I was quite desperate to do the MSc and to pass it, and here I was going on some sort of…well, I don't know what I was going on really (laughter) but, on the other hand, it was quite exhilarating in the sense of *not* knowing and more and more developing that reflective self. Because I think it did grow enormously.

Kim: You did?

Liz: Yes, I don't think I will ever be the same again, and I don't want to be. I suppose it's that I think I recognize in the dissertation. If I wrote it now it'd be very different.

Kim: Yes it would.

Liz's dissertation became a reflection of her journey of becoming more of who she knew herself to be. She felt strengthened by the process and, although she was unsure of where her future paths might lie, she knew she had changed.

In the following chapter I take this topic a stage further, trying to unpick exactly what is involved in this process of change, while also engaging at a theoretical and experiential level with what is meant by heuristic inquiry.

*Chapter 8*

# Heuristic Inquiry as a Vehicle for Growth and Development

Heuristic inquiry is a process that begins with a question or a problem which the researcher seeks to illuminate or answer. The question is one that has been a personal challenge and puzzlement in the search to understand one's self and the world in which one lives. The heuristic process is autobiographic, yet with virtually every question that matters personally there is also a social – and perhaps universal – significance.

(Moustakas 1990, p.15)

This chapter explores two counsellors' experiences of engaging in heuristic research and its contribution to their personal and professional growth. It focuses on how reflexive conversations encourage the emergence of what Rosanna Hertz (1997) has called 'reflexive knowledge' and enable researchers and participants to co-construct meaning. It also shows how the research supervisor can help, and the impact of the research process on the person's life and their client work.

## Counsellor/researcher roles and relationships

As counsellors and psychotherapists we usually accept that we are changed by the encounters we have with our clients: we are impacted upon in their process of change and our relationship with them can open us up to parts of ourselves hitherto unknown or only dimly known (Etherington 2001a; Grafanaki 1996). In supervision of our practice we reflect upon those relationships and perhaps come to know and develop ourselves still further.

As qualitative researchers we enter into relationships with participants for different purposes that also provide opportunities for change and growth, in ourselves and our participants, whether or not they are/have been our clients (Etherington 2001a; Gale 1992; Hart and Crawford-Wright 1999; Rosenthal 2003; Skinner 1998; West 1998; Wosket 1999).

Counselling training provides us with skills, theories and understandings of moral and ethical issues that we can use to inform the process of building and maintaining a range of relationships in different contexts, including research. I also bring to my role as researcher my curiosity about the world and the human condition. All of these are necessary qualities for any social science researcher.

Sometimes students arrive on research training courses believing they have to leave behind all the knowledge and skills they have acquired through counsellor training. They think they have to be 'academic', by which they usually mean 'intellectual', 'in my head', 'scientific'. They are often pleasantly surprised to discover that reflexive research training uses and values all that they bring with them and seeks to develop and add to that – not to divest them of ways of being they have come to value. Indeed, counsellor training gives us a great advantage as novice researchers compared to novice researchers in other disciplines.

It could be argued that as counsellors/therapists we do not need to adopt a *new* role of 'researcher' because every encounter with our clients is itself a re-search activity. Indeed, narrative therapists refer to the people who consult them as 'co-researchers', positioning themselves in those relationships as 'not knowing', in contrast to the 'expert' position adopted by some therapists (Freedman and Combs 1996; Payne 2000; White and Epston 1990). However, I believe that although there are many similarities between my roles as therapist and researcher, there are also differences. The main difference is that as a therapist my purpose is to assist my clients re-search (into themselves and their lives), and in my role as researcher the positions are reversed: they are there to assist *me* in discovering something about a topic or concept that *I* am curious about. As a counsellor people seek *me* out: as a researcher I seek *them*. This inevitably influences the power dynamic although it would be disingenuous to deny that the researcher is nonetheless in a powerful position.

## Research as a vehicle for change and development

We have come to recognize that the choice of research topic often has personal significance for the researcher, whether conscious or unconscious (Devereux 1967). Indeed, some methodologies, such as heuristic inquiry described by Moustakas (1990, 1994), *require* us to have personal connection with the topic of inquiry, which inevitably leads to 'self examination, significant personal learning and change' (Stiles 1993, p.604). Walsh (1996, p.383) states: 'Unlike practitioners of quantitative methods, we can learn as much about ourselves when conducting research as we can about the persons with whom we collaborate'.

Increasingly researchers create methodologies to suit the purposes of their research from a range of approaches and methods that reflect their personal views of reality and their beliefs about how we know what we know. Frequently these approaches are underpinned by a heuristic process of discovery that becomes a vehicle for personal growth and development. However, heuristic inquiry is not the only methodology that provides a vehicle for growth: there are other stories I will tell in later chapters about autoethnographic, narrative, life story research that also impact on the researcher's growth, the common theme being reflexivity.

One of the questions I asked participants in this study was: What has been the impact of doing research on you personally and professionally? I was curious to see how people interpreted the question and where it led.

## Methodology

The word 'heuristic' come from the Greek word *heuriskein*, meaning to discover or find. However, it seems to be a word that means different things in different contexts. In the context of this book it refers to a process of inquiry that leads to discovery – a process that developed out of humanistic psychology. Heuristic inquiry derives from phenomenology and seems to attract researchers in the field of counselling and psychotherapy who are interested in exploring the 'essence of the person in experience' (Moustakas 1990, p.39). Moustakas described six stages – not implying a linear process but rather stages to enable the researcher to locate themselves and guide the research. He named those stages as:

- *Initial engagement:* when researchers begin to connect with their interest in the topic, and find and connect with participants. They may also begin to engage with the literature;

- *Immersion:* through interviewing, transcribing, listening, analysing reading, communicating;

- *Incubation:* a period when the research is 'put on the back burner' for a while, creating space for new understanding to unfold, or emerge through ideas, dreams and images;

- *Illumination:* new insights and understandings develop, perhaps through recognizing structures or patterns and themes;

- *Explication:* articulating and making sense of the material;

- *Creative synthesis:* the researcher produces a synthesis that depicts her integration of the data, reflecting personal knowledge, tacit awareness, intuition, and understanding of meanings.

These stages can be seen to echo more general theories of the human creative process that encourage us to reflect on, and connect with, tacit knowing, images, dreams, hunches, ideas that come between sleeping and waking, intuition, out-of-body experiences, synchronicity and exceptional human experiences (Braud and Anderson 1998). These aspects of experience are gathered along with data collected through conversations with participants, journal writing, and a range of relevant materials that may be offered by participants, all of which is filtered through the researcher's own experience (West 2001).

## My heuristic inquiry into Rachel and Paula becoming reflexive researchers

In the following section I offer the reader an opportunity to enter into my mean-ing-making process by presenting parts of my conversations with two of my earliest research participants. By using reflexivity, sharing my thoughts and images, and by asking curious questions as they arose between us, I undoubtedly influ-enced the kind of data that were gathered. In the conversations depicted below we are mirroring something of the processes that are being described, and thus a mul-tilayered story is created.

I will present parts of the conversations with my intermittent commentary in response to the text. Aspects of these conversations that have resonated with me will be different from those that resonate with you, the reader, because you and I bring different things to our reading: our histories, our perceptions and prior knowledge. Those aspects that resonated with me have formed the stories or themes that emerged as I immersed myself in the data. This kind of thematic analysis is sometimes said to reflect a realist epistemology, when themes are believed to represent an underlying truth about the 'subject' and the data are seen as a window onto the person's reality. This is not what I intend in this chapter; rather I see the stories as constituting the storyteller's reality.

I have selected and re-presented stories in both conversational and stanzaform (so that you might notice the difference and your preferences), in the hope that they will provide you with access to the lived experience of two women and allow you to consider how I came to analyse and make sense of what I heard.

## Rachel's story

I met Rachel for the first time when she was deeply immersed in a study of how one of her clients and herself were experiencing 'change' in the counselling process. As a psychology student she had been trained in traditional research methods and dis-couraged from including herself in the research. During her MSc in counselling research training she was introduced to new paradigm, reflexive methodologies and began to explore 'who am I?' in terms of her view of the world, her beliefs about how knowledge is acquired, all of which needed to be congruent with her approach to her study. Her exploration of different methodologies led to adopting a 'complex, quilt-like bricolage, a reflexive collage or montage' (Denzin and Lincoln 2000, p.6) – a methodological approach that challenged all her previous research training and created a sense of disequilibrium.

### 'I've seen the image of what I am'

Rachel:   What came out for me were some memories that I had forgotten – about my earliest experience of being back in this country – because I was born abroad...my heritage is mixed... The research process brought this about in

> my trying to monitor my experiences and bring into focus things that were on
> the edge – on the periphery – things which have an influence, maybe subcon-
> sciously, on what I am, who I am, how I think, how I behave – all of that…

She went on to say that by bringing into focus the 'things that were on the edge'
she could name them and, by naming them, they 'moved forward' and 'other
things took their place'. I asked her what she had named so far.

Rachel:    (Pause) I've kind of, I suppose, named – well not named as such – I've seen the
image of what I am – to acknowledge the fact that: 'Yes, I am – a 57 variety…

Kim:    What do you mean by that?

Rachel:    A mix – really.

Kim:    A mix in terms of you as a person – or methodology – or what?

Rachel:    Wee-ell it's me…it's recognizing that I'm feeling – I wouldn't say *very* comfortable – but reasonably comfortable with not belonging in any one
place…although part of me always *wants* to be rooted in some particular spot.
I could apply that to the research methodology – it's been a terribly frustrating
journey in trying to not fall into the trap of saying 'Yes, I'm definitely that' and
then trying like hell to mould the whole thing to fit that particular thing. And
again, there's that connection between me the person and me the researcher. I
think me the person has always tried to do that and it's only recently that I've
realized – 'Oh shit, I don't belong in that camp, or that camp, or that camp. I'm
actually a mix of the whole thing' and I suppose the research has reflected that.
That, if you like, has named it. The research has named who I am.

Rachel talked then about how difficult it had been to let go of her need for
certainty and how being in a heuristic process required her to trust 'tacit knowing',
immerse herself in the data through writing a journal, 'in-dwelling', reading
around the topic, and her engagement with the participant's material and her own.
Heurism required her to allow a period of 'incubation', during which she simply
had to trust that she *was* getting somewhere, even when it didn't feel like it; to wait
for 'illumination' when things would begin to make sense (which had not yet
happened at the time of our conversation) and would lead to her being able to
explain to herself and others what she had discovered; and to trust that eventually
she would be able to create something that represented an integration of the data
that reflected her personal knowledge, tacit awareness, intuition, and understanding of meanings, in ways that would meet the criteria of an MSc.

## 'The fear that's attached with not knowing'

Ruefully she told me there were times when she wished she had stayed with a more
traditional approach, developing a hypothesis that she could set out to prove or
disprove, beginning from Rachel's sense of:

Rachel: ...knowing already what the outcome might be... That would have been a *far* easier way of doing it, instead of tying myself up in knots – which is what I have done... It's become quite a frustrating, convoluted process, and part of me would have appreciated it if I had just gone the way I originally thought I might have. ...I think to do that would have meant compromising quite a lot of me and ended up with me writing about something I didn't believe in or didn't believe had any significance to me – which is generally not how I am.

Kim: When you said about it being a convoluted process I had an image of this passageway with all sorts of twists and bends – where you can't see round the next corner...

Rachel: That's exactly what it is... I do like to have some sort of view of where I'm trying to get to. At least I can plot my way along. This is just like – in your imagery – there is no light and I am just touching the walls and working my way along it.

Kim: (enthusiastically) That sounds like a real process of discovery!

Rachel: (vehemently and laughing). Yes, it might well be and it doesn't actually make it any easier!

Her vehemence made me realize I had missed something important. So I backtracked and reflected her feelings.

Kim: No, no – it sounds very scary as well.

Rachel: It is very frightening. One of my fears is that at the end of the day I might end up with something that is – nothing – almost. I know that's not rational...but that's how it feels. I suppose it's something about the unknown – the fear that's attached with not knowing.

All this resonated closely with my own experience when I had been deeply immersed in a heuristic process with my ex-clients (Etherington 2000). I had felt out of control: there was so much data, so many ideas and thoughts and images and no understanding of how it might all come together – and the fear that it might not! It was a theme I was to hear over and over again from other participants who had engaged in a heuristic process. I then asked Rachel how the research had impacted on her and her life.

## 'I don't think I've fundamentally changed...'

Rachel: Well, I'm on my own...since I started all of this. And I'm very happy to be on my own... I'm not withdrawn but I've become quieter...more reflective... I don't know whether it's been part of the impact of the research: but it feels as if – this doesn't sound reasonable or rational either – but it kind of feels that it *needed* to happen. I don't think this [research] process would have been possible had I had...somebody else there, another adult there... With [my partner]…there was this covert need, or disappointment, if I wasn't doing or being there for [him].

As she talked I remembered how I had also felt the need to withdraw into a very private space as a result of my heuristic study – not for the same reasons but rather to experience myself as a separate human being and to face my fears of being alone (Etherington 2000). Rachel went on to describe how her partner had become resentful about her work and how she began to change.

Rachel:   …I don't think I've *fundamentally* changed – it's that I'm beginning to recognize that these aspects of myself have *always* been there but have never really been heard or have never been given the chance to come through because of whatever else was going on.

I asked her if the changes she had experienced in doing the research were similar or different to the changes she had experienced in herself through her training as a counsellor.

Rachel:   …the certificate and various other courses…were basically course oriented, achieving various modules…and not paying too much attention to the personal aspects, the self-development aspects – whereas the research is almost the other way. The emphasis and the value has been on *me*, what *I'm* doing, what's happening to *me* as I'm trying to work this out… And that's about…allowing *it* to dictate to me, rather than *me* dictating it from the positivist angle.

I wondered if the personal development she experienced through her reflexive research process was similar to or different from personal therapy and she responded by explaining what happened when she was doing her research:

Rachel:   …when I write down something I'm experiencing…and look at that, I'm aware of the split of experiencing it and *not* experiencing it – just watching myself experience it. In personal therapy – I don't do that. I give it to someone else to do it. And I'm aware that when they don't do it I get irritated…

Kim:      The thinking part of it? Thinking about this experience you're having?

Rachel:   Yes and making the connections *for* me…when I'm writing in conjunction with research and something pops into my mind, I'll *push* it in there without thought to grammar or anything else – just pop it in to see what happens. As I'm writing it down I'm already analysing it…because it's all done very quickly – there's no boundary between the two. I think in my therapy…I don't do that – I say 'This is for you to do, you're my therapist – that's your job – it's not my job to do that. I'm here to give it to you and you can do the rest.'

Later in the conversation I asked Rachel if she thought her practice would change as a result of doing her research.

## 'I'm asking clients. . . just to allow themselves to do it. . .'

Rachel:   Oh I think that's already happening. I am being *less* cognitive although I still do put an importance on cognitive processes. But I think I'm asking clients not to work with [only] their intellect – to try and suspend it, not discard it but just to hold it and to be able to explore…just to allow *themselves* to do it… They might like to sit there quietly and think about what it is they are feeling or experiencing… And if they can't do that then that's fair enough – but just to give them the choice of doing that, whereas maybe I didn't do that [before].

She seemed to be saying that her experience of staying with her fear of 'not knowing' in the research had enabled her to encourage her clients to stay with *their* 'not knowing', and that she was more able to stay alongside them as they experienced themselves more fully and found ways to make sense of their experiences.

As our conversation drew to a close I asked Rachel how she had experienced our conversation. She referred back to the image I had offered of 'a passageway with all sorts of twists and bends' and referred to it as an 'intestinal tract, the large intestine and the small intestine'. She said the image had helped her 'name' her fear. This reminded me that fear is often experienced as a 'gut' feeling: stomach cramps, diarrhoea, frequency of urination. It seemed as if she had connected with a 'felt sense' (Gendlin 1969) that had perhaps shifted as we talked.

## Paula's story

Paula had been awarded her MSc about six months before I first met her. As we talked I was struck by her use of poetic imagery; it was as if she was constructing meaning through images and metaphors as she went along, so her words at times, were slow and faltering.

Colleagues who read earlier drafts of this part of the chapter told me they felt bored as they read the conversations. I found this hard to understand because I knew that my response in the moment had been far from bored. After returning to the tapes I decided to represent her words in the first part of her story in stanza form advocated by Gee (1991), Leftwich (1998) and Speedy (2001). In a later part of her story I revert to reporting our conversation in prose. The reader might be interested to observe the impact this difference makes on their reading. The stanzas are presented using natural breaks and hesitations to shape the lines. My own input is placed on the right hand side of the page.

Our conversation began by Paula describing how she chose her methodology and her excitement at discovering Moustakas's work on *Loneliness*:

## 'Jumping in at the deep end'

That was the catalyst for me.
I thought
'I don't know how I'm going to do this,'

because I'd never done research before
I'd never *attempted* anything like this before
   but when I read his [Moustakas's] book on loneliness
my connection with heurism
was immediate for me
   very immediate…


Later she referred to this as 'jumping in at the deep end' and reflected that maybe that had not been the best way of approaching it. She went on to describe her experience of being in the process.

## 'It almost feels like a journey'
   I go all over the place
I go along different roads that I've never been before.

It's like you sleep, eat and breathe it
   That's what it is for me.
A lot of my thinking was done very early in the morning
when I woke up.
I was aware I was there
in the bed,
birds outside singing
(it's very quiet here)
I would start going back,
   and coming back.
A bit like this
(moves her hand from side to side)

                              Like being on the edge of consciousness,
                              as if you've just woken up?

Yes.
It's a lot clearer
at that time of the day.
Because it feels like the rest of the world isn't there:
   there were no distractions then.

It was always on my mind.

I'd be thinking about what had been said on the tape
and thinking
'Yes, that was what it was like for me'
   I was swinging between
         the present and the past.
Because I was doing heuristic research, I believe
you have to look at yourself as well…

It was like going into another place
especially early in the morning.

## 'Another world...doing research'

It invaded my life when I didn't want it to:
It had a great impact on my family
and my home life.
    I had to be dedicated
    If I was going to get this right
    I needed to put the effort in.

It actually answered lots of questions for me
I thought I'd dealt with years ago
but there were lots of things that came to me
that I hadn't realized.

I wouldn't be frightened of research now
    even though it was very painful for me
because I had to resubmit my dissertation.
I had to dig even deeper than I did
the first time around.

But having done it
    it's almost like another world
    another world altogether
doing research.

## 'I'm not ACADEMIC'

I feel like I've been stretched
because
I always say I'm not academic.
I left school with nothing
and...all my learning as a counsellor
has been in the last ten years.

I never had any qualifications
so for me it's been a struggle
and when I was at university
    because I sometimes struggled with the work
my tutor would say to me
'Listen to your own voice
because when you do that you're great.
Don't think you have to be academic
because when you listen to your own voice you *are* academic!'

Yes, yes. It comes from inside *you*.
It's not someone else's voice.

Paula intimated that the personal development she had experienced through doing
the research was more profound than she had experienced from being in therapy.
Being focused on her own responses as she filtered her participant's tape through
her own experiences meant that she was in control of her own process.

It means
that I've
   [found parts of myself]
I didn't know I had
So that's given me more confidence.

Because when I go to therapy
   (not so much now but a while back,
   and I'm sure our clients do this)
there were parts I would hold back
to please my counsellor
and not let those dreadful things out

perhaps *too* much.

Protecting the therapist?

Yes. But as a researcher
and
being *triggered* into being allowed
to go back further into yourself
there isn't any need to protect.

It's almost as if the research participant is
   stimulating you to…
   your self-discovery.

There are two of me in there:
There's one that's in the here and now
   the researcher,
putting it down on paper,
and there's another part
that's the 'client',
being allowed to say what's going on inside…

         So you don't have to *be* the client
         you can hold onto your position of power
         as the researcher
         and what you're doing can be stimulating
         and challenging to your personal growth?

Yes.
I've never really looked at it quite like that
but that's true.
It *is*, it's as if you are allowed to go there
   if you *want*.

That's powerful isn't it?

## Being tuned-in with myself and my clients

It's made me more aware
[with my clients].

I thought I knew it all.
It seemed to open me up even more.
   It's almost like I am 'fine-tuned' now.
   It's as if I hadn't tuned the radio in properly before
I'd found a better station if you like.
(both laugh)

                                        It's coming through clearer?

                                        So the process of doing the research has really helped
                                        you with your client work?

In some ways it has changed my practice
I might invite clients to try going back
   a bit quicker than I would have before.

It has *allowed* me to take a walk backwards a bit more
with the client
I think it's helped me tune in better
   to myself *and* my clients.

I think it's made me a better counsellor
   in some funny way
and that's about knowing *me* better

I think I was an OK counsellor before
it's made me more relaxed,
it's made me more open

                                      I really liked that image you used about the radio
                                          being tuned to another line,
                                            a clearer line
                                      and you just said again about how you've cleared
                                      those connections
                                        to parts of yourself.

                                      It sounds, from what you are saying now,
                                      that you are hearing your clients better
                                      …you've tuned yourself
                                      to the same programme as them
                                      so that you are hearing them
                                      more clearly somehow.

I think there was part of me
that wasn't quite so flexible before.
I was flexible,
   to a degree,
but this has made me…

It's like when you start going to the gym
you get sore joints and aching muscles
   but you keep doing it don't you?
But if you keep doing it for a long time
you get really flexible.

It feels like the research has given me
a really good work-out,
    it's really moved things
so that I can go with it more.

                    Yes, and you said before
                    that you felt like you'd been stretched.
                    This physical image of going to the gym
                    and having a good work-out
                    is like what you said about
                    being stretched into going beyond
                    where you can normally go to.

You think you can only go so far.
I don't think that any more.
When I submitted my first dissertation
I thought: 'I *can't* do any more.
    I can't dig any deeper than this'
and then I had to do it again
and it was quite…
earth shattering.

## Role of research supervisor

Paula went on to explain the role of her supervisor in her re-submission. She had previously employed a supervisor who was not attached to her course because she lived so far away from the University. But for her re-submission she chose to be supervised by one of the course tutors.

As a research supervisor myself, I was very interested to know exactly what it was about supervision that had made the difference to her experience.

### 'Drowning in my own material'

Paula:   I think it's more to do with the person rather than having someone who knows the course – but it may be a combination of the two. She was able to say something like: 'there's something missing here', without giving me the answer. She'd explore a few things, she'd tap into where I was and how I might add some more or look for something else… I think she stretched me, she made me – she didn't *make* me – she *allowed* me to look in other areas. *She* was digging around as well, if you like, she was *with* me, she was tuning into me, she tuned into what I needed to be able to move on.

Kim:    A bit like you were saying before – *she* tuned into *you*?

Paula:   Yes, yes… She wasn't *just* being with me where I was – she was trying to push me beyond that…I *needed* someone to push me and I thought I'd been pushing all along.

Kim:      Yes, well you obviously had been but maybe there was yet another layer for you to reach?

Paula:    Yes, there was…

Kim:      So what do you think you added [to the dissertation] to make the difference?

Paula:    I actually thought I [had been] a bit *too* centred on where *I* was instead of looking at…other people's work and how that re-inforced what I was doing. Almost like I became too engrossed in where *I*…*too* heuristic if you like.

Kim:      You got lost?

Paula:    Lost, yes, lost. That's a good word. Yes I felt lost. I felt like I didn't know where I was going – almost like I was submerged – drowning if you like… I actually felt like I was drowning in my own material.

Kim:      Right. That's really graphic. So what did your new tutor/supervisor do – what did you do – that helped with that?

Paula:    Yes, she tried to guide me, steer me – like she was steering me *up* rather than me going *down*.

Kim:      You were drowning and she was steering you up?

Paula:    She was pulling me up and saying 'Hang on. Have a look round and see what else is here.'

Kim:      …like throwing you a lifebelt so that you could pull yourself up to the surface.

Paula:    Oh, absolutely. I feel quite emotional (her eyes fill up) because there's only one other person who was like that – it's funny isn't it – only one other person. That was a schoolteacher I had at school – Mr White. I still remember him. He encouraged me and I moved from a B class to an A class. That's exactly what came to me when I was with my supervisor. She did that. Yes.

Kim:      She brought you up to the surface again so that you were in a position to look around to see what you could find to ground you?

Paula:    That's right. She was wonderful. I said to her once 'You must be a Christian;' she said 'I am.'

Kim:      You'd been saved.

(shared laughter)

Paula:    Yes. I never thought of that!

Paula went on to say that she believed she had to resubmit because when she wrote her first dissertation she was still 'drowning' in her own material.

Paula:    Because I thought that was what I needed to do. But…it caught me unawares…

Kim:      What do you mean when you say 'I thought that was what I needed to do?'

Paula:    I thought that heuristic research involved total submersion and it's not that – it's about being able to submerge and come back.

Kim:    It's interesting that you are using that word 'submersion'. I think what Moustakas says is 'immersion'.

Paula:    Oh. Yes. That's strange isn't it? So perhaps my thoughts were that I needed to drown! (Laughter).

Kim:    Or maybe it [the water] just came up too quickly and you didn't have a chance to catch your breath?

Paula:    Yes. It could be, yes. Because right at the beginning I had this immediate response: 'Oh I want to do this, this is the one' – straight away – instead of saying 'OK it feels like the right one – let's just put it to one side a minute and let's check the other things out as well'. It's almost as if I jumped in at the deep end.

Kim:    …So are you glad you did some more?

Paula:    Yes. If I'd left it there I'd always have been angry, frustrated and felt cheated and for the wrong reasons. So having done that bit more, got my lifebelt, having stopped drowning, got out and done some more – I'm glad I did 'cos it's a much better piece of work and I'm proud of it.

## What leads to personal growth?

The conversations above show us glimpses of two women's experience of research that changed them as a person and as a counsellor. Aspects of a heuristic process that contribute to the depth of experience have been described as focusing; in-dwelling; making connections with body–mind experiences, tacit knowing and intuitions, images and felt-sense.

### Clearing a space for focusing

Before we can focus on something in-depth we need to make space in our lives. Rachel described the necessity of 'clearing a space' in which to focus on her research without distraction from her partner. Paula also comments on this in an unreported part of her tape. Moustakas describes this beginning phase as akin to the preparation made by an artist before embarking on creative work and says that until this is done the rest of the work cannot happen.

Douglass and Moustakas (1985) point out that we need time if we are to focus on an experience in order to identify qualities that are not fully conscious. As we reach deeply inside ourselves we can connect with creativity and originality and discover aspects of our experiences that are not yet verbalized, but rather known at a tacit level.

Ferguson, in the introduction to a revised version of Gendlin's work *Focusing* (1981) describes focusing as moving 'inward, drawing on information from the deeper, wiser self' that is held in a 'felt sense' within the body that involves 'whole brain knowing', connecting our left and right hemispheres and leading to a sense of release that accompanies a new understanding of something that was previously unclear. This seems to connect with Rachel's description of what happened when she began to focus on things that were 'on the periphery' and Paula's description of connections she was making on the edge of sleeping and waking early in the morning.

## Developing an internal frame of reference

All of this contributes to an internal dialogue with our selves, connecting us with the sources of our research question and enabling us to develop an internal frame of reference. Carl Rogers (1951) taught that when we experience empathic under-standing of our frame of reference this can lead to growth and change. When, as in heuristic inquiry, the researcher is both subject and object of the inquiry, through paying attention to tacit knowing, intuitions, images and felt-sense, we can experi-ence empathic understanding of our selves, by our selves, as well as empathically understanding our research participants.

Paula's increased ability to 'tune in' to herself and her clients seems to have occurred as a direct consequence of engaging in a heuristic process. Rachel, too, expresses how she came to know herself better through the process, gathering up parts of herself that she knew had always been there but not clearly connected to. Both women express an increased selfconfidence that stemmed from an increased trust in their ways of knowing and in their competence to work with clients.

The concept of 'in-dwelling' is a conscious and deliberate process that allows the researcher to follow clues, hunches and intuitive ideas, to examine the details contained within them and expand their meanings. This can lead to new insights and understandings.

## Transformation

Moustakas (1990, p.13) recognized the link between his research methods and personal growth:

> Through an unwavering and steady inward gaze and inner freedom to explore and accept *what is*, I am reaching into deeper and deeper regions of a human problem or experience and coming to know and understand its underlying dynamics and constituents more and more fully. The initial 'data' is within me; the challenge is to discover and explicate its nature. In the process, I am not only lifting out the essential meanings of an experience, but I am actually awakening and transforming my own self. Self-understanding and self-growth occur simul-taneously in heuristic discovery.

Reflecting on aspects of these conversations that explore the differences and simi-larities between personal growth that occurs through research, counsellor training or personal therapy, I noticed that Paula and Rachel both seemed to indicate that the research process had had the greatest impact on their growth. Both indicated that they were task-focused during counsellor training. Heuristic inquiry had provided them with a vehicle for self exploration that was also the 'task' (the research dissertation).

Rachel told me that while in therapy she had wanted to hand over the task of making connections to her therapist and was disappointed when that did not happen. During the research process she relied on *herself* to make the connections between all aspects of her experiences – experiencing *and* thinking as she wrote it down: 'there was no boundary between the two'.

## Balancing objectivity and subjectivity

By being both subject and object of her research, Paula experienced herself as therapist, client and researcher; she thought she was therefore more in control of whether or not, and when, she allowed herself to be 'triggered' into her own material. As it turned out she became 'flooded' with her own feelings and was unable to think. This kind of methodology has been criticized as encouraging self-indulgence and lack of objectivity. And it is clear from Paula's comments that she believed she had become *too* deeply immersed in her internal world and wondered with me if she had interpreted 'submersion' rather than 'immersion' as a necessary part of the process. Her second supervisor was able to lead her towards a more objective stance that grounded her, balancing her feelings with her thinking by inviting her to come 'up to the surface' and look around her, engaging her with the literature and suggesting that she re-focus *outside* her self. Gendlin (1981, p.165) observed:

> Focusing is not an invitation to drop thinking and just feel. That would leave our feelings unchanged. Focusing begins with that odd and little known 'felt sense', and then we think verbally, logically, or with image forms – but in such a way that the felt sense shifts… Thinking in the usual way, alone, can be objectively powerful, but when put into touch with what the body already knows and lives, it becomes vastly more powerful.

Researchers and supervisors need to understand that subjectivity is not an end in itself and that heurism invites us to filter our participants' experiences *through* our own, *not* to supplant their experiences with our own. It is clear from Paula's moving story of her relationship with her supervisor that if her first supervisor had had a greater understanding of the methodology she might have been able to throw Paula a 'lifeline' earlier in the process, before her personal material threatened to 'drown' her, and she may have been better able to keep her head above water throughout the powerful process in which she was engaged.

★     ★     ★     ★

This chapter set out to demonstrate how a research process can be a vehicle for personal and professional growth. My exploration provides a glimpse of the evidence that I have begun to accumulate on these issues. Several other participants have echoed these stories and indicate that growth was experienced as a result of undertaking research that required them: to create a space in their lives; to let go of structure and embark on a journey into the unknown; to reflect on self *and* others; and to move beyond cognitive processes into connecting with body, mind and spirit through exploring our felt-sense and tacit knowing. The parallels with good therapy are clear.

The underlying ontology (ways of viewing what is) and epistemology (ways of knowing) of heurism has been criticized as imprisoning the data, and its methods as aping realist approaches (Martin 2003). It has also been criticized for its inward focus that does not address 'the more outgoing dialogic and culturally embedded relationships between researcher and researched' (Speedy 2001). Heurism is a methodology of its time and as such it raises these issues in the light of developments since the 1990s when narrative and reflexive approaches have begun to proliferate. When used as part of a bricolage (as Rachel and Paula did) these issues can be addressed by examining the interfaces and tensions that are created between methodologies. Narrative methods invite us to examine our responses to the data in terms of culture, gender, history and context. Reflexivity encourages us to explore our own construction of identity in relation to the data, our participants and our selves and provides a bridge between our internal and external worlds.

My conversations with the two women graphically describe, through the powerful use of images, what it can be like to engage with a heuristic process. For both women the journey was difficult *and* rewarding, leaving them with a sense of having grown and developed personally and professionally. Through the process of research they were helped to re-collect (which is more than remembering) aspects of themselves that had not previously been known, thus increasing self-confidence and strengthening their connection with a sense of identity. I am left with questions for further exploration, questions such as: why is the research process more of a vehicle for personal development than personal therapy for some people; are people more likely to choose heuristic research because it is a safer way of facing personal issues than being with a therapist; and how are the changes people make in themselves during research the same or different from those made through counsellor training?

For some heuristic researchers it may be helpful and supportive to engage in personal therapy during the research as well as ensuring access to good supervision. If our research topic triggers us into unprocessed material of our own, not only might the quality of the research suffer but we, as researchers, might suffer too (as I learned to my own cost: Etherington 2001d). Ethical principles of 'non-maleficence' apply to researchers as well as participants (Etherington 2001a). Research is not a substitute for therapy, even though it can be therapeutic, just as counsellor training is not a substitute for personal counselling.

*Chapter 9*

# Keeping a Reflexive Research Journal

I realized that writing was private, that the paper would not snarl at me, frown at me, burst into tears, or be horrified. I could say what I liked, and unsay it, or say the opposite if I liked.

(Bolton 2003)

Journal writing has been recognized as an important aspect of qualitative research in general and reflexive research in particular. Usually we think of our journals as a private space in which we can log our uncensored thoughts and feeling about our lives, relationships, activities and interests. This kind of privacy allows us to explore, without inhibition, aspects of our selves that we might be reluctant to share with others. In this way we can create a coherent narrative that helps us to develop a sense of who we are, while still remaining uncertain and open to change.

Many training courses encourage counselling and psychotherapy students to use journal writing to monitor their growth and 'to develop their own "internal supervisor", extend and maintain awareness of self and others and continue to integrate all aspects of their learning from the course and outside it' (Johns 1996, p.90). So when counsellors become researchers their use of a journal may already have become part of their reflective practice.

## Noting our presence as researchers

Keeping a journal as part of reflexive research can help us to focus on our internal responses to being a researcher and to capture our changing and developing understanding of method and content. We reflect on our roles, on the impact of the research upon our personal and professional lives, on our relationships with participants, on our perception of the impact we may be making on *their* lives and on our negative and/or positive feelings about what is happening during the research process. We can capture our dreams that might inform the research even while sleeping, or poems that reflect the essence of something barely known to us and provide new insights, or conversations with colleagues about the research, or cartoons, drawings or doodles that represent events, people, or telephone conversations, photos of places or people that may have become part of our research journey – indeed anything that might be useful to reflect upon to inform our process or use as data. The journal can provide a means by which we can make the most of the complexities of our presence in the research setting, in a methodical and regular manner (Holliday 2002) or even in an unmethodical and irregular manner.

## Noting communication and bias

Using the private space of a journal to record and process our thoughts and/or feelings can enable us to 'clear' or free up our communications with participants if they become stuck. Unacknowledged negative thoughts and feelings may block our ability to hear participants clearly or may influence how we make sense of what we are hearing. On the other hand, being aware of our thoughts and feelings can help us to notice our biases. Ely *et al.* (1997, p.350) quote Jane Marsh, who asserts: 'A bias that we are aware of, a passion deeply felt, may be an entrée into the experience we are studying'. They go on to say: 'This is what Bernstein (1983) calls an "enabling", not a blinding bias. The difference between the two would seem to lie in self-awareness.' This seems to be a very good argument for writing a journal as a way of reflecting and processing our internal and external responses and behaviours.

## Writing our selves

Keeping a written historical record of our research can also help to free up our writing and provide a framework for the writing of a 'self-narrative' or a story about the writing process (Richardson 2000, p.941). Writing a journal can help us expand our vocabulary, our habits of thinking and train us to attend to our senses – what we see, hear, and sense in our bodies – all of which are needed for reflexive monitoring.

Sometimes we can engage participants as co-researchers through inviting them to keep a journal to capture *their* involvement with our study or as an ongoing method of data collection. Janesick (2000, p.392) refers to these as 'documentary tools' that may become part of an interactive communication. They might take the form of letters or emails between participants and researchers or maybe another form of interactive writing that contributes to co-constructed findings on the project (Etherington 2001b, 2002a, 2003).

An example of this kind of journal writing in research is reported in a book written by Irvin Yalom, a psychotherapist, and Ginny Elkin, his client (Yalom and Elkin 1974). Yalom invited his client, who was a writer experiencing writer's block, to journal her experience of each session immediately afterwards. He also kept a journal of each session, noting his feelings, thoughts and what was left unspoken. After six months of therapy they exchanged their journals and read what the other had written about the journey so far. Therapy then continued for a further six months while they continued to write.

Rich and multilayered stories emerged through these journals that served several purposes. They provided: a set of qualitative evaluative data about the therapy itself; a therapeutic tool, in that the practice of writing enabled the client to overcome her writer's block; by revealing themselves to each other through sharing the journals half way through the year, they reached a depth that might not otherwise have been achieved; and a book that became a tool that other therapists could use for their own learning.

For researchers who are similarly blocked about writing, the practice of journal writing can be a rehearsal for writing the final dissertation or research report.

## Catherine's journal

Catherine was an MSc student using heuristic inquiry to study the lived experience of mothers whose sons had been sexually abused. Her own sons were abused by a neighbour almost ten years before she began her study, and her desire to write a dissertation on this topic was fuelled by her recognition that although society now acknowledges more readily that there are thousands of abused children, the mothers are still 'hidden', through 'mother-blaming' discourses, shame, lack of services for their support and a mother's need to protect her child from further exposure and abuse. A mother who tells her story is also telling her child's story unless, like Catherine, she uses a pseudonym.

Catherine's journal became an important resource for processing her confused feelings, painful memories and thoughts as she progressed through her journey. It also became an important data source as she captured the heuristic process. She offered me parts of her journal for this book.

---

*Sunday 17 February 2002*

This is a time of inner conflict and questioning of the validity of my research topic. I am aware that through conversations with people, sermons, prayer, listening to tapes, radio programmes, etc. I am gradually recognizing and trusting my way forward.

*Saturday 23 February 2002*

Sister Susan led a quiet morning at church. I liked the tale she told of a man waiting eagerly to watch a butterfly leave its cocoon. It was a very slow process and therefore, to hurry the process up, he put the cocoon close to a lighted candle. It did quicken the process but when the butterfly emerged from its cocoon, its wings were not properly formed and so it could not fly. Similarly, we can short-cut our research process or we can allow the process to happen within us, giving it the time it deserves, enabling us to emerge at the right time.

*Saturday 2 March 2002*

I start my research journal today as I find myself in a place where I *know* that I am ready to start writing with clearer vision somehow. I feel peacefulness within, compared with the confusion, conflict and helplessness that I have been feeling. Moustakas (1990) describes this phase of heuristic research as 'initial engagement'.

I have been experiencing my whole being as if thrown into an unknown and unfamiliar turmoil. I was unable to articulate what was happening for me, both verbally and through writing. This felt distressing as my natural outlet is to write. I felt as if I was being tossed about by an unexpected and powerful wave. I felt overwhelmed with a sense of helplessness as, ravaged and thrown unforgivably, I felt unable to gain control and equilibrium; choking among the disturbed churned sand and salt water; being taken over until the force continued to its conclusion…and then calm. Calm and a sense of order eventually arrived, but even now the journey of discovery continues to be rather like that of a roller-coaster ride. The highs are exciting, exhilarating even, but the lows can bring confusion, self-doubt, panic, despair, and for me a time of wandering in the wilderness. My faith has been important to me throughout my research and was a key part in my decision whether to undertake my study or not.

*15 July 2002*

Where to start? To enter into a heuristic process feels like letting go of the tight grip that I endeavour to keep; letting loose my desperate clutch to the root of a tree as the river attempts to sweep me away in its powerful current. I let go and allow myself to be carried along on a journey into the unknown. Entering unfamiliar waters feels scary, uncomfortable and chaotic. I like order in my life; it helps me to feel safer somehow. But this process throws up disorder and yet is able to bring with it new discoveries, new insights. I experience frustration, confusion, excitement and satisfaction. It takes me a long time to feel able to trust in the process but I think that finally I *am* believing in it. As I reflect on my process so far, I recognize how necessary it has been for me to work through the issues that I have. I have immersed myself in my study, reading a wide range of books relating to my topic. My co-researcher's life becomes a part of my world and I produce a large quantity of creative writing in stanza form that attempts a re-telling of her lived experience.

*8 September 2002*

I believe that no amount of teaching and reading about the heuristic process could have prepared me for the *lived* experience. I am *in* the process and I am only now beginning to trust that 'not knowing' *is* OK! That was always difficult to accept. Have faith, the process unfolds naturally, without force and new discoveries are made. Letting go of control feels challenging but that is what I must do. I reflect on the pressure that I placed upon myself to *keep on* being immersed in my study, with no breaks.

However, my concerned husband persuades me to fly to Barcelona for five days. It feels a great relief to leave my research behind and visit the fantastic sights of Barcelona and spend time with him. The heuristic process is expensive in attention, time and energy and therefore understanding families and friends are essential!

*14 September 2002*

My trip to Barcelona provided me with an incubation period. I took the opportunity to invest my time and energy in other pursuits and interests and returned home feeling refreshed.

> During this incubation it is important to put the research aside and get on with other tasks in one's life. Physical activities can be a great help such as gardening, walking or cycling. It is important to trust these tacit processes. At such a time it can feel like one has accumulated a mass of data but is unable to make any sense of it. (West 2001, p.129)

Barcelona came at an appropriate time as I felt overloaded with thoughts, ideas, information, and felt confused regarding what to do with it all. On my return I felt resistant to indulge once more in my work. However, following a peer group meeting I experienced an overwhelming enthusiasm to immerse myself in my study once more.

*Saturday 12 October 2002*

Methodological process – IS THIS THE *'RIGHT'* WAY?

During my tutorial yesterday some of the haziness that has taken up residence in my mind became clearer. This was regarding my methodological process. Right from the beginning I have been recording my feelings in this journal: they range from complete despair to wonderful exaltation. However, I had not entirely grasped the relevance or value of them – how these entries would become part of my methodology in the final dissertation. It occurs to me that this might be how I capture 'tacit knowing'. Polanyi (1983) considers one type of tacit knowing is involved in the way we find our way in the dark. He says,

> ...for example – entering a theatre after a movie has begun. We grope in the darkness but then there are flashes of light. We 'feel' our way along, picking up subsidiary clues and combining them with our sense of the focal qualities of space, shadow and light. We develop a sense or meaning of where we are and thus are able to locate an empty seat.

There was a part of me that knew the value of my process but it was not until yesterday that the light went on – *illumination.* I recognized that *my* personal journey *is* a part of my methodology. I now feel somewhat puzzled that I had thought this was to be recorded yet bracketed off from the study.

I am in a heuristic process, I know this much! I am immersed in my study: it is my constant 'companion', if you can call it that! It has frequently felt more like an enemy. My feelings of confusion and disorder sit uncomfortably: it all feels such a mess! I strive to seek order and structure but there is none. To be reminded that this is expected, this is how it *should* be, comes as a huge relief. I'm aware that I constantly ask myself the question: 'Am I doing it *the right way?*' Whatever my process, that *is* the right way, *my* way. I re-enter my lonely bubble in which I become enveloped once more, oblivious to external interference. Moustakas (1990) recognizes that loneliness is, 'a capacity or source for new searching, awareness, and inspiration...when the outside world ceases to have a meaning' (p.92). Time vanishes as I get swept along allowing the process to take me over.

## An interruption to the Masters stage: what PhD students had to say about journal writing

During the period I was writing this book I invited a group of my PhD students to spend a day at my home during the summer break from university to share their learning and make contact with each other. I hoped they might find this supportive on their journey. Spontaneously they suggested that the conversations we had during the day could be taped and later gave me permission to include some of those conversations in this book. At one point early in the day the conversation turned to journal-keeping and Peter began by saying he had kept a journal for about 20 years.

Peter:    I love journals because I like having somebody intelligent to talk to who really understands me (laughter) but what I find is awful is that I only write it when I'm miserable or low or confused or…I mean I do force myself sometimes to say, 'had a lovely day' or something like that, but in my research journal… It's being afraid I'll lose the shape of what happened, because part of my research is *about* the process and when I've sorted something or it's no longer a problem, it just goes… I dictate it actually. I dictate it.

Ruth:     You dictate your journal?

Peter:    Yes, because I speak more easily than I write.

Kim:      I'm just wondering about the different purposes that journals serve.

Nell:     I didn't even call it a journal. I write every morning but it's just for me. It's a way of connecting with me…   And I just write. I just have a little notepad and I scrawl away and it's mostly incoherent and then – what I did until I met Kim was – after [filling] a few of these [notepads], half a dozen or something I chucked them away.

Kim:      I wept when she told me.

(laughter)

Nell:     Just the look on your face made me think 'I'll have to rethink this'. But it's illegible anyway. It's just me and it's not performative at all. I'm angry about the idea of it ever being performative. This is so much me: just clearly working through, hearing myself, slowing myself down, just taking the time. I think it's made a lot of difference to my life and I've made big changes in my life since I've done it. But since starting this PhD I've been trying to work with it differently. So instead of doing that, occasionally, particularly if what's going on for me is researching, I'll either write into the notepad and then maybe type up after-wards anything that's relevant from it, or now, a couple of times, I've even written it directly into my laptop – which is very different. And a little while ago for the first time I brought some [of it] to a narrative research group meeting here and shared it. People actually heard my morning writings for the first time – so it's been a whole process of going through, what does that mean and…

Ruth:      How did that feel?

Nell:      I don't know yet. It was about a month ago – maybe a bit more than that. I think I'm still processing what that means. It felt like a real big difference – valuable – and I think what I really want is to know how can I keep all those things going? Similarly with research – there's a real value in keeping hold of some of it – knowing what's relevant – and sharing what's relevant and getting the feedback from that. But there's also real value in having this daily practice that is actually a kind of a writing meditation. And I want to keep all of it and keep all of it going.

Ruth:      There's probably enough in that for a PhD alone! (shared laughter)

Nell:      I'll do it on that. 'Stuff interviews – I don't like transcription!' How about that? (Laughs)

Peter:     I discovered, when I was reading Daniel Stern's stuff on mothers' memory, it just kind of tweaked something inside me and I think – probably because I was a war baby – and for other reasons – that probably it just didn't happen, that reflexivity. I had two sons of my own and I've got quite a strong feminine side in me so I just naturally would mirror back. I didn't have to think about it, I just did it. And it seemed terribly important to me. And I think the diary for me probably does that, it kind of makes what I'm feeling real and gives me a way of making me visible. So when I lose touch and become mildly psychotic, just *reading* the diary, I find I've sunk back into myself, you know, whatever was in the diary.

Ruth:      I think I use mine differently. When I started this process I started writing a kind of online journal which was not daily, but sporadic… I feel like I've got two very distinct, separate voices: one's a kind of 'academic' voice (I call it like my Meccano set voice – hammers ideas together) and then there's this much more emotional, experiential one. And so when I really lose confidence, a way of getting back in touch with myself is to write a more fluent one. But I have a critical voice in that too. It will come in every so often, saying: 'Well, what's the point in this?' or 'This is just avoiding doing what you should be doing.' So I don't use it all the time. But I still go back to it.

           But what I have found that I've really loved doing (and this is relatively new) is including bits and pieces, playing around in a very scrawly way, creatively with ideas and so on, and I don't feel my critic comes into this bit. So I put dreams in it, but also things I need to do to get finished on time, which of course I break all the time…

           I read that one last night and I thought 'Well, I've already broken four of those!' So I have to keep using it as a way of disciplining myself. But I use the other one much more than this one (takes her journal from her bag): this one is about thinking multi-dimensionally, and knowing I've got a very bad memory, and if I don't jot down a concept I'll not remember I've ever read the thing. Whereas if I have a metaphor I'll be able to remember 'oh yes that's in that article'.

Kim:       So what's the other one?

Ruth:    The other one's much more…it's written in sentences. It's written with an emotional theme in it, whereas this one here is just…there might be little bits of 'Where am I now in the process?' but it's mostly becoming [a place where I make notes] – things I've just read on postmodernism. It's like it's a map of my mind.

Viv:    Mine started out as [a place to record]…some concept that I wanted to remember or something that just clicked for me. But it's very jumbled. It's an odd mixture of things that I've read or ideas that I get from say watching something on television or reading in a paper, but it's also *a space* where, in the writing process, I discover things. So I start off with some kind of intuition, but actually in the writing more will come out of it than I had known before I started to write: so it's a space where I discover things.

        But it's also quite chaotic. It's like a file with scraps of bits of paper in, and even if I sometimes copy the things that I've jotted down on bits of paper into there, I still hang on to the bits of paper because I want them in their original form and with the feeling that went with them, and somehow that is in the writing itself. So I have thought of copying them neatly in a systematic way into it, and occasionally I do transfer things that I don't want to lose, but I've got a file packed with pieces, scraps of paper, different shapes and colours, that represents the kind of chaos of what I actually feel a lot of the time. This (she holds up a book) is probably a little more systematic and it's probably a little more legible.

Kim:    I'm very envious of you all having these journals because actually I've got about three, but I hardly ever use any of them. That's not entirely true – but I don't do it in any systematic way. Backs of envelopes are just as likely for me to be where I'll capture things. And they're all over the place, and every now and again I'll come across one or… What I generally tend to write down are dreams, or images, I capture those, but not necessarily all in one place.

Ruth:    Is it important for you that they aren't actually gathered together?

Kim:    I haven't really thought about it, but I do know I've got a journal beside my bed and I've got another one in my office. Actually I read the one in my office the other day. I wrote some stuff in it many, many years ago, that's really quite interesting to read now (for this research project). But I don't sit down to write in my journal, I'll write on screen. I'll open up and think 'Where am I in this process?' and then I'll just put something in. But not regularly, just when the spirit moves me. It hasn't become a discipline and yet it's one that I value, I don't understand why. I haven't thought about not doing that or doing it, it's just the way it is.

As I reflected back over this conversation I marvelled at the many and varied purposes of journal-keeping named by the group and I have listed them below as they appear in the PhD students' dialogue.

Practical purposes:

- to 'jot down a concept'
- to keep notes on 'things that I've read or ideas'
- 'things I need to do'
- 'as a way of disciplining myself'
- 'thinking multi-dimensionally'
- 'I put dreams in it'.

Creative purposes:

- 'playing around in a very scrawly way, creatively with ideas'
- 'a space where, in the writing process, I discover things'

Self purposes:

- 'makes what I'm feeling real and gives me a way of making me visible'
- 'little bits of where am I now in the process?'
- 'a way of getting back in touch with myself'
- 'working through, hearing myself, slowing myself down'
- 'a way of connecting with me'

Metaphoric symbolisations:

- 'a kind of writing meditation'
- 'having somebody intelligent to talk to who really understands me'
- 'represents the kind of chaos of what I actually feel'
- 'it's like it's a map of my mind'

## 'If I have a metaphor I'll be able to remember'

Several of the group spoke about using very spontaneous approaches to their journals to capture their ideas through the use of metaphors. Metaphor has been described as 'the magic wand that enables pattern to be communicated' (Williams 1999, p.20). Through the use of metaphor we can communicate what is abstract – that which we perceive or know (tacitly or intuitively) but for which we have no direct translation into words.

When we capture images or metaphors through our journal writing we can use them to remind us not only of the facts but also of the feelings and felt senses that surround them. Metaphors and images act as bridges between sensory processes, cognition and feelings, thus connecting us with ourselves (and others) on many levels. Metaphors activate a series of psychological associations and start the mind working at an unconscious level, without the paralysing interference of conscious thought. This can open up a space that has special value because metaphor represents the language of the right brain, and allows us to expand into the unknown part of ourselves to connect with 'gifts not yet exploited' (Godin and Ooghhourlian 1994, p.189).

★    ★    ★    ★

In this chapter I have explored the different ways of using journals in research and their importance, particularly in reflexive research, as a tool for making the impact of our presence in the 'field' conscious and transparent. I have shown a portion of a heuristic researcher's journal that became part of her data and how that clearly captures the essence of her process over several months.

The group conversation highlights the many different ways of using journals, and the point that there is no right or wrong way. We all have our own ideas and practices that range from the practical to the creative, and many aspects of ourselves can find their way onto those pages. Some of those aspects have been captured through highlighting the purposes described and the metaphors used by members of the group.

*Chapter 10*

# Autoethnography

In using oneself as an ethnographic exemplar, the researcher is freed from the traditional conventions of writing. One's unique voicing – complete with colloquialisms, reverberations from multiple relationships, and emotional expressiveness – is honoured. In this way the reader gains a sense of the writer as a full human being.

(Gergen and Gergen 2002, p.14)

On the final day of the research training unit for which I am a tutor, students who have completed their dissertations present some aspect of their work to others, including their peers, prospective students who may be currently at an earlier stage of training, and staff members. This gives them an opportunity to experience something akin to a conference presentation but in a familiar and informal (and perhaps less frightening) environment. It is an essential part of their training as a researcher. They are invited to choose their topic, perhaps taking one small part of their research, and to be as creative as they like during a half-hour slot.

Back in 2001 Mel, a student who had undertaken an auotethnographic study (Rees 2001) asked me to play a taped farewell message to her peers on the final day of the course. As a result of her research she had decided to spend a year travelling the world and by then she had left on her journey. The tape captures her research experience so well that I asked if we could use it to give the new cohort of students a sense of what could happen. I present the contents of the tape below (with her permission), while recognizing that, although it is a rich depiction of her 'lived experience', it lacks the full power of the impact of hearing Mel's voice, her inflections and pauses, the lilt of her musical accent and the fast pace of her speech. The written words are not everything.

I want to begin by apologizing for my absence – I wanted to be there on the last day but my life is heading in another direction at the moment and so I'm off on my travels and I'll probably be in India when this tape is played. However, I want to offer something to the group in terms of my research project and particularly the reflexive process which has, to a large extent, helped me follow my dream now.

As most of you are already aware, the focus of my research changed several times during the first few months so that it wasn't until May that I decided on my final title: *The Rainbow Journey: An Autoethnography of Personal Growth Through Addiction Recovery and Becoming a Counsellor.* Initially the topics I considered were related to my work with drug addicts, thinking I could combine qualitative and quantitative research methods, something I thought would be required to meet the academic standards for an MSc. I believed that to achieve credibility it was important to produce some statistics or comparative data whereby I could address the issues around reliability and credibility.

As I engaged in the research process I followed the six stages of the heuristic cycle and entered a period of immersion. I looked within myself to see how my own experience of addiction and recovery related to the research I was then contemplating with clients. This was of interest although it didn't inspire me. As I looked within I found myself asking: how did I get to where I am today? How did I achieve and sustain recovery?

As I searched for answers I felt a strong shift in my energies, a new enthusiasm that I had not felt before – one that compelled me to look further. Being in that place – within – felt far more congruent with where I was on my life's journey. I didn't want to externalize and intellectualize everything any more. I needed to be true to my feelings and felt that if I couldn't be, then maybe it was not the right time to be undertaking an MSc in counselling research. Then I remembered something that Jane said to the group back in April, something along the lines of, 'If anyone doesn't want to actually go out and conduct research [on other people] that may be OK too'. So I didn't go 'out there'; I went 'in' instead.

After talking this through in a tutorial with Kim I decided to tell my story of addiction and recovery and the story of my personal growth through counsellor training, believing the two to be inextricably linked. I wanted, and needed, to tell my story. I felt that it would help me to gain a better understanding of what I'd come through, and that an autoethnography could help me to write the final chapter in my story of addiction and thus achieve further closure.

However, I was concerned that I might be labelled 'self-indulgent', so I had to balance this with any potential benefit for others. I believed that this would be the case because my story might help others to gain insights into drug addiction and recovery, as well as highlighting the personal growth possible through counsellor training.

I didn't know what my story would be until I wrote it. At first I thought the main focus would be on becoming a counsellor; then, that it would be about the nature of my addiction; and yet again, that it would be about my recovery. My focus kept shifting, but in the end I couldn't plan it; I just had to feel it and write it, trusting what I wrote would ultimately reveal where any emphasis lay.

After I had written my story I was quite surprised to see that the emphasis was not on any of the aforementioned issues – yet it was also on *all* of them. Though I leave it to others who read it to make their own interpretations, mine was that, underpinning my journey of addiction, recovery and counselling training, was what I realized became the core theme of my search for meaning and the importance of spirituality in my life. It has made me realize that I am still searching and that this is the most important thing for me. And that is why I am off travelling. I don't expect to find answers in the places I see nor in the people I meet – I know they lie within me. But it is so hard to find the quality of time I need for my search while I am so caught up in the business. I need some time out.

Counsellor training, and undertaking this research, have both shown me how important it is for me to be congruent with my values and beliefs. I'm so glad this has been brought into my awareness. I don't have to compromise myself anymore; I can be true to my heart, mind and soul.

I have to say that the reflexive process has not always been an easy one. Fortunately at the outset I recognized this may be the case so I engaged in counselling as a client for the duration of my research. It has been important to have this safety net, as well as the other support I have received on the MSc course, especially from tutors and peers.

At times I felt like I was going mad. I looked so deep, and for so long, that my head felt like fried spaghetti. I think my style of reading had a lot to do with this for I'm the sort of person who can read a book and it can change my life. I used to swallow books whole, fact or fiction: they could massively impact upon my life. An example of how this had a negative effect on me was on reading a book by Karen Horney called *Neurosis and Human Growth*. After a couple of chapters I convinced myself I was completely neurotic and almost convinced myself that I needed to have a nervous breakdown!

As result of the research process I have now learnt a new style of reading whereby I look more critically at what I'm reading: not just taking it all in but being a lot more discriminating. I realize now that some books are not good for me personally – or the time isn't right for me to read them. So I now know when it's time to put them down and stop reading. I've learned a lot through this research: academically, professionally and, most of all, personally. It has been an incredible upward, inward and outward spiral of growth. It has been the catalyst which has propelled me forward on another leg of my journey: physically, emotionally and spiritually.

I hope others may reap similar rewards and I wish you all the very best for the future. Take care.

*Lots of love, Mel*

During Mel's journey around the world she kept in touch with me through email, from internet cafes, friends' computers and public libraries. As I was writing this I re-read those emails with message headings that read: An incredible day!; Hi!; Bye from NZ; Back on land; An interesting stay in Bali. Along with stories of swimming with dolphins, pot-holing, meeting new friends, one of her messages was about thinking about doing a PhD when she returned. Out there in the world her researcher self was still alive and kicking.

## What is autoethnography?

Autoethnography is an autobiographical genre of writing and research that has been described as a 'blend of ethnography and autobiographical writing that incorporates elements of one's own life experience when writing about others' (Scott-Hoy 2002, p.276); a form of self-narrative that places the self within a social context (Reed-Danahay 1997). Autoethnography is a word that describes both a method and a text.

Ellis and Bochner (2000, p.739) describe the process of how researchers create autoethnography:

> As they zoom backward and forward, inward and outward, distinctions between the personal and the cultural become blurred, sometimes beyond distinct recognition. Usually written in the first-person voice, autoethnographic texts appear in a variety of forms – short stories, poetry, fiction, novels, photographic essays, personal essays, journals, fragmented and layered writing, and social science prose. In these texts, concrete action, dialogue, emotion, embodiment, spirituality, and self-consciousness are featured, appearing as relational and institutional stories affected by our history, social structure, and culture, which themselves are dialectically revealed *through action, feeling, thought, and language.*

Ethnography, has traditionally focused on the 'other' as an object of study, typically spending time observing people in other cultures and societies, but in more recent times, influenced by feminism, postmodernism and an increasing understanding of the role of researcher reflexivity, experimental methods have been proliferating among sociologists, anthropologists and more generally across disciplines such as communication studies, psychology, women's studies, management and organizational studies, theatre studies, literature, health sciences, education and sports science (Bochner and Ellis 2002; Ellis and Bochner 1996).

Ethnography places an emphasis on exploring the nature of particular social phenomena, and increasingly in more recent times, working primarily with unstructured data, investigating small numbers of cases (maybe even a single case) in depth and detail. This may be followed by interpretation of the meanings of the data and critical reflections upon the purposes and motivations of social actions (Atkinson and Hammersely 1998). These studies might be represented in a variety of creative ways, including art, photography and other audio and visual means, or performed through poetics, stories, theatrical and dramatic presentations (Bochner and Ellis 2002; Ellis 1995; Ellis and Bochner 1996; Ronai 1995).

Bringing the 'self' (auto) into the field of ethnography has attracted counselling and psychotherapy researchers and practitioners, who are increasingly using autoethnography (Cooper 2001; Etherington 2000, 2003; Karma 2003; Kneeshaw 2000; Law 2002; Rees 2001).

As counsellors and psychotherapists we have been taught to think about the cultures and family systems within which clients operate. Likewise we have been trained to examine how our own culture and family systems impact on our life stories and on our relationships with others. However, autoethnography does not merely require us to explore the interface between culture and self; it requires us to *write* about ourselves.

In the world of psychological therapies a tension exists about self-disclosure that is related to the philosophical and theoretical beliefs that underpin approaches to training. Traditionally, psychoanalytical and psychodynamic therapists do not disclose themselves to their clients, except perhaps in terms of transference or counter-transference, whereas those trained in humanistic approaches would see self-disclosure as part of being more present in the real relationship with their clients, characterized by congruence – a value espoused by person-centred and humanistic therapists. As a therapist who was trained in a humanistic model based on person-centred philosophies, and who increasingly uses narrative approaches (Etherington 2000) to assist clients to tell and re-tell their stories, I use self-disclosure when assisting in the co-construction of the preferred stories sought by those who consult me (Freedman and Combs 1996; White and Epston 1990). As I listen to the stories they tell, I make my responses to their stories available to them in a way that can enrich the therapeutic endeavour and become an integral part of 'mutual creative meaning-making' (Shaw 2003, p.59).

Autoethnography therefore feels a familiar and useful way of conducting research, and has provided a methodology that legitimizes and encourages the inclusion of the researcher's self and culture, as an ethical and politically sound approach that takes into consideration 'the complex interplay of our own personal biography, power and status, interactions with participants, and written word' (Rossman and Sallis 1998, p.67).

## Challenges to autoethnographers

However, autoethnography has its critics, some of whom have vociferously attacked the methodology as self-indulgent, solipsistic and narcissistic – criticisms that have given rise to articulate and persuasive challenges to these attitudes and credible disputations of those points of view (Mykhalovskiy 1997; Picart 2002; Sparkes 2002), while also recognizing the potential for autoethnography to fit all of those descriptions if the researcher approaches the methodology without understanding its purposes sufficiently, their own motivations or without the skills to ensure that the outcome is of aesthetic, personal, social and academic value (personal communication with Jane Speedy).

From a slightly different perspective Janice Morse criticizes and questions the ethics of autoethnography in an editorial of *Qualitative Health Research* (2000, p.1159), saying:

> With due respect to autoethnography, I usually discourage students from writing about their own experience. There are many reasons for this. First, the narrative is rarely their own. It includes information about others who are, by association, recognizable, even if their names have been changed. As such, writing about others violates anonymity. If these 'others' do not know about the article, it still violates their rights, for they have not given their permission and they do not have the right of withdrawal or refusal the informed consent provides.

These issues are raised earlier in this book when I discuss Catherine's work on being the mother of sexually abused boys (Chapter 7). Caroline Ellis also addresses these concerns in her paper about her relationship with her mother (Ellis 2001), showing the complex ethical struggles that arise when using autoethnography. As she struggles with these issues she concludes:

> You have to live the experience of doing research on the other, think it through, improvise, write and re-write, anticipate and feel its consequences. In the best of situations, all of you feel better at the end.

She acknowledges the muddle created by trying to decide

> what it means to ask and give permission to write about others. This muddle, however, is closer to the truth of my experience than a contrived clarity based on prescribed rules would be. And for me, that's good enough for now' (p.615).

In my own view, a major ethical requirement is that we make our attempts and struggles transparent in just the way that Caroline has.

Perhaps the simplest way to provide anonymity for family members, or those close to us who might be recognizable in our personal stories, is for the author to use a pseudonym. However, in academic circles this disadvantages authors who cannot then be credited for their work – work that is sometimes relied upon for tenure or promotion. Neither can they present their work at conferences. Indeed it may be only from a position of the 'safety' of an established career that this kind of writing can be undertaken without fearing these costs and, even then, the fear for reputation can impede the ability to be open about ourselves (Bond 2002).

Kathryn Church, in speaking directly to professors of sociology during a conference discussion on autoethnography, and reported by Flemons and Green (2002) in Bochner and Ellis (2002), addresses these points:

> I think tenured professors are the ones who need to be assuming the position of vulnerability and writing difficult stories. I myself wrote an autoethnographic tale about a breakdown experience, and I think there has been a tangible cost to me in writing that tale as a person who has not succeeded in making entry into a university position, who has not been legitimated in those ways that you already are. I think there is a direct link between the telling of that tale and the outcome in terms of my personal and professional life. So, those risks I think we need to lay on the table. My purpose in writing a breakdown experience as a social science text is to socialize the experience and to help people understand that what it is that I have lived through is not just me, it is profoundly social, it is common, it is always among us. And this is why the risk is so important. (p.167)

It seems there is a real risk that others might pathologize us if we expose our vulnerabilities in writing and research. My own experience of writing about my self in my research has been personally enriching, even though I may have been pathologized (see Jim's comments in Chapter 2). Alongside that, feedback from others has been affirming and encouraging, and certainly not pathologizing. I know that writing in this way has changed my sense of the experiences I have written about and strengthened me in the process. However, it is also true to say that I did not take those risks until I had achieved a PhD and reached a stage in my life and career when the risk seemed less important than the value of being known for who I really am.

## Personal responses to writing and publishing autoethnography

Taking the point made above about the cost to academics of writing under a pseudonym, the cost can also feel profound for non-academics, as the following story shows.

In 2003 I edited a collective autoethnography, written mainly by therapists, including myself. Those stories became a narrative inquiry into *Trauma, the Body and Transformation* (Etherington 2003). Each contributor volunteered their story in response to my advertisement that asked for contributors who: (a) could write well; (b) had had some form of childhood trauma that had been experienced in some way in their bodies; and (c) had found ways of transforming their bodily experiences.

I carefully guided authors through the process of informed consent, including an invitation to use a pseudonym, pointing out that, in telling their stories, they would inevitably be telling the stories of others who were involved with them. Having considered the ethical issues, all but one author decided to use their own names. Once the book was published I invited them to give me feedback on their experience of writing and of seeing their stories in print. The person who had used a pseudonym – Ginny Mayhew (2003) – wrote:

> I think I have written to you before about the amount of stuff that was brought up for me during and after writing my chapter. Old stuff revisited and new stuff revealed. But what has been a major impact for me has been the use of my pseudonym.
>
> As soon as I realized I could not hold out any longer, that the book was to be sent off, I had a feeling of dread, anger, sadness. I'm not sure but it's a familiar feeling for me: one of not having done my best. I think, too, the help you gave me at the end was so useful I kicked myself for not asking for more at an earlier stage.
>
> I think a lot of my feeling had to do with my relationship, in that I was afraid of upsetting my husband. I asked him to read my story and to help me. He was an English teacher and I had heard him help my daughter with her essays, as to ways of composing and putting things, so I was a bit thrown when he only corrected my work grammatically.
>
> When I thought about it, I wondered whether he was feeling upset, vulnerable, jealous (he tried writing himself when he retired). I just knew he was not 100 per cent in favour. So I decided to use a pseudonym. As soon as I did that it felt wrong, and when the book went off to press I knew I didn't like the idea. I thought of asking to have it changed but I had already caused you enough delay and hassle so I didn't.
>
> When the book arrived I just didn't want to know. I didn't open it for several days and I haven't re-read my story. I no longer felt it was true. It could just have easily been made up. So far I haven't let anyone read it.

I have since spoken to my husband about my feelings. He said he was proud of me but had felt relieved when I used a pseudonym.

So that's where I am at the moment. I have now purchased ten copies of the book but what I shall do with them remains to be seen.

Sorry to be a bit of a wet blanket. My feelings have nothing to do with the book as a whole. I think it a great credit to you and I do hope it will be successful.

*Ginny*

I replied:

Thank you very much Ginny. I can quite understand what you are saying. You would, no doubt, have a different, but maybe equally huge reaction if you HAD used your name. Who knows? If the book goes into a second printing we could ask for your real name to be used if you want that.

I'll keep in touch and show you whatever I write about the process before using it. I hope some day you'll feel proud and good about it.

*Kim*

⋆　　⋆　　⋆　　⋆

Dear Kim

Thanks for the feedback. I purportedly used a pseudonym for my husband's sake so I was surprised when he told me he doesn't want me to show it to my family of origin. This leaves me with mixed feelings of shame and injustice.

Then your offer to change my name for a second printing surprised me and helped me to be in touch with other feelings – something about fearing standing out, of being front stage. Not sure I could take it on. And I recognize that as a pattern I have followed all my life.

Heigh-ho, I need more therapy I guess!

*Ginny*

⋆　　⋆　　⋆　　⋆

## Collective autoethnography

Ginny's story was part of a 'collective story' (Richardson 1990) that has the potential to transform the reader as well as the writer, and to challenge societal and individual attitudes. Sparkes (1998, p.78) suggests that, in presenting individual stories, we create a challenge to the limitations of available narrative by providing new narratives, that on hearing them, legitimates the re-plotting of one's own life. Likewise, collective stories also have transformative possibilities at a socio-cultural level.

My own intention in creating a collection of autoethnographic stories was to *amplify* the individual voices of those who had found ways to transform their bodily expressions of trauma; to help draw attention to stories not yet told; to create the possibility of making previously unrecognized connections; and to create a sense of community, thus breaking through the sense of isolation and alienation that is frequently experienced as an aftermath of childhood trauma. I also hoped that the stories would in some way inform medical practitioners and open their hearts and minds to the need for them to listen to patients whose underlying trauma was being expressed through bodily symptoms and to understand how they might use their power to create alternative services, thus challenging the restricting influence of western medical thinking.

However, I was not entirely convinced that my presentation of these stories would be taken seriously by those in positions of power within the medical community, so it was with great delight that I read the following email from a colleague in Cambridge who was working with medical students:

> It [the book] certainly set me thinking about my experiences which are manifold of hypochondriachal pain for which western medicine finds no pathology, so thanks for that…I wanted to be able to recommend it to the medical students, and I may, but I'm not sure if they will be able to engage with it at their age and stage.

I responded:

> Thank you for your feedback on the book. I hope your doctors *will* read it – it would have helped me (and all of us) if *our* doctors had read something of the sort – maybe saved many years of suffering too.

My friend's response some weeks later was:

> It is now in the departmental library at Cambridge University!

## Autoethnography as healing stories

Writing about aspects of our lives can become a healing endeavour (whether for research purposes or otherwise) that strengthens our connections with our body, mind and spirit through sharing our experiences and newly discovered self-knowledge (Bolton 1999; Bolton *et al.* 2003; Etherington 2003; Hunt 2000; Hunt and Sampson 1998). We know that writing stories of traumatic experience has been shown to produce physiological changes that contribute to gains in health and feelings of well-being (Harber and Pennebaker 1992; Herman 1992; Pennebaker 1988, 1993).

Writing stimulates and facilitates the motor and sensory regions of the brain, and can help us recover additional fragments of former experiences (Penn 2001). Half-known aspects of our selves can be accessed through the metaphors we use in our writing as we 'reach intuitively into some part of ourselves that is outside our notice – still unnamed but there' (Penn 2001, p.45). In telling our stories we are also re-affirming and re-educating our selves, our experiences and our lives and creating new stories.

Writing autoethnography involves us in a kind of 'recollection', which is more than remembering. It is:

> …remembering from the viewpoint of a fresh perspective… It is an opportunity to rewrite the family history by giving a different outcome, to recapture the original self (the acorn) and to reinvent the mature self and its culture. (Zohar and Marshall 2000, p.186)

We tell different stories for different purposes, and at different times, for different audiences. Sometimes these differences are blurred, and something written for one purpose may serve unexpected and altogether different needs that we may have held outside our immediate awareness. However, it is important in research that we remain focused on our main purposes, even though other issues may emerge that attempt to divert us. Janice Morse (2000, p.1159) describes this as a kind of 'conceptual broadsiding' that occurs when personal experiences derail the inquiry, unwittingly moving the research away from its focus. However, sometimes when this happens the researcher might choose to change the focus of the study, with all the additional work that this involves, recognizing through the process that a more important topic has emerged and can now be followed. These new topics, arrived at through an heuristic process and leading to deep connections with the researcher's own life, can become the most fruitful pathway towards healing and transformation (see Mel's story at the beginning of this chapter and my conversation with Liz in Chapter 7).

## Autoethnography as witness

Arthur Frank (1995) suggests that in order to reclaim our 'selves' (that might have been lost through illness or trauma) we need to make our selves available as an audience to our self-story (p.65). 'Reflexive monitoring is the perpetual readjustment of past and present to create and sustain a good story.' In the process of paying attention to our history and experiences while writing autoethnography, we may enter into a creative process that helps us remember and re-collect aspects of our experiences that may have been known tacitly or intuitively without knowing *how* we know. Frank sees these kinds of stories as 'a moral opportunity to set right what was done wrong or incompletely' (p.132). The research enables us to 'speak' of events that may have silenced us when they were happening, thus bearing witness or giving testimony.

When we give testimony to experience through writing our stories, we bear witness to the past and challenge the idea that terrible experiences are too awful to be told (Frank 1995). We also create a possibility for change and a better future.

Although there have been other stories that bear witness to the suffering caused by the holocaust, Ruth Barnett's story in *Trauma, the Body and Transformation* (Etherington 2003) is a glimpse of the kind of story that is less often heard, a story of someone who *escaped* from Germany during the war. Hers is a story that bears witness and gives testimony to her experiences of being brought to the UK to escape the Nazi regime in 1939 and of her subsequent fostering as a small girl of four with her seven-year-old brother. She responded to my question about the impact on her of writing her story and seeing it in print:

It certainly did impact! But it was not the first time of writing my story. I wrote several versions before, starting with the 1989 Reunion of Kindertransporte when Bertha (our 'mother hen'!) asked us to send our stories for an anthology she intended to publish – and she did. Since then I have written several versions for different books or articles and I include bits of my story in papers I give now. I think the nub is in the 'bits'. Which bit of my story am I going to tell? I am conscious of this question each time I go into a school as a 'live witness' to tell and discuss my story with children and teachers. Which bits will they want to hear? Be able to hear? Benefit from asking questions about and discussing?

You asked for something new, focusing on trauma expressed through the body. This was something I had neglected. Although I was aware of psychosomatic aspects in my work, I did not really apply this to myself. I had a mental image of myself as being a very healthy kid throughout my childhood. Right now I have the thought that this 'no serious illnesses happened to me' parallels my pre-story image of 'nothing happened to me because I was rescued'.

I wondered whether I actually had a story that could fit your book, and that's why I started with 'nothing actually happened to me'. I made notes on what illness and body manifestations of distress I could remember and astonished myself with memories I had not called upon for years. I read through some of my old diaries and was surprised at the number of days I had off school with colds, headaches and tummy aches – classical psychosomatic communications which of course no-one picked up!

Yes, the effect of writing my chapter for your book was to extend the details of my story. This reclaiming of memory and filling out my story has been going on for 14 years since 1989 and I don't think it will stop.

*All the best, Ruth.*

## Validity, reliability and truth

Autoethnography and other postmodern research texts 'trouble' familiar rules for judging the quality of research. Laurel Richardson (2000, p.934) has suggested that we need to find 'deliberately transgressive' ways to judge quality that are commensurate with ways of knowing that underpin qualitative research methodologies. She suggests that we change the central image normally used to measure validity, reliability and truth (the triangle, i.e. triangulation) and use instead the image of a crystal:

> Crystals grow, change, alter, but are not amorphous. Crystals are prisms that reflect externalities *and* refract within themselves, creating different colours, patterns, and arrays casting off in different directions. What we see depends upon our angle of repose. Not triangulation, crystallization… Crystallization, without losing structure, deconstructs the traditional idea of 'validity' (we feel how there is no single truth, we see how texts validate themselves); and crystallization provides us with a deepened, complex, thoroughly partial understanding of the topic. Paradoxically we know more and doubt what we know. Ingeniously, we know there is always more to know.

She goes on to list the criteria she uses when reviewing social science papers for publication and I have adapted these below:

- *Does the work make a substantive contribution* to my understanding of social life? Does the writer demonstrate a deeply grounded social science perspective and demonstrate how it is used to inform the text?

- *Does the work have aesthetic merit?* Does the writer uses analysis to open up the text and invite interpretive responses? Is it artistically shaped, satisfying, complex and interesting?

- *Is the work reflexive enough* to make the author sufficiently visible for me to make judgements about the point of view? Does the author provide me with evidence of knowledge of postmodern epistemologies that convinces me of their understanding of what is involved in telling people's lives? Am I informed how the author came to write the work and how the information was gathered? Have the complexities of ethical issues been understood and addressed? Does the author show themselves to be accountable to the standards for knowing and telling participants' stories?

- *What is the impact of this work on me?* Does it affect me emotionally, intellectually, generate new questions, move me to write or respond in any other way?

- *Does the work provide me with a sense of 'lived experience'?* Does it seem to be a truthful, credible account of cultural, social, individual or communal sense of what is 'real'?

As each of us struggles to write this kind of research we will no doubt go on adding to these ideas, recognizing that as we learn from each other's experiences, there will be new stories of validity to be told.

I notice that more and more researchers and authors invite responses from their readers. Perhaps we are coming to recognize that the value of autoethnographic writing can best be known when we hear the responses of those who read it as they resonate with what is written from a place of recognition within themselves. One such reader responded to *Trauma, the Body and Transformation* by email saying:

---

Hi Kim,

I didn't get showered and dressed on Saturday until 2.30 p.m. (when my grandchildren arrived), and yesterday (Sunday) it was nearly 4.00 p.m. – I couldn't put the book down until I had finished it! It was disturbing, sad, inspirational, but for me certainly the most gripping aspect of it was the gift of learning that was on every page. I thank you and the other authors for sharing your painful learning with me.

Each story was so well written – I could only stop to eat or drink or go to the loo at the end of each story. I was so held by each person's story that to put the book down mid-story would have felt abusive and disrespectful.

I was enlightened and encouraged by the wonderful diversity of their pathways to transformation and at the empowerment their pathways created but I despaired at times when I thought about how those pained, wounded children and adults had lived for so long with their unbearable hidden hurt. I felt breathless with fear and cried for them (and for me) as they excruciatingly identified the source of their pain. Later in their stories I shed tears at their agony as they worked through their painstaking release from the torments and fears of the past.

I marvel at the resilience and courage of all the authors who acknowledged and confronted the unhappiness and devastation of their childhood experiences and worked their way through to a healthier self. I'm sure there are happenings in the stories that will resonate for many people as they have done for me.

I took comfort from the way that, despite or through their pain, all the authors have come to a place of giving without bitterness, where the cycle of pain is not perpetuated. Instead they and you offer hope for future generations by the caring, giving work you all do.

Thank you Kim (and your fellow authors). The book is wonderful!

*Marie*

---

Braud's work (1998, p.219) encourages me to read her response not only as a powerful and personal response from a fellow human being but also as an affirmation of the validity of that work:

> When feelings of excitement, surprise, and delight are supplemented by feelings of awe and gratitude, researchers can be assured that they are being true to the experiences that are being explored and that their approach and findings are valid.

In the following chapter you can examine your own responses to one woman's autoethnography in relation to the criteria for validity that I have outlined above.

*Chapter 11*

# Using Creativity in Autoethnography

The new experiential research…is similar to some contemporary art…in which the artist's life becomes the work of art.

(McLeod 2001, p.154)

The story contained within this chapter is an autoethnographic account of becoming a reflexive researcher written by Sue Law whose Masters dissertation was based on a personal journey. Sue called her study: *Hope, Hell and Highwater: an autoethnographical journey from addiction to recovery* (Law 2002).

Sue is an artist and a counsellor, both aspects of herself that she was able to call upon in creating her study, in which she used painting and poetry to depict her powerful and illuminating stories.

## Art as a mode of inquiry

By creating paintings that depicted her journey, Sue provided tangible represen-tations of her experience with which we as 'audience' were able to interact at levels beyond that reached by the written word alone. Creative depictions give data a life and dimension that convey the visual, intellectual, bodily and emotional qualities of the experiences being studied. Sue's paintings reached me on a visceral level, the colours, shapes, forms and the movements all portraying her passage through the darkest parts of her life and out again into the light of her life today. Others too have described art 'as embodied inquiry – sensuous, emotional, intimate' (Bochner and Ellis 2003).

> To use art as a mode of narrative inquiry was to move towards a new research paradigm in which ideas became as important as forms, the viewers perceptions as important as the artist's intentions, the language and emotions of art as important as its aesthetic qualities. The product of research, whether an article, a graph, a poem, a story, or play, a dance, or a painting, was not something to be received but something to be used; not a conclusion but a turn in a conversation,

not a closed statement but an open question, not a way of declaring 'this is how it is' but a means of inviting others to consider what it (or they) could become. (Bochner and Ellis 2003, p.507)

Although not everyone will resonate with the experiences being portrayed through art, it is the researcher's task to present their data in formats that maximize opportunities for the audience to respond to the stories in personally meaningful ways, whether through dance, performance, photographs, video or other creative means (Braud and Anderson 1998).

## Poetry as inquiry

Sue also offered poetry as a means of communication. Poetry needs few words to capture experience. Her poem graphically portrays her feelings and experiences of powerlessness, stigma and shame, all of which are the focus of her dissertation:

'A bottle of sherry please'
I say to the assistant in Alldays.
It's eight in the morning
And I'm already jittery
She raises her eyebrows at me
And I suddenly feel paranoid
'It's for a leaving do today,
I nearly forgot' I explain
She says nothing
What does she care anyway
Miserable cow.

Another poem shows us a different aspect of her experience as a social worker, seeking for help outside her immediate community where she is known, showing how labels and medical power can reflect societal attitudes.

'Why should you be treated differently?
After all you are only
A common drunk'
He asks the question
But it is not really a question.
He rolls it out languidly
As if enjoying it
Sending it across the desk
Then leans forward after it
Staring at me.
I experience his contempt and coldness.
I open my mouth to explain
Desperate for him to understand
But I'm silenced by his stare.
My shame fills the room
I look at the floor. He has control
And I have no control at all.

Most conventional research tends to stay with traditional means of representing data but nowadays poetry is a familiar and often used creative format (Bochner and Ellis 2002; Richardson 2000). Poetry is sometimes reified as a literary art form that is beyond our personal capability but poems can also be appreciated as vehicles to convey meanings. Angoff (1994, p.xi) describes poetry as

> the response of our innermost being to the ecstasy, the agony, and the all-embracing mystery of life. It is a song, or a sigh, or a cry, often all of them together. Thus we are really all poets.

For some people it is easy and natural to find a creative source within that inspires us to learn more about ourselves and our world. As we reach inside to find words and form, we begin to express our thoughts and feelings through language, rhythm, metaphor, sound and imagery that invite us to use both hemispheres of the brain. It allows us to *feel* our thoughts and images, and to *imagine* and *think* our feelings (Stainbrook 1994). Even the shortest poems, perhaps a few lines, can distil the core issues. Lerner (1994) quotes Myra Cohn Livingstone, who says:

> Poetry humanizes because it links the individual by its distilled experience, its rhythms, its words to another in a way which no other form of communication can. Poetry also helps to ease the aloneness which we all share in common. (xi)

## Sue Law's story of using art and poetry in autoethnography for a Masters dissertation

> There are still times when I have to pinch myself in order to appreciate fully the opportunity I had in being able to use painting and poetry within my study. It was a powerful and transforming experience for me. However, I did not set out to do this. It was something that evolved as part of the reflexive process.
>
> I had difficulty in starting my dissertation and procrastinated a great deal. When I did start writing my good intentions to produce meaningful text slid away into word doodling and then into doodling without words as little drawings grew around the edge of the sheet of paper.
>
> I came to love writing at school, inspired by my English teacher who also introduced me to poetry, opening up a creative world of vibrant and powerful word pictures. But this time it was different. I felt daunted by the prospect of trying to balance the academic with the personal and write about *myself*. It was challenging to say the least. It also required some fearless self-scrutiny as I shone the searchlight within myself and out into the world.
>
> Carrying out an autoethnographical study meant laying bare my experience, knowing this would evoke some sort of response in the reader. How could I make this real, credible and something which would grip the reader's interest? Most importantly I wanted readers to use it to reflect upon their own world. Smith (2000, p.13) says, 'personal story told as research is still new enough to evoke transformation among its audience'. At best autoethnography can provide valuable and unique contributions to the understanding of

persons. At worst it can be what Behar (1996, p.13) describes as a boring revelation, one that fails to move the reader.

I wanted the story for my study to be an interesting read. A story that moves heart, belly and head (Bochner 2000, p.270), bringing readers evocatively into what it felt to go through the experience (Ellis 1996, p.152). However, the first draft of my story was a dull read, a catalogue of events. I wrote another, not much better. I showed two friends who asked, 'Where are you in this? How did it feel to succumb to alcoholism, to have hallucinations and be called a common drunk by the psychiatrist?'

I realized I needed to change the format so that instead of describing chronological events and generalizing about how I felt, I needed to immerse myself in the memories, placing myself back into those situations, using emotional recall. I decided to return to therapy in order to support me in the process. To have my therapist hold a mirror up to my experience enabled me to feel again, on a deep level, not only the horror of my descent into alcoholism and my despair and shame, but also my journey back into the light again and the beginning of a new sober life.

As a child I loved to lose myself in drawing and painting. My parents were both artists so it was natural for me to express myself this way. When I left school and started at art college in the early 1960s I started writing poetry and the beat poets such as Allen Ginsberg and Jack Kerouac reached me emotionally. Theirs was poetry of rebellion and existential bleakness and yet it contained a great deal of energy, rhythm and creativity.

Art college in the sixties was an exciting place to be, artistically and culturally. I studied classical representation of form in life drawing, still life, portraiture and landscape, benefiting greatly from this foundation of learning. But I also learnt to express myself freely using form, colour and texture in whatever way I wanted. I was especially influenced by the symbolists and expressionists, all of whom sought to evoke an ultimate response to the unattainable mysteries of the human psyche (Butler, Van Cleeve and Stirling 1994).

I am often asked how I go about creating my art works and whether I have an end product in view. The answer to that is I do have an end view or vision but I don't know exactly what it will look like because it is an evolving process.

I began the MSc with a blank canvas on which to create my autoethnography, and I knew that form, colour and texture would be achieved through standard text, using what Richardson (2000, p.931) describes as 'the literary criteria of coherence, verisimilitude, and interest'. I did not imagine that I would literally have a blank canvas – in fact eight of them – on which to create these things.

In terms of the research as a whole, it was both *intentional* and reactive and, as Blom and Chaplin describe: 'An organic plan emerges to take us forward in time, yet it only becomes articulated as we move' (Blom and Chaplin 1988).

Looking back now as I write, it is difficult to say which came first – the poetry or the paintings. I think it was the poetry. However, I believe the 'seed' of an idea of using art in some way had already been planted in my head. Sifting through the literature prior to writing my study I came upon John McLeod's

(2001, p.153) invitation to consider art as a metaphor for qualitative research. He suggests both the researcher and the artist have *constructed* (author's italics) the representation that is being presented. McLeod invites the reader to select their own piece of art to act as a metaphor for them. I was drawn to the work of David Hockney and his book *That's the Way I See It* (1993) in which he describes a series of paintings, stating that

> These simply grew more complex. I soon realized that what I was doing was making internal landscapes using different marks and textures to create space so that the viewer wanders round.

I began to immerse myself in the heuristic research process and started keeping a journal in which I jotted thoughts, feelings and ideas accompanied by doodlings, both idle and not so idle. I then experienced a dream in which I was in a room with lots of packing cases. Somebody whom I did not know was there with me and we were unpacking. Suddenly in one of the boxes I discovered an autobiography written by someone recalling their experiences of war, and it included both writing and drawings. I thought I shouldn't be looking at something so personal and wanted to put it back into the box.

Reflecting on the dream I realized that I was looking at *my* 'book' that had been written and not yet written – as in my research project; already written because my primary source material was the life story I had written during my stay in the treatment centre. In the dream my attention was drawn to a page on which a flock of birds were rising into the air. Some of the birds had been shot and wounded by the random firing of guns engaged in war. The birds had been inadvertent casualties. Some had escaped, some had been killed, and some wounded. *I* was one of the wounded birds and here was my first painting.

Thus inspired, I decided to paint a series of canvases to run alongside my writing and to illustrate the prose (see pages 156 to 158). I included photographs of the paintings to illustrate the text. I also decided at this time to have my poetry printed in red among the black text. Painting alongside writing was a unifying process in which I discovered that my personal (artistic) and researcher self were, and are, one self (Bruner 1993).

When I paint a picture I use whatever method and medium will convey 'what is'. Denzin and Lincoln (2000, p.6) tell us, 'The product of the interpretive bricoleur's labours is a complex bricolage, a reflexive collage or montage – a set of fluid interconnected images and representations'. The eight pieces of artwork I created for my study were indeed a set of fluid interconnected images. The first one was of the birds caught up in war; the second was a self-portrait in black and white, depicting my depression; the third depicted my entrapment in alcoholism; the fourth my experience of having hallucinations in the middle of the night; the fifth depicted shame; the sixth, riding out the highwater of initial recovery (see the front cover of this book); the seventh, return and forgiveness; and the final one was a collage made up of images cut from photographs of the first seven.

I feel I should say that I agonized over my paintings, trying to capture the vision, but the truth is I didn't. In the past I have had my fair share of agonizing over my artwork, with the inevitable tearing-up of paper or abandonment of canvases. But most of the paintings for my study were carried out rapidly once the representation was ready to be put onto canvas. The only preliminary workings were a few sketches. There was one picture I spent too long on and it suffered because of being over-worked. Most of the paintings were done in one 'sitting' once the outline had been drawn on the canvas. A few of them were painted in the middle of the night when preoccupation with their images and an urge to get on with them over-rode my need to sleep. The night can be a good time to work when concentration is focused so acutely. I sometimes wondered whether being able to create so quickly negated the piece of work and rendered it 'artless' but I did not think this for too long. I had created the image I wanted and needed to leave it be.

I lived with my paintings growing around me like the magnificent seven, which may sound a bit grand (and arrogant) but they became my companions and I was pleased with them and the way they were becoming an integral part of my study. Having them photographed was like taking the family to the studio. Seeing them bound with the text and poetry within my 'book' was, and is, difficult to describe. It was exhilarating and, to be honest, it was marvellous.

I was invited by Jane Speedy at the University of Bristol to present my work at the British Association for Counselling and Psychotherapy Research Conference in May 2003 as part of the autoethnographic strand. It was very exciting, albeit scary, sharing my research, reading my poetry and showing my paintings.

What have I discovered from writing this mini-autoethnographic account of using paintings and poetry as part of the process of becoming a reflexive researcher? Well, firstly, I have discovered just how important both have been throughout my life. They helped me to find meaning in my life and provided me with a vehicle of expression at times when I could find no ordinary language or when words were simply not enough. Currently I am involved in running an 'art as therapy' group which has reinforced for me just how important creative expression is for mental health.

How do I feel about writing about writing about myself? When I first began I found it difficult to 'hold' the task, and as Kim said: 'Multilayeredness can get out of hand!' I hope I have indeed conveyed how it felt to be a reflexive researcher using paintings and poetry. Giancola (1992, p.7) describes readers as being 'like artists who connect the two-dimensional dots on the page and in experiencing they create a three dimensional image with their gaze'. Well, I hope I have made enough dots to enable you as reader to create images of your own.

*Figure 11.1: I was one of the wounded birds*

*Figure 11.2: Self-portrait — my depression*

*Figure 11.3: My entrapment in alcoholism*

*Figure 11.4: Hallucinations – middle of the night*

*Figure 11.5: Shame*

*Figure 11.6: Return and forgiveness*

# Talking to the world
## (from Mel's conversation with me)

I kind of feel,
this research just made me want to talk to the world
    but I don't know quite what about
and I don't know who would want to hear me,

it has given me a voice,
I've found my voice and I do want to use it now,
I'm just not sure how, really.

But writing, the actual…,
my story
and doing this research has made
    – talking about self love –
has made me realize that that's been missing
a lot in my life and is only now really coming in,
and that's something I really want to foster and nurture

and that's one of the reasons why
I'm taking this time out,
it's for me,
and so I just want to have the experiences of…

I said in my dissertation
I didn't know how to play as a child,
I didn't play with others
and as an adult I played on drugs,
and now,

it's almost like
I'm taking a year out of my life to play
and I don't know whether it'll be physically,
emotionally, spiritually, whatever…,

I just feel I've got the biggest best playground
you can imagine in the universe
and it's out there
and I just want to go and experience it now.

I feel like I've read and read for this course,
courses before,
for the last years I've been reading and reading
and now I actually want to go out
and just do it,

whatever it is.

Part 3

# The Doctoral Stages

In Part 3 I focus on the stories of doctoral candidates and some of the issues that become prevalent during this stage of their journeys towards becoming reflexive researchers, using themselves as an important tool in their research. As such they need to process their experiences of doing research, their relationships with participants and what they are discovering about their topic within the safety of a supportive supervisory relationship.

I begin this part with Chapter 12, which focuses on the supervisory relationship, using extracts from my own diary during this phase of my life, showing some of the dilemmas I experienced in forming a supervisory relationship within a culture that did not share my values or seem to understand my needs. The second part of this chapter uses a conversation between one of my own doctoral students and myself that was the basis of a conference presentation at which we invited discussion of the expectations and hopes that underpin this relationship. The last part of this chapter shows what one of my participants experienced as supportive and helpful in his relationship with his supervisor.

Chapter 13 focuses on a conversation between a group of doctoral research candidates and myself, and shows how our personal connections with the topic of study, when sufficiently understood and processed, can enrich our research once we are ready to move beyond our own story, see how it connects with the wider world, and use it to think with other people about their stories. This chapter also illustrates how, by telling our stories and having them witnessed, we can begin to re-author our lives and allow new meanings and identities to emerge.

Chapter 14 follows with a re-telling of the story in the previous chapter from a different perspective, allowing the reader into the private and public world of a disabled doctoral candidate, and showing the kind of struggles she faces as she engages with her programme of learning. This is a multilayered reflexive story, dealing with the interfaces between home, academia and the world as inhabited by a person who has experienced illness and disability and how all of that impacts on current and future plans.

Chapter 15 raises some important questions about what we can do to avoid becoming *over* involved with our participants' stories and how reflexive research might require us to maintain some distance from our participants, while also remaining closely engaged and aware of how we are affected by the stories. At best, reflexivity occurs in the creative space between objectivity and subjectivity, allowing something unique and dynamic to unfold.

The same theme is developed in Chapter 16, based on stories told to me by a doctoral candidate whose research focus is on the body, both as the topic and as an important tool for her research. The importance of the body is often unrecognized by researchers, and her stories show how much our physical reflexive responses inform and guide our actions, understandings and beliefs.

This leads to Chapter 17, which deals with further considerations of using reflexivity in heuristic research as a tool for recognizing ethical issues that can emerge in our relationships with research participants. The story in this chapter was written and offered as data for my study by a doctoral candidate who recognizes how his relationship with his own story has changed and developed over the duration of his study so far, and as a result of immersing himself in other people's stories alongside his own.

So Part 3 tells more of my own stories; uses conversations between myself and participants, some of which are arranged in stanza form to show *how* they were told; group conversations that were held for a different purpose; diary extracts; a research presentation; pieces written specially for this book; and in between all of this, my own academic voice links theory, experience and stories into a meaningful whole.

*Chapter 12*

# The PhD Student–Supervisor Relationship

Most PhD students get on well with their supervisors – and if they don't, they usually find someone else to work with. But the relationship remains perhaps the most fraught aspect of post-graduate life.

(Budd 2003, p.2)

Doctoral candidates can spend many years doing their research, depending on whether they spend three years studying full-time or up to six years part-time. For those who choose reflexive methodologies, their relationship with their supervisor can be crucial to their success.

However, the quality of this relationship has been found to be fundamental to completion rates for PhD students more generally across the social sciences. In 1990 the Economic and Social Research Council (ESRC), a body that provides much of the funding for social science PhD research in the UK, became concerned about 'poor completion rates amongst social science students, in comparison to those of their natural science and engineering counterparts (Rothschild 1982; Swinnerton-Dyer 1982; Winfield 1987)' (quoted in Hockey 1995, p.200).

In response to these concerns, the ESRC funded research to establish what might be contributing to this state of affairs. Between 1990 and 1991 interviews were undertaken with PhD supervisors at nine UK higher education institutions to gain an understanding of the process of PhD supervision in the social sciences. One of the findings was that frequent breakdowns in the relationships between PhD students and their supervisors was a contributing factor. It was recommended that there were good grounds for introducing training programmes for PhD supervisors that included an examination of the relationship between both parties and the factors that influence it (Burgess 1994; Hockey 1995).

Historically, academics have 'metamorphosed' into becoming PhD supervisors by reason of their seniority and status in their field, and this has meant that supervisors have learned by trial and error, sometimes at great cost to the students (and themselves). Budd, in an article in *The Guardian* in which he writes about the training of academic supervisors, says:

> Most academics have only ever seen one other supervisor in action – the man or woman who guided them during their own postgraduate days. When they begin supervising, they draw on their experiences, whether good or bad. So people who suffer disengaged, absentee mentors will often try to micro-manage their own students. (Budd 2003)

Although recognized as experts in their chosen field, some academics have limited understanding, few skills, and little inclination to take on the more relational aspects of the supervisory role. Sometimes those who did so found themselves becoming over-involved in a way that caused stress both for themselves and for their students. However, some universities clearly expected supervisors to 'offer advice to the student on academic (and personal) problems' (University of Bristol 1993, quoted in Hockey 1995). In his discussion of these issues Hockey (1995, p.208) suggests that supervisors:

> need to be guided in how to empathise with their charges' intellectual and emotional problems, while simultaneously achieving enough social and emotional distance so as to be able to effect the intellectual tasks of guide and critic. They need to be encouraged to be more self-reflective about the nature of their supervisory responsibilities and how these are managed. The capacity to balance empathy, objectivity and self-reflexivity is at the centre of effective counselling.

There seems to have been little research from the perspective of PhD students on the quality of their personal relationships with their supervisors. A notable exception is a qualitative study undertaken in the USA (Schlosser *et al.* 2003) of 16 third-year counselling psychology students, 10 of whom were satisfied with their relationships and six of whom were dissatisfied. Their experiences differed in several aspects: (a) the ability to choose their supervisor, (b) frequency of meetings with their supervisor, (c) the benefits and costs of the relationship, and (d) how conflict in the relationship was dealt with. Those who had positive relationships with their supervisors said the relationship had improved over time, while those who were dissatisfied said their relationships worsened over time.

Another study, using reflexive action research, was undertaken by academics at the University of Auckland's School of Business (McMorland *et al.* 2003), who believed that there needed to be a greater involvement in individual and collective reflection on the practice of PhD supervision among the community of academic supervisors and students. In particular they noted that 'while there is growing interest in research *about* higher education practice, and supervision in particular, few studies inquire into practice from the inside'. This realization led to a period of action research involving PhD supervisors and candidates over two years. As an outcome of these meetings the researchers suggested that:

> much greater intentionality has to be paid to the multiple and complex relationships that exist amongst students, staff and institution if the PhD endeavour is to be a fulfilling creative enterprise for all. (McMorland *et al.* 2003)

They advocated that staff and students needed to develop skills and courage in reflecting on their own capabilities, to develop skills in peer learning and peer engagement, and to strengthen a culture of learning across multiple role relationships.

One useful outcome of this kind of research is that there has been an accelerating trend in higher education institutions to develop supervisor training programmes. Since 1995 I have been involved in providing part of that training, focusing on the PhD supervisor–student relationship and incorporating many aspects of the studies named above. The knowledge that I bring to these courses is derived from my own experience of being a PhD student, as well as having supervised PhD students in more recent years. I have also gained a great deal of learning through the conversations I have had for this study with people at the doctoral stage of becoming reflexive researchers.

I begin with my own story and follow with the stories of other participants.

## My story

This part of my story is told through excerpts from my diary from the end of September 1992 to the end of February 1993. The taught aspect of the Masters had ended in July 1992 and I had handed in my dissertation on 28 September 1992. The following day I registered for a PhD.

For several months prior to the point at which we join my diary I had been negotiating with the university to get to this stage (see Chapter 6), and I had been accepted as a PhD student on 2 July 1992. In the meantime, I had been searching the literature in preparation for my new research into *Adult Male Survivors of Childhood Sexual Abuse*.

As readers may note, my diary shows the parallels between my experiences of sorting out supervision for my PhD and issues related to power, gender, age, choice and negotiation – issues that are commonly faced when attempting to form and sustain any kind of relationship. My learning from this experience was painful and profound.

---

*29 September 1992*

Registration for PhD at Senate House! Informal meeting at Social Sciences Faculty.

*7 October 1992*

Drinks at Social Policy Department to meet other new students. I hate those kind of gatherings so I just showed my nose and then went. I've been allocated a supervisor who works in a social policy dept. Not sure if that's the best thing for me. Trouble is there are no counsellors with PhDs around here who can supervise me. I asked if I can have my Masters tutor as a supervisor and there's a possibility she can be second supervisor but I don't know if she'll want to do that because she isn't very interested in research.

## 15 October 1992

Went to meet research group where my PhD supervisor hangs out. It was a beautiful day and a lovely setting and I enjoyed meeting the women who were employed there as researchers (while also doing PhDs) but it was obvious that they weren't happy in that environment. At lunchtime everybody sat around on sofas eating French bread and cheese, olives, etc. – all very elegant. I met with my supervisor, who seems a nice enough person (I'm probably old enough, at 52, to be his mother!).

By the end of the day, having met most of the group, I decided I couldn't possibly do a PhD there. The attitudes about male abuse expressed by the senior man were so far removed from my own that I felt very uncomfortable. I felt very upset when I left and wondered what I could do about any of it. I felt like giving up the idea of doing a PhD. How do you reject a research supervisor? He seems OK himself – it's just the company he keeps! How much do those attitudes brush off? He also seemed to want to sit a bit too close to my shoulder (metaphorically speaking) and seemed to think he should draw up an agenda of what I should do and when I should do it. I am an independent learner – the two years on the MSc have taught me that, if nothing else!

## 17 October 1992

Very friendly letter from Pam (not real name), one of the women who is doing a PhD whom I met on 15th. She said 'I hope the experience wasn't too traumatic'. I had spoken to her about my misgivings when the women described how they had their work returned with CRAP or RUBBISH written across the page! I couldn't believe that they could put up with being treated like that. She is supervised by my supervisor *and* the top man, and she wrote:

> Although they are both very good at what they do, they can also be hypercritical. I think it's important when you are trying to do something as consuming as a PhD to try and keep a sense of humour and always keep at the front of your mind that supervisors are there for your benefit – they are not gods – and you can take or leave their advice as you want. …From my perspective, I sincerely hope you don't give up the idea of doing your PhD as I feel we really need good women researchers in this field in order to present a balanced sensitive approach in child abuse. I would love to talk to you about this and about many other things.

She asked if we could arrange a meeting, and I wrote back suggesting a date. I really appreciated her letter. It validated my experience and helped me to think about it in a more balanced way. However, I did rather get the impression that the women, in general, were hoping I would stick with the group because they saw me as a 'strong' woman who might fight some of their battles. I really don't want to have an up-hill struggle – doing the PhD will be hard enough without having to battle on that front too. It's really tempting, though, as I would love to be working with a group of women. But maybe it's too high a price to pay? I don't know what to do about it.

## 30 October 1992

Pam came to see me at home. We got on really well together, even though she is much younger than me. She is a full-time researcher doing her PhD part-time, and she spends a lot of time searching the literature for her 'day job'. She offered to send me articles she comes across related to my topic. We talked about the supervisors. I really don't think I can stay with them.

## 12 November 1992

I've had several phone calls from my supervisor who seems to think I should be letting him know what I'm doing (every week it seems!). I pointed out that I didn't really work like that and that I would contact him when I needed to. He seemed a bit surprised by that and insisted we make a date to meet in late January. Reluctantly I agreed. I don't know how to deal with this. Who am I supposed to talk to about how I feel? He is my supervisor and I can't really talk to him about him!

## 14 January 1993

Went to a PhD seminar (joint social policy and social work) about supervisors' relationship with students! The speaker was a female professor who had sent out one of her papers to be read before the seminar. I really liked her style and what she said about the relationship. As she was talking, I kept thinking 'Yes, but what if that's not what your experiencing?' I tried to say something during the discussion that followed but I felt like a child telling the teacher about somebody else being horrid to me! So I think what I said was too cryptic to be understood. It's made me realize how difficult it is to sort out this kind of thing when there is a power differential – real or imagined! But a PhD supervisor *is* powerful.

At the end of the seminar I talked to the Graduate Studies Officer (GSO) who was there and said I wasn't very happy with the supervisor I had been allocated. She seemed to understand and said she would look into the possibility of finding someone else. That was a relief! I expect I just have to wait to hear from her.

Speaker asked for feedback on the paper she had sent us to read ahead of the seminar so I think I will write to her.

## 19 January 1993

My letter to the professor:

> You asked for some feedback about the article you presented at the PhD seminar group last Thursday evening. For me the paper was a useful way to focus my thoughts and ideas about the relationship I have with my own supervisor. I found the way you included your own experience of being a supervisor/adviser allowed me to become clearer about my own understanding and expectations of the relationship.
>
> As you could probably hear, I have been struggling with trying to find a way to communicate my anxieties about my relationship. I wonder if such an article could include something about the possibility that problems might be felt on either side, and that a preliminary meeting might provide an opportunity to test out the 'chemistry' and clarify expectations, thus giving an opportunity for either one to choose not to work with the other. Perhaps a contract could be set up, which included ongoing evaluation of the relationship to provide an opportunity for difficulties to be discussed and any re-negotiations to be made.
>
> I wonder, too, if some consideration of the mature student might be mentioned, and of the advantages and disadvantages this could bring to the relationship.

> On the whole, I found the article interesting, useful and easy to read. I very much enjoyed your personal style of writing, especially as I had not met you in person. I felt I had met a bit of you through your writing. I was reminded of something Carl Rogers wrote: 'What is most personal and unique in each of us is probably the very element which would, if it were shared or expressed, speak most to others'. I hope these comments are helpful.

> I felt a bit nervous giving feedback to someone who was so senior but I genuinely thought she would be open to it and welcome people's comments.

> ### 26 January 1993
> The planned meeting with my supervisor is in three days and I still haven't heard from the Graduate Studies Officer (GSO) about a new one. Am I supposed to go ahead with the meeting? What do I say to him? The GSO said she would explain to him about the change, and I had been relieved about that, but I don't know if it's happened yet and when I tried to ring her she wasn't there so I couldn't find out anything.

> ### 28 January 1993
> Went into the university to talk to one of the academics working on child abuse and asked her, in desperation, if she could be my supervisor. She said she'd talk to the GSO about it. As I was leaving the building I saw the GSO who asked if I'd got the message she'd left on my answerphone this afternoon (after I'd left the house) to say the professor to whom I'd written had offered to be my supervisor! I was delighted. I told her about the conversation I'd just had with the other person and she said she'd sort it out. She also said she'd contact my current supervisor and let him know about the change. I explained that I was supposed to be meeting him tomorrow and therefore it was urgent for her to contact him before then.

> Later that evening he rang to ask for directions for tomorrow! I tentatively asked him if the GSO had spoken to him today and he said 'No. What about?' So I was in the difficult position of having to explain to him that he was no longer my supervisor. There was quite a long silence and then he asked 'Why?' I tried to explain how I had been feeling, and I don't remember much about the rest of the conversation. He seemed really upset. So was I!! It was a horrible thing to have to do but I knew it was necessary for my survival.

> ### 26 February 1993
> First meeting with new supervisor. What a difference! She emphasized that this was *my* PhD and that I was responsible and in charge! I know this is going to be OK. I asked about the possibility of me having a second supervisor (perhaps my MSc tutor) and she said she didn't think having two supervisors was helpful as it sometimes meant that students were pulled in opposite directions. She did, however, say that she would speak to her about the possibility of offering me emotional support if I should need that.

My relationship with my new supervisor proved to be successful in the main. Each time we met I left her office feeling affirmed and respected for my knowledge. Her style was empowering and intellectually supportive. The emotional support I had hoped for by requesting a role for my previous MSc tutor was never set up, and there was a period during the summer of 1993, when I was interviewing men about their experience of sexual abuse, that left me suffering from vicarious traumatisation (Pearlman and Saakvitne 1995). I have described this in more detail elsewhere (Etherington 2000).

Although doing the interviews during the summer suited my purposes because I had more free time (my practice always slows down and university courses are not running), with hindsight I realized it also meant that my supervisor and other supportive people were not available. One of the costs of having a supervisor who is highly respected and in demand throughout the academic world is that they might be absent from their home university more frequently, and for longer periods, than a less high profile academic.

I particularly valued the presence of my supervisor during the upgrade from MPhil to PhD student (an assessment half way through the process) and the viva examination held as part of the final assessment (during which PhD candidates meet with the internal and external examiners to 'defend' their work). During both those assessments she sat quietly in a corner and made copious notes of what was said. Without those notes I would not have remembered much of what had occurred, as my stress levels were fairly high. I also valued her presence on both those occasions as we sat outside the room while the examiners conferred about how I had performed and decided whether or not my work had reached the standard required for a PhD.

PhD students need to become 'experts' in their chosen field, and they cannot do so if they become trapped in a position where they view their supervisor as the only expert – a state of affairs that is sometimes encouraged by some supervisors who might feel unable to let go of that position. The model I am proposing is one of power-sharing, both parties being able to acknowledge their expertise, albeit the students being at an earlier stage of development. Nigel's experience of supervision, which follows, seems to have been of this kind.

## Nigel's story

Nigel Copsey is a Team Leader for the Department of Spiritual and Cultural Care at the East London and City Mental Health NHS Trust, a Christian Minister and a humanistic psychotherapist. Nigel had completed a PhD just before we met to talk about his experience of becoming a reflexive researcher. During our conversation I asked him about the support he received while he was undertaking his PhD, and he began to talk about his supervisor and what he had found to be valuable in their relationship.

Nigel:   Well, I'll tell you things that were most important to me. Firstly, Michael is very affirming…about what you've done…so that the comments he makes about things that need changing and altering are very much from a position of affirmation. I got the feeling with him that he was really interested in what I was doing. So the fact that he was interested, the fact that he was supportive and affirming enabled me to respond to his criticisms in a very [positive way]. I felt that all of his comments and criticisms were justified, and they were coming from a place…, not of being critical for the sake of it – they were constructive. But they all came from that first of all, the affirming of the good of what I'd done…

And another thing that was really helpful was that Michael was always incredibly responsive to things. So that if I sent him a draft by email it would come back incredibly quickly. I wouldn't be sat here a month, two months later, thinking: where the hell has it got to? I never had to wait too long. And also, if I was up against it, as I was sometimes, because we had some personal situations at home when my mother in law, who had been living with us for a long time, was dying and I got behind in terms of my schedule and my deadlines and things were getting a bit tight, Michael was incredibly responsive to that.

So that even when I was feeling up against it, in terms of time-tabling things, he would get back to me very quickly. So it was that willingness to be responsive to my circumstances.

What other things? I think also that it's good to have a supervisor who is very creative in ideas. I mean Michael was very good at coming up with lots of ideas. What was very good was… I was very aware of my methodology – more so than Michael, because I had been the one that had really gone into it, but Michael had *enough* knowledge of action research to follow what I had done and still be incredibly supportive in terms of looking at the methodology. He had enough knowledge of the whole to be able to support me. So, I think also he was very good at pointing me at different things to look at which were helpful…

Kim:      Giving you sort of guidelines…

Nigel:    And tips. He was very good I think at giving me tips in terms of what was going to be needed, what was going to be looked for by the examiners.

Kim:      Yes. It sounds like you were very lucky.

Nigel:    Oh I was! I thought he was absolutely brilliant and I found his whole way of being, and willingness to be so responsive, very supportive.

Kim:      It's really important to be so supportive during that process, isn't it? And so you had your supervisor to support you, you had your peer groups to support you, you had the course to support you. Anything else?

Nigel:    Well, I've also been in individual therapy. There were quite often things which came up that touched me personally. Because the model of the doctorate was so anchored in my work, there were personal things that came up around that, and I think that having personal therapy did at certain points help, especially when I was trying to challenge part of the system within the NHS. Some of the action plans that were coming up, and how that was then affecting me personally, in terms of when I wasn't being heard in challenging the system – and so personal therapy was an element of the support.

## Negotiating the student–supervisor relationship

The following section is taken from a conversation between myself and Nell Bridges. Nell is an MPhil/PhD student who began her PhD in September 2002 and I am her first supervisor. She also has a second supervisor, like most of the doctoral candidates in the department. She has an ESRC grant for three years full-time study. As an experienced counselling practitioner and trainer, Nell is skilled in communication and assertiveness. She is also accustomed to contracting supervisory relationships, both as a counsellor and supervisor. We used the following presentation for a conference held at the University of Bristol in the summer of 2003 (Bridges and Etherington 2003). We began by introducing ourselves to the 'audience' and explained that we were going to read to them our (edited) conversation, while Powerpoint highlights, capturing themes, were transmitted onto the screen behind us. These highlights focused on exploring the expectations and hopes of the relationship in terms of themes such as: inspiration, honesty and respect, limits and boundaries, mutuality and power-sharing, challenge, managing difficulty and change, checking out responsibilities, and negotiating times to meet.

## Expectations and hopes

### 1. Inspiration

Nell:     What I want in a supervisor is somebody who feels…, inspiring is the word that came to me. That my research is an area that you're interested in, not one that you're disinterested in, but that my work matters to you… The feeling that what I'm doing matters and it links with your interests, and so when we meet that there's a kind of buzz between us. Something between us that actually makes me want to go off and go 'yes!' So I want to pick this up and read that… And if there's something you've heard of, somebody's doing this or somebody's published that, say to me, 'Have you read this, have you seen that?', to kind of keep that going between us, for that to be mutual. I think would be lovely.

### 2. Honesty and respect

Nell:     And there's the honesty thing.

Kim:     Honesty about…?

Nell:     If there's anything you're worried about, I want you to say so. That, if I'm working with you in a way that you think isn't OK for you, you're honest about that, so I know what the deal is. For instance, how often is it OK to email you? What can I expect back if I send you some stuff, and if I don't hear back from you, when is it OK to hassle you and say…? You know, those silly but practical things…so I'm not here thinking: 'I haven't heard anything for two weeks but…' Or whatever. At what point is it OK to say, 'Did you get that?', or 'Did you think about it?', or 'Could you give me some feedback?' or, …you know. Apart from a total black hole, I can work with a lot of variation, as long as I know what it is I can expect.

## 3. Limits and boundaries

Kim:     So if I'm bogged down with some work that doesn't allow me to have time to look at what you've sent, I can email you and tell you that.

Nell:     Yes, tell me that.

Kim:     And let you know I will get round to this in two weeks' time.

Nell:     Yes, two weeks' time, two months or whatever.

Kim:     If you don't hear from me for three weeks then please jog me again.

Nell:     Fine, that sort of thing, so that I know. It's so like counselling, it's like 'What's the deal here? …'

Kim:     I think we're quite fortunate in that we're used to making these kind of contracts in counselling…that we do really plan for things in advance.

Nell:     I think as counsellors we're also used to hearing somebody say what's not OK, and I think a lot of people who aren't counsellors think that some things are rude, that we wouldn't think of as rude. So if I ask you something and you think 'No, that's not really on,' for you to be able to say to me, 'Sorry, I don't see that as being part of my role,' or whatever, or 'That's too much to ask,' or 'I don't want to do that.' I want you to be able to do that as well.

## 4. Mutuality and power-sharing

Kim:     Yes, I think that's right. I'd rather have that too. And it also goes the other way, I would prefer if something's not OK for you, for you to feel that you can come and say, 'I really didn't like it when you did that,' or, you know, 'I would rather that didn't happen again,' or 'Why did that happen?' and we can talk it through and sort things out before they get worse. Is there anything that might stop you doing that?

## 5. Challenge

Nell:     So far not. So far I'm really comfortable with you and I think I could… I know that sometimes I can be upset by people, and I don't quite know it at the time, and it takes me a little bit of time to think, 'What was going on there?' And it can be a couple of days afterwards and I'd think 'That's what it was.' As far as possible I'd like to do things there and then but I know I'm not always aware enough to do it there and then. It sometimes takes a little bit of processing, time for reflecting.

Kim:     And then after that you can do it?

Nell:     Then I can do it, yes.

Kim:      I'm just wondering what other factors might be important to notice at this stage. For me it's an ongoing process. Our relationship is something that we'll probably work out over time and as things happen. If we are open to talking about them, then we can keep re-establishing and re-negotiating or keep it alive if you like. It's not a once and for all thing.

Nell:     Great.

Kim:      We're going to be fairly closely involved with each other for three years. And that's quite a chunk out of anybody's life, isn't it?

Nell:     Oh yes, yes. And this kind of work…because so much of it has such personal meaning, there's all of that as well. And that kind of raises my good old Rogerian stuff – the core conditions. I prefer to have that in as many relationships as possible, not for you to be my counsellor but for you to have warmth, empathic understanding and a good, honest, as far as possible, transparent relationship with me. And with the stuff we work with.

## 6. *Managing difficulty and change*

Kim:      Now what shall I do if I get fed up with you? And what if you get fed up with me and you want to have a different supervisor?

Nell:     I think what I would expect, if anything started to happen along those lines, is that we would try to work with that as soon as the first problem came up. So it would take a lot for it to get to that point. I'm trying to think of ways that it might happen. What's coming straight to my mind now is another experience I had with a counselling supervisor. And I had to stop that supervision, and that involved her solicitor reassuring me that she wouldn't practise again. So I would never say again, 'Oh no that won't happen.' I think we need to deal with problems as soon as possible as they come up, if they do. But if something happened – like if my research took a twist somewhere different, or if we had a boundary problem or whatever – I'd talk it through with you and we'd work it out. And if it meant that I'd go on to somebody else, we'd sort it.

## 7. *Checking out responsibility*

Kim:      Sure. And I'd support you in that and try to help you to find the right person, and I wouldn't take offence (laugher). Yes. I had to change my own supervisor after the first little while, it was never going to work, there was no hope for it from the beginning really. But it was difficult because in those days we didn't have anybody in counselling who had a PhD and who was in a position to supervise me, so I was always going to have to go outside and not feel quite as understood in terms of our field. The person I was offered was not an empowering person, he sat on my shoulder and… I don't work like that. Like you, I'm an independent worker. And while we're on the point, I'm assuming that you will take responsibility for asking for what you need, and that I won't need to come chasing after you to say, 'Are you OK?', or 'Do we need to meet?' But you will know when you want that, and that you can give me reasonable warning and that we can negotiate a time that's good for both of us. But the bottom line is that *you'll* know when that's needed and you'll take responsibility for that.

Nell: And I guess if there's information you have, things I can't ask for because I don't know they exist. It may be that something's been published or some event is on or something like that. Anything you know that would be relevant and useful to me, if you could send it.

Kim: That would be my responsibility, yes. And I do see my responsibility as being to give you time that's not distracted by phone calls and callers, and that when you send me stuff, I'll let you know when you can expect to have something back from me, and that you're not kept waiting too long. And that the feedback I give you on what you do is respectfully conveyed. I think until you know where you're going, we don't quite know quite how often you'll need, I don't think we can say in advance how often we'll need to meet.

## 8. Negotiating time to meet

Nell: No, at the moment I have no idea. But there'll be regular stuff anyway, because there's the CLIO, and I will be seeing you at that, and I don't know about the monthly narrative research group – how that will turn out, if I will be part of it, or be able to come to subsequent meetings here.

Kim: Yes, I think it would be very good if you could because it would give you…, I mean it's going to be quite a frequent…, I don't know how you feel about how often you want to make that journey.

Nell: Well there may be some meetings when it just won't fit but as far as possible I'd like to. But I don't know what feedback you got from the group, when you were asked if it was OK for me to come.

Kim: Nobody said…, nobody's responded to that question so I can only assume it's OK with them…

Nell: Too late – you've had your chance…

Kim: I can't see for one minute that they would have any objection. It was really me being respectful of the group that made me ask them.

Nell: So you're going to be a present person in my life anyway, those two things, the meetings for CLIO and the meetings for this research group…

Kim: And I'm sure we'll fix our meetings around that.

Nell: I'm a good person at email contact, I like email.

Kim:     We did quite well in the beginning when you did your ESRC grant application, didn't we. From nothing we became regular correspondents by email, and I like that too. I'm quite happy with just popping up and saying hello, just to make contact.

Nell:    Fine.

Kim:     So I think it should work out quite well.

## Responses from the audience

After the presentation we invited responses from the audience, and a lively discussion followed. Our intention in presenting this conversation was not to provide a model to be emulated or for it to be seen as the 'right' or 'only' way to establish this relationship, but rather a way of stimulating further conversations that would create opportunities for learning, both for ourselves and for those involved as audience. We were not disappointed.

Many of the audience were overseas students, and immediately one of them observed that from the conversation between Nell and myself it was difficult to recognize which speaker held the power in the relationship. Indeed, one person commented on the fact that the 'student' seemed to be making all the 'demands' – which was not how I experienced it at all. This comment led me to think about how the beliefs held by Nell and I, as counsellors who ascribed to feminist principles concerning power-relations, might be very different from those held by students from other cultures.

Sheila Trahar (2003) recognizes the dilemmas faced by students from different cultural backgrounds (particularly those from a Confucian heritage) who may perceive academics as authority figures and 'experts'. In such cases, the behaviour demonstrated by Nell and myself might have been considered 'improper'. By attempting to redress some of the power issues inherent in the role of supervisor my behaviour could be seen as confusing and unhelpful – students might want me to hold onto the power invested in the role of supervisor. Trahar quotes Wu (2002, p.389), a student from Taiwan, who said:

> One's unspoken demands for more pedagogic control somehow feels infantile, or in bad taste, and one feels vaguely uncomfortable about them but can never discuss them because of local culture, which is taken for granted and unquestioned.

Trahar goes on to ask if we, as the dominant culture, might be transferring to our teaching/advising of students from other cultures our beliefs about what contributes to good teaching, without questioning if it might indeed be 'best' for them.

My own learning experiences, referred to elsewhere in this book, have influenced my behaviour as a teacher and academic (and PhD supervisor). During my training as a counsellor my learning involved experiential and discursive teaching practices that enabled me to develop as a critical thinker whose point of view and experience was valued. I was encouraged to communicate my feelings, needs and questions, and this helped me to gain confidence that my emotional, intuitive and tacit knowledge was as important as my intellectual and cognitive abilities. Sound though these principles are, their philosophy is based upon modernist traditions of individualism, which places the learner at the centre. Trahar (*op cit*) asks how this translates for those whose cultural values are more collectivist, 'Where more emphasis is placed on group rather than individual good, and where success may involve significant others, the family, peers, society as a whole'. She goes on,

> Such questioning leads me to recognise my move from a liberal humanist position towards a more critical postmodern approach to adult learning theory, where the relationship between the individual and society is both recognised and celebrated (p.3)

One of the limitations of my study for this book is that none of my participants is from overseas. Sadly this is a reflection of current counselling training programmes, although this is beginning to change. Students from ethnic minorities are severely under-represented currently on our Masters research programme, although at Diploma level the balance is beginning to shift, and in time, I hope, some of those students will filter through to the research unit. My learning through this presentation, and the thinking that ensued from it, is that, as a supervisor, I need to be constantly aware of the potential tensions that might exist between my personal values and beliefs about the supervisor–student relationship and those of the doctoral candidates I supervise. By recognizing the influences of cultural socialization and the needs of the group (organization or institution), as well as the individual, tensions created might co-exist and lead to creative and illuminating relationships.

*Chapter 13*

# Connecting Doctoral Research Topics to Ourselves

Storytelling is for another just as much as it is for oneself. In the reciprocity that is storytelling, the storyteller offers herself as guide to the other's self-formation. The other's receipt of that guidance not only recognises, but values the teller. The moral genius of storytelling is that each, teller and listener, enters the space of the story for the other.

(Frank 1995, p.18)

Students who sign up to study for a doctoral degree might be studying full-time for three years or part-time for up to six years, so the topic of inquiry needs to be something that can sustain interest and energy over a prolonged period. In the field of counselling and psychotherapy many doctoral candidates choose to focus on a topic that has some personal meaning for them, knowing that this connection will develop and grow over time and keep them engaged in what can sometimes be a difficult and lonely process.

My own choice of topic – male survivors of childhood sexual abuse – was of interest to me on several levels. In my work as a trainer, during the early 1990s, I had been asked about the impact of abuse on men who were just emerging out of the shadows to identify themselves as victims. But this topic was also of interest to me in more personal ways. As a female who had personal experience of abuse I had considered studying the experiences of other women but decided against that on three counts. First, research on sexual abuse had always focused on females, and there was already a body of literature emerging as women were increasingly telling their stories; there was little known about men. Second, I believed that by studying men's experiences I might begin to understand them better. Having grown up as the only girl among seven brothers I was not much interested in men. After all, you can have too much of a good thing! My experience of growing up in an all-male household had not inclined me to feel much compassion for the male species but as my therapy was progressing, and I was exploring my relationships with masculinity, I felt the need to challenge myself about some of my attitudes and take the risks involved in examining the lives of men more closely. And the final consideration was that, by studying men, I was putting my own experience at a slight distance, not wanting to identify too closely with the participants' experiences, and thereby risk losing perspective or balance.

Our personal history, when it is known to us and processed in ways that allow us to remain in contact emotionally and bodily with others whose stories remind us of our own, can enrich our role as researcher. Our 'empathic resonance' (Spiro *et al.* 1993) allows us to hear the others' experiences without the need to defend ourselves against that knowing. Likewise, if we are exploring topics through research, which are part of our own history that is *out* of our awareness, we are in danger of using our participants vicariously to explore their issues as a way of avoiding facing our own. This puts us at risk of over-identification, which might lead to overinvolvement and biases that are out of our control. It also puts us at risk of harming our participants.

For these reasons, tutors on our research programme normally explore students' personal reasons for choosing the topic of their inquiry at the early stages of the process. Because our students are mainly counsellors or psychotherapists, it is expected that they will have undergone personal therapy, which will have opened them up to understandings of where these connections might lie within themselves. This exploration is normally done in one-to-one tutorials. However, a group of doctoral candidates I supervise recently expanded this process to include each other in their explorations of how they came to be interested in the topics they chose to research. My intention in inviting them to tell their research stories was partly a response to my own experience of feeling quite isolated as a doctoral student – something I had always vowed I would work to avoid for others I might be supporting through this stage of their research life. They invited me to use our conversations from this day for my research so a tape recorder was hastily set up.

When we tell our research stories to others, the listeners can find points of entry into those stories that might help us (and them) deepen our understanding. Each listener brings with them their own history, and by offering their personal resonance to the storyteller they can contribute to a process of co-construction of new stories that offers the teller and the listener new ideas and perspectives, thereby thickening existing stories and enriching the learning. Because storytelling is a social activity, this learning is available to all parties involved.

On a hot summer's day in 2003 the doctoral candidates for whom I was a supervisor gathered at my home. This was the first time they had met as a group, and they decided to tell the stories of their research journeys to each other as a way of making connections, of capturing how they might tell those stories at this point in time, and to receive feedback from others. All of them were interested in reflexivity, narrative or heuristic inquiry.

The story below was told by Viv Martin, who had registered to do an MPhil/PhD six months earlier. The other group members were further along the research pathway: Ruth was about six months from completion of an EdD; Peter had successfully up-graded from MPhil to PhD; and Nell, the only one who was studying full-time with the help of an ESRC grant, was about nine months into her period of study.

I have selected Viv's story from among others that were equally powerful, partly because, in spite of the anxiety she expressed about sounding incoherent, there was a clear shape and narrative form that I could use for the purpose of this book. Her story also included all of the other group members in some way, so I was able to honour each individual's contribution to the stories that unfolded. Also, as the member of the group closest to the beginning of her journey, her story focused closely on the theme of this chapter.

Hers is a moving story of how a woman who had suffered a serious and life-threatening brain tumour decided to study for a PhD, and how her previous learning and life experiences influenced her decisions about how she was planning to conduct her research. Her story begins hesitantly, as she struggles to find words. I have gathered her stories under headings that indicate different aspects of her telling: *The Introduction*, where she reflexively comments on the process of beginning to tell her story; *The Illness Story* contextualizes her current story against the background of a remembered past and the source of her research story; *A Story of Healing*, in which she recounts something of her spiritual beliefs and ways of knowing that now inform her choices; *Stories of Writing and Research*, where she moves more hesitantly into newer stories that are helping her construct new realities and find new meaning as she tells them; *Emerging Stories of Methodologies*, as she begins to share her ideas of how she might go about her research; and *Self/Other Stories*, that show how, having reached a stage of understanding her own journey so far, she recognizes that new learning will be found in other people's stories that will extend and stretch her knowledge. The last part of her conversation becomes a co-construction as she invites the other members of the group to contribute from their positions as witnesses to her stories and shows the impact on her changing sense of identity of the listeners' resonance with her stories.

Viv's words are arranged on the left of the page, and the words of other group members are on the right, with the name of each new speaker indicated. In this way the storyteller is central and the witnesses are peripheral, including myself as researcher.

## The introduction

Having said that I'll go first
I have that 'caught in headlights' sort of feeling
and I can't start.

(pause)
Erm.
I would not be here today…,

I would not have ever envisaged
that I would be thinking of,
be starting a PhD and the strange…

Had I not been ill
then I would have done my Diploma around that time
and I would have probably gone on and done a Masters.
But being ill has led me in such a different direction
and negotiating the transition from my self-concept before I was ill
to where I am now
has been through writing really,
and it's been such a big process of discovery and…

(long pause)

I think I need to kind of talk about…
    I suddenly feel quite self-conscious
I think I need to tell a little bit of the illness story
and how that has led me into writing and research.


## The illness story

So it was in '93, around this time of year
I developed a kind of pins and needles on the side of my face
which moved down my arm
and I was referred to a neurologist
and taken to hospital for a week for tests
    angiograms and MRI scans
which revealed that I had a swelling deep down in the right thalamic region,
at the top of my brain stem,
which had haemorrhaged.

They didn't know exactly what it was,
but it was too deep-seated to remove and too deep-seated to do a biopsy.

Things looked pretty desperate
because it was still haemorrhaging.

So it was decided to leave it and see what happened
and from September '93 through the Christmas
I deteriorated quite badly
and lost all strength on my left side
and finally the risks of
    at that point
    just having a look at it,
were worth taking because…

But then once I was taken to hospital again,
    and even in the week I was in hospital,
I lost a whole sense of my left side really and I was in a wheelchair,
and I was clearly going to die…

There really didn't seem to be a way through it,
so the risks of surgery were worth taking and they removed it.
And I was not expected to…,
I was not expected to survive the surgery.
There was a very strong chance that I would die during surgery,
or most definitely have quite severe left-sided disability.

So, to the surprise of the medical staff,
I survived it and with less disability than they expected.

That's only one of the stories.

## A story of healing

The other story that went on through this
was that when I was first diagnosed,
one of the patients on the ward came up to me and said:
'You're not going to believe this
but my sister's a healer and she feels she can help you.'

It was strange because the evening of the diagnosis,
    before hearing this,
I'd asked Tony, my husband, to ring a friend of ours in the north-east
who is a healer and he wasn't in.

Tony had left a message for him
and then the next day this patient came up to me
on the ward and said 'My sister's a healer and she feels she can help you.'

So I saw the sister, Brenda, and just as soon as I met her
I knew there was a way through:
and medically there really didn't seem to be a way out of it,
but I just had…

I knew I'd have to go through the whole process
but I kind of knew that I'd get through it.

I mean, there were periods of absolute despair
and there were periods of looking at my children and thinking
'I'm not going to see them grow up.'
    really, really
but then, underlying all of that was
this kind of strong sense that I was going to come through it.

And when I was then referred on to a surgeon who said
    as surgeons do
he went through the risks in…
    it was great actually because
    he was just so straight and to the point.
    And I loved it because I could…

He went through…
catalogued all the different risks and

I said: 'And death?'
He said: 'Yes.'

So I knew that the risks of surgery were huge
and I knew he could do it.
I knew.
That was a deep intuitive…
I had no doubt about it.
So the process of making sense of it all…
    having entered into counselling training
a couple of years before that meant
    that I had friends who were counsellors.
    And I had good friends anyway who…,

so I was able to work my way through what had happened.

## Stories of writing and research

Well, there was still more,
and really it was almost exactly a year after it happened
that I started writing about it.

And the writing was…
I learned things about it and didn't even…,
and also found the writing so fulfilling.

Well, it ended up as a book.
    I hadn't set out to write a book.
It was published in '97.
I did my Diploma from '98 to 2000 and wrote a paper
looking at the kind of marginalization that you can experience
when you're hospitalized:
looking at it from the perspective of person-centred theory
and also looking at my own writing process from the perspective of person-centred
theory.

And I found that really valuable
    to write about it all again
but taking a step back and from within a broader social context.
To locate my own experience as someone who's positioned as a patient
and looking at it from that point of view.

But when I was doing my Diploma,
the bits that I loved were the extended essays.

My second year placement was at Warwick University which I just adored,
it was just wonderful
    I loved that client group and it was…
    I loved that too.

Both of my extended essays were on spirituality and person-centredness:
    I feel a real passion about that.
    I feel it's…

I feel very incoherent, really incoherent.

But it kind of all links together for me.

Nell: It's making sense to me if that's any help.

Is it?

Nell: Mm, it doesn't feel…

Thank you, yes.

I suppose with that,
it was quite validating because I knew, I knew,
I gained confidence in my writing
and I knew that I could write in an academic way
and one of the things that I now know about myself is
that I can write in a way that integrates my intellect and feeling.
I can do that.
I feel good about that.

When I was doing my Diploma
I had a feeling that I wanted to do research.

I didn't want to just go straight on and do a Masters.
I wanted the freedom to do what I wanted to do.
And while I was teaching my counselling evening classes in two groups,
at different times,
I had encountered four students;
   – one who'd had major heart surgery when he was in his early teens;
   – one who had had major back surgery as a child and had spent a lot of time in hospital;
   – another student who had cancer and a mastectomy while she was on the course;
   – and another student who'd had a kidney transplant.

And on hearing their stories
in the context of teaching a person-centred course,
I had just a sense of…
there's something here…

I became very curious about different experiences of illness
and started to think
'Well maybe…
I've loved writing my story but I'm actually ready,
I don't want to write about me any more,'

or I didn't need to do that in the same sort of way.
But I still had a sense of connection to the area of illness
and, in a sense, it was still about me;
it was part of my longer process of trying to make sense of it all,
but within a community of other people who have experienced illness.

When I told you, Kim, the story about the students
and you said something like:
'All of them have had major surgery, very different kinds of surgery'
that just kind of clicked.

I feel that I'm moving towards… (pause)
I don't know how it would work
but I had a kind of germination of an idea of approach to research
and Kim, you mentioned Sally Lockwood's MSc
so I photocopied it and read it.

## Emerging stories of methodologies

One of the things…
    – I feel really hesitant about saying this
    – because I feel silly and I don't know that it's a good idea
    – or whether it would work
but I think one of the things I would quite like to do
is maybe work in some kind of focus group way,
but using some of the person-centred art therapy things that I've done,
and maybe say,
    I don't know, over six sessions
    (that's just arbitrary),
work with a particular group of people
who knew what I was wanting to do and,
I suppose,
had done some of the reflection that you do on yourself
in counselling training,
but people who'd had maybe different forms of surgery.

So not necessarily thinking
    I mean I haven't even said anything to the previous students
but it was that that got me thinking of possibly talking to them
to see if they were interested;
but also maybe seeking some people through the counselling journal.

But rather than just interviewing,
actually having a series of sessions
in which people told their stories in different ways
and responded to each other,
and maybe following that up
with some kind of more in-depth individual interviews.
And I don't know,
that's where I'm groping my way towards at the moment.

## Self/other stories

It was through writing the paper
that went into the *Auto/Biography* journal
that I came across the term autoethnography which I've never heard of
and Kim, when she read it she said, 'Oh, autoethnography'.

I'd never heard the term and I've been reading a lot of Carolyn Ellis since.

I found that quite validating 'cos actually,
it's all right to write about yourself,
it's not purely self-indulgent!
It can have beneficial effects in a much wider ways.

But I'm not sure where my own story
and my own reflections on that will fit in
or relate to hearing other people's stories.

I feel quite unclear about that
and where those kind of boundaries would be.

That's kind of pretty much where I am at the moment.
Yes I do feel ever so incoherent,
I feel quite nervous and I feel quite exposed.
Thank you for letting me ramble.


## Witnesses' stories

Nell: It didn't feel like rambling.

Peter: I was going to say:
I think it would be really good
to listen to this [tape recording]
actually and then you would know
that you don't ramble,
because you've actually given
a very clear picture
of where you might go – by speaking.
And maybe speaking is quite an important way for you
because I felt engaged with you every second.

Thank you Peter.

Ruth: I just wanted to say
it didn't sound incoherent to me either.
It felt a bit like you were
searching around for the take-off point.
That's really where I thought you were.

It didn't sound incoherent but that
you just didn't know quite where to…

Nell: But the story of your illness felt to me
like you *knew* this,
you've worked with this.
Then there was the move
to your work with the students
and that moment of bridging,
the link, accepting *your* experience,
just as your experience
and how that then connects up
with other people's experience.

That sounded like a real change
but a real, coherent change with direction.
And then,
as you got up to decisions now,
about where you go from here,
that felt less certain
but it didn't feel incoherent.
It felt like 'Dare I say this?
I'm not sure about this,
I haven't gone through this myself much yet.
I haven't practised it' but...

Ruth: It felt like you were stepping out,
not knowing quite what
you were going to say
because you haven't actually said it yet.

I felt very frightened
saying it because...yes.

Peter: I'm really curious about who you thought
    I'm not asking you the question
    in case it's private
but I felt really curious about
who you thought
was going to slap you down.

Didn't feel like it was in this room.
It felt somewhere there was
this quite important sense of...,
and the bit that made me nosy was when you said
about doing drawings and things.
So it felt like *working with* people
                with illness narratives
rather than just a narrative,
'cos you seem to know [already]
what you need to know about the narratives.
And maybe it felt like the healer in you
    you told us about the healer,
    who wanted to do some healing –
and I felt in my belly,
    I always feel things here
    because I actually had half
    my stomach taken away
    and nearly died
and I thought
'Well this woman could heal me.'

It didn't have that form of words
and it's not something I'm asking of you
and I don't want that to be in the way

of what I'm trying to say to you,
but it felt like there was an impulsive ache  here
and I just thought how *daring* that woman was
to come up to you and say:
...my sister...
And you could have said 'Get lost!'
couldn't you? or frozen her out,
and it felt like was something you knew,
wanting to move towards something...

That is a real gift Peter thank you,
because as a teacher
I know I'm good at it [teaching]
because I engage, I risk something of myself and in my writing.

It's quite hard saying that.

In a way I know it's healing.
I know the healer in me
but I appreciate having that recognized
and thank you.

Kim: I had an image of angel cake!
I thought:
'Why am I thinking about angel cake?
Oh angels again.'
(to the others)
Viv had previously talked with me
of the importance of angels

Peter: Or layers.

Kim: Yes, it was the colours.
As you were telling me the story
at the beginning when you were struggling
because you thought you might be incoherent
I had a sense of it being
because there were so many stories
that were all part of the same story
and to articulate them
you had to separate them out,
but actually that was rather unreal
because they were all
so much part of each other,
and I had this image of angel cake.
Layers of pink and white and...

Peter: I can connect with that too
because there's something very childlike
about the colours
and there's something Viv
about your innocence in what you were saying
that I loved.

I felt I wanted to protect that innocence
and I hoped you wouldn't turn it
into something clever.
Otherwise it'd stop being profound.

Ruth: The point where I felt most…moved isn't kind of the right word – but kind of caught in a point, was when you talked about how Kim had reflected that what was in common, was surgery. I thought 'Nobody really knows about that'. People know their individual experience, whether it's going through an appendicitis…but nobody *really* knows about that, and I thought: 'Wow it's just very important.' And it's something to do with that kind of point, point of the knife, but also the liminal space that people go into before surgery and the whole world of anaesthesia. I thought: 'God, if you could in any way allow people to access, probably things they don't even know that they know,  it would be… I don't know what it would be…, profound maybe is the word.'

## My brain works

I think part of my motivation is that I have a deep sense…

I've got deep crevices and holes in my skull
and if you look at an MRI scan,
I've got a big black hole in the centre of my brain and,
    I've said this to Kim before,
    I have a deep need…,
much, much deeper need to use my brain now,
a need to prove that even though I have a damaged brain
my brain works.
And there's a little bit of a 'use it or lose it' sort of feel there as well,
but I think it's more my sense of myself
as having a very damaged brain and my kind of…
    this is part of my north-eastern roots,
    – my mum and dad,
    – very determined and stubborn

I need to use my brain.

Peter: possibly about damage to your spirit.

(Viv looking puzzled)

Peter: Well it's like you are aware of the hole in your brain, but I kept hearing your self-doubt and I kept thinking as a mere outsider, 'Why?' And it seemed to me that this research has got ever such a high potential for you to yield whatever the damage in your spirit is that makes you doubt yourself.

I don't see that as damage in my spirit,
and I think the self-doubt is rooted
in my childhood and my schooling.
Yes, my schooling particularly has not been good enough,
    – those kind of messages – and in fact,
in some ways,
my confidence in my intellect has grown, paradoxically, since my illness.
I think I'm probably more confident in my intellect now
than I would have been before my surgery.

Kim: Why is that?

I think because, to a degree,
I've been driven to use it and actually,
by using it I've realized things about myself.

I've realized that when I write,
I can write in a way that can be moving and powerful,
but intellectually rigorous too,
and I didn't know that about myself until I'd done it.

> Ruth: I think the metaphor of a black hole is a very powerful one, whether it ends up in the title of your thesis or something around that, because it's a metaphor or image that resonates with me but for different reasons. I just think it's an amazing one, even to toy with that as one of your images.

Yes, thank you.
I appreciate you picking up on that
because it's one I've used before
but I haven't recognized it almost.

> Ruth: Feels very deep, which is the word you kept using alongside it.

Yes

> Peter: I'm still fascinated by the... I was thinking to myself, what is it I like about her, and I like your hair. I think it's probably just me, but it's also something about you. Then I realized that your hair was covering the crevice you told us about.

Thank you.
Deep, deep crevice – then holes.

> Peter: Then I rebelled and I thought: well I still like her hair.

> Ruth: It's like a crown.

> Peter: Well I don't know, there's a bit of 'fuck you' about it. I kind of, my guess is, that's what will get you through your doubts.

Yes, absolutely.

> Kim: It also speaks to me of fun, which is another part of you I think will be very important as you go through all this...the sense of fun that you have that I've seen.

That's another part of me that I like,
the fun and the slightly rebellious thing...

★　　★　　★　　★

As Viv told her stories many things were happening: she was re-telling her illness and healing stories for a new audience, from a new perspective, and for a new purpose – as the context and background against which she could tell her research stories. She had told her illness and healing stories many times before and in different ways, including her published book. As we listened to her talking, we were probably filling in the gaps in her story from our own experiences and histories and we were reflexively responding to the feelings, thoughts and images her stories were evoking. As she reached the point of a natural break, Viv indicated this to us by saying 'thank you for letting me ramble', thus inviting the rest of the group to respond. From this point the story entered a phase of re-authoring when other people's responses were offered to reflect back to Viv some of what we noticed that then became part of Viv's new stories and of ours. Her responses to our reflections, in turn, led her to tell new stories of her newly emerging sense of identity as 'someone who needs to use her brain' and someone who likes fun and being 'rebellious'.

All of these stories challenge our ideas of disability. Viv's are not tragic stories but stories of hope, resistance and transformation. Her illness, surgery and subsequent disability has opened up her mind and heart to think about how she might use her experiences to develop herself, discover new abilities and teach others about the many levels she has touched during this part of her life. This is what Frank (1995) refers to as a 'quest story': a story that is told by those who have 're-turned' from a journey and accepted the 'boon' of knowledge and the insights that came through making that journey, which they now want to pass on to others. In passing such knowledge on Viv bears witness to her own suffering and that of those closest to her. Quest stories may also become *manifestos*, which require social action and point up the need for change. Writers of such stories do not want to go back to the way it was before; they want to use the suffering to effect and change others, and the society in which they live.

The past is reinterpreted in the present and takes on a new meaning. Stories like these can easily become 'escape' stories about 'rising above it', phoenix-like, but the antidote to that is the underlying story of chaos and distress that prevents us from romanticizing severe illnesses. Viv would have preferred that it had not happened, but as it did, then she will use her experiences in the best ways she can. Frank (1995) reminds us that the phoenix remembers nothing of his former existence as he rises from the ashes but Viv has not forgotten her suffering and does not deny her current condition. Renewal is never complete, she bears her scars in awareness and often with pride and in doing so she reminds others that they too can heal. The telling and witnessing of such stories provides us with a moral opportunity to set right what was wrong, or at least to know it for what it was. McLeod (1997) says, 'A story is not merely a chronicle of events. A story is an account of events set against a landscape of moral values' (p.153).

★   ★   ★   ★

In the chapter that follows Viv re-tells some of these stories: she writes in her own words about what is happening to her as she commences her doctoral studies. She shows the reader how her disability affects her and what it is like for her to be a disabled research student, including some of what she found helpful and/or hindering along the way. She allows us to glimpse some of her fears, frustrations and hopes, set against the cultural, financial and historical backdrop of the NHS, university life, home and the era in which she lives. Technology now plays an important part in most people's lives and for disabled people it has opened up new possibilities. But technology needs to be available and mastered if it to be of use. Viv's disability severely affects her ability to use a computer but with a professional assessment of her difficulties and what she needs to overcome them, she is freed from those constraints.

This is the story of one woman – a local story in postmodern times that can be set against 'grand narratives' of the modernist era. The 'grand narratives' in which illness and disability have been embedded are usually identified in terms of the 'medical model', seeing disabled people as 'patients' with symptoms that need to be 'cured'. However, a challenge to these views emerged from within the medical world as other professions developed, bringing ideas from psychology and sociology to put alongside the medical model. In turn psychology and sociology were themselves changing and applying these changes to health and social care (Cooper, Stevenson and Hale 1996). Further developments ensued with Engel's biopsychosocial model (1977), which was accepted by both academics and practitioners as a model that could provide an holistic understanding of the individual's experience of health, impairment and disease.

Against this background people with disabilities claimed their right to tell their own stories and speak for themselves, and did so powerfully, thus influencing social policy and political campaigning for equal rights of access to all walks of life, including higher education (Barnes, Mercer and Shakespeare 1999, p.2). Disabled people have been marginalized and excluded from mainstream education, and as their voices were heard calling for access to education at all levels, including higher education and life-long learning, this began to change.

Postmodernism brought to our attention that disability is a social construction, challenging the 'individual model' and the 'medicalization' of disability in which it was seen as a personal tragedy. The 'social model' emphasized instead the need to recognize that impairments people sustain, whether from birth or occurring later in life, do not in themselves necessarily create disability. Rather, disability sometimes occurs within a social context and within disabling environments that create barriers for people who have impairments (Swain *et al.*1993). However, this model too has its critics from both outside and inside the ranks of disabled people, who have argued that it does not resonate with some disabled people's experience of impairment, especially that of women and those who feel that the distress and disability they experience from their particular impairment would be little affected by changes in their environment or in society itself (Woolley 1993).

New stories are continually emerging, and increasingly disability is understood in terms of the *relationship* between impairment and the physical and social environments. Disability can be defined in these terms as: (a) an individual problem, (b) a social construction, and (c) a social creation (Oliver 1993).

Bearing all of this in mind, as you read the following chapter I invite you to use Viv's stories to reflect upon the social context and identity of the teller and how in telling and re-telling stories, new meanings are created, new identities are formed, and contexts are changed.

*Chapter 14*

# Stories of Liberation and Independence

To think *about* a story is to reduce it to content and then analyze that content. Thinking *with* stories takes the story as already complete; there is no going beyond it. To think *with* a story is to experience it affecting one's own life and to find in that effect a certain truth of one's life.

(Frank 1995, p.23)

## Viv Martin's stories

This is my story of how it feels to be a student with disabilities starting a PhD. It is very hard to know where to start because if I hadn't been ill, and ill in a way which interrupted my previous conceptions of self, with the losses and the transformations that entailed, then I would not have even thought of doing a PhD. And so, for me, doing a PhD and experiencing disability are not separate; they are deeply linked. Although I did not foresee the direction I have taken, I look back to about five years ago and realize that at some intuitive level I was preparing for this.

I will say something about the nature of my disabilities and the illness which led to them. Then I will focus on my lived experience of taking on something that feels hugely daunting in many different ways, as well as exciting and potentially liberating; something which is full of contradictions and paradox; something full of old scripts, dominant stories, rebellious stories, and 'unique outcomes'. I will tell the 'jacking it all in' stories, as well as the 'maybe I am good enough' and the 'I can do this' stories.

If you were to look at me, I don't think you would see disability. If you were to spend some time with me, however, you would notice that sometimes my concentration wanders; you might notice my engagement and enthusiasm, but you would also see me disengaging with tiredness in my eyes. If you were to see me walking, and watch carefully, you would see my left side moving more slowly than my right, sometimes dragging, sometimes bumping into things. You might notice my left hand moving like a mechanical grabber, the kind you saw in fun fairs in the 1960s, awkward and clumsy; or

195

you might see me burn my left hand and become aware of it a split-second too late. If you saw me in a bookshop or library you might see me take a book from a shelf and not know where to put it back. You might see me coming out of doorways and turning right when I wanted to go left.

I had a swelling in my brain which haemorrhaged and was removed in 1994; the effects weren't anything like as severe as they were expected to be. I am relatively mobile, and my speech is all right. On the other hand, I experience a permanent pins and needles and burning sensation on my left side; my sense of touch is impaired; and my fine motor control is poor. Therefore I can no longer write with my previously dominant left hand. I have a slight spatial and visual memory problem, and I tire very easily. But I am 'extremely lucky to be alive'.

In order to give something of the feel and sense of my lived experience as a research student with disabilities, I have included extracts from my journal written over the first six months of my research journey.

---

*13 January 2003*

Registered for M Phil/PhD today – what a tornado of doubts and panic. Is this a huge mistake? Have sense of being swept up by events; I never expected this to happen. Feel I have gone about this the wrong way round, so when potential research supervisors said this research idea was possible, and more than that, I was overwhelmed. I didn't expect to be taken seriously. I didn't expect my writing to be rated. When I wrote about my illness it was just to 'make sense of my experience' to 'prove I had a brain'. It's not like I've worked my way through the system. I've gone round the houses and come in through the backdoor. So, what right have I to be doing this? Who do I think I am? When I said to Pauline a few years ago, 'I quite fancy doing a PhD', she said quickly 'You don't have to be intelligent to do a PhD'. I countered quickly with: 'Well, obviously. All you need is to be motivated and prepared to work hard', which I knew I was, I am – but what a put-down! Maybe it was hard for her to think I might be intelligent and maybe it felt important for her to put me in my place. But, yeah, I have got the right to do this.

But when I went to register today, I asked myself: What am I doing here? Who am I fooling? They're sure to find me out. Even though I got a good degree I have not travelled the conventional academic path and I feel a fraud. But at the same time I know my determination and my refusal to give in – my 'awkward bugger' self, rooted in the North East and in my family of origin – is a source of my strength.

*20 January 2003*

Meeting of narrative research interest group in Kim's house. Very scary, but maybe I'll get there. Reassuring that K said she rated my writing. Feel vulnerable but know if I express it and it is truly received, then that is transforming: I will find my own strength. It is in the tension between the knowing and the not knowing, between the fragility and the strength, the hopeless and the hopeful, the giving in and the carrying on, the retreat and going forward. If I express it and I am understood, I can go on. I can take the risk. I will 'feel the fear, and do it anyway'.

It's a very huge effort, both physical and emotional, to go to Bristol, but also see my learning/discovery/development (as researcher) as being about relation-ships. They are central to me, to my sense of self – belonging, being accepted, finding stimulation, affirmation and validation – all of this activates my own capacity for discovery and creativity (as well as my capacity to engage with others in ways which are affirming). But I find the distance and the difficulties of travelling prevent me from engaging as much as I would like. My disability e.g. the knowledge that I can't run if I'm feeling threatened or feeling unsafe returning home late at night, is scary. I don't know where this leaves me. I know I need to cope with my initial anxiety and hopefully come through it. I swing between engagement and excitement, on the one hand, and fear and doubts, on the other. Feel huge doubts at the moment – just want to shelter at home.

### 19 February 2003

Arrived for third of research training unit. Saw disability/access person. She thought it might be worth applying for disabled student's allowance and having needs assessment. Sounds like good idea but feel a bit ambivalent.

### 20 February 2003

So tired I can barely think. Day went fine. Fifteen people in the group, all doing educational research. My own project of exploring the illness narratives of others feels quite different. I sort of held my own as far as I can tell. Had bit of panic later – got lost on way back to where I was staying. Felt very frightened and not safe; when I'm tired spatial problem is much more pronounced. This experience is certainly clarifying my needs in relation to my disabilities. All feels a bit much though – terrifying, exhilarating, interesting, intensive, utterly exhausting. Ring those I love and burst into tears. Feeling of intense pressure in head, struggling to focus on reading, concerned about getting lost. Am I pushing myself too hard? A bit scared and worried – don't want another haemorrhage. Check strength on left side. Seems OK. Might ring Dr Anderson.

### 6 March 2003

Talk to Sue in Rome doing her art history research and loving it. She's a real inspiration for me. realize how determined I am. Important to have my own difficulties acknowledged (e.g. access unit) but not to allow either myself (or systems) to prevent me from doing what I am capable of. Confidence has sort of grown. As I tackle assignment and grapple with ideas – yes, feel huge 'neuro' drain on energy but also know that in 'neuro' terms, or any other, I don't have to accept language of deficit.

### 20 March 2003

Down in Bristol for autoethnography day. Stay in hotel on Square – expensive but worth it. At least I won't get lost! Decanter of sherry in room – text Ali to tell her; her reply – 'sounds like something out of *Inspector Morse*' – really makes me giggle. Being on my own I become aware of reclusive tendencies as well as bit of adventurous spirit and liberation. I like being on my own and am also afraid. Like time and solitude, but frightened of distance and separation. Echo of awful fear of separation when it looked like I would die – fear of being forever cut off from family and friends. Aware that journey out of illness is journey through this 'separation anxiety' – illness as experience of regression – just coming to realize extent of that. Being here in Bristol, though scary, is important and necessary. Research path is not just looking out, but looking in: investigation is also step towards transformation. Also feel sense of wanting to 'make a difference' – to 'illuminate understandings' of doctors, and challenge 'results culture' of NHS. I know that in such a culture I was 'lucky' to have surgery at all: in fact young Senior House Officer later told me my operation was so risky that no other surgeon would have attempted it. Mr Meyer was definitely a surgeon with courage.

*25 April 2003*

See Dr Anderson. Told him about symptoms – pressure in head, etc. Expect him to say 'Don't waste my time'. Shocked when he says, 'In the light of your history, we'll do an EEG and an MRI scan'. Told me not to overdo it. Know from experience it will be a while before appointment comes through – will try to put it on 'back burner'. But shocked.

As I go over the appointment in my head, as I process it, things he said start to emerge: 'It's nearly ten years. You've done really well'. I know I have, but implicit in that statement is the idea that I was not expected to live this long – that ten years is better than expected.

He told me he would be retiring on 20 June, said he hadn't envisaged it. Suggested it was to do with changes in NHS. I wished him well and said I was sorry that he was going before he had planned to, and in this way. Feel huge sense of loss, tears fill my eyes as I write. Hate this bloody government – that a person of Dr Anderson's wisdom, humanity and experience should be driven out. He'll be really missed, and not just by his patients – also by his colleagues.

*12 May 2003*

In Bristol: Liked Ali's metaphor of Tate Modern: groping in the dark, finding reference points. In doing this, I'm learning about subtleties of disability and effects of illness – living out transformation making meaning and discoveries. Find Moustakas on heuristic research appealing – that it seeks to illuminate a topic that has personal resonance as well as wider social/cultural implications.

Staying at university accommodation. I like it, apart from walk up hill – but probably good for me. realize how slow I've been to get going, blocked initially by my fears and doubts. Very aware of contradictions – physical challenge of hill, yet determined to do it – need exercise, have become lazy slob. Very real fears about health grounded in reality, yet drive to 'prove' myself. Will utilize 'awkward bugger' configuration of self!

*13 May 2003*

Train home.
Spring sunshine.
Horses, sheep,
May blossom – reminds me of Mam
Hawthorns in May, shades of green, depth of colour, texture, richness

Coming into Birmingham,
through Bournville – rich, green and alive,
nature, life and growth.
Not the stereotype people have
beautiful, vibrant, friendly,
mix of cultures and class
realize how much it is home
roots in Durham, home in Birmingham
Sense of possibilities

*15 May 2003*

Feeling that everything we experience in life is part of the process that leads us to where we are and who we are now. The Alchemist tells the traveller: 'Everything you need to know, you've learnt through your journey'. How I need to remind myself of that.

The writing process: I have gradually come to realize that writing is not just an external expression of something within, but a process of discovery, of finding meaning and of coming to know what, at some level, I do know, of actively and creatively engaging in that unfolding process. It is almost as if it is in the telling that the story reveals itself and the meaning emerges. Philip Pullman says: 'I never start with a theme – it has to emerge, when the story itself shows me what it's capable of saying' (Pullman 2000).

### 5 June 2003

Experience of needs assessment for DSA – very positive. Felt like first time I could detail my specific difficulties, have them recognized and understood – but that I was also related to as a person with capabilities and equal rights – not just clichéd talk, but genuine recognition of my rights to an independent life, to be able to do things for myself – not patronizing or condescending. It was straightforward and focused on identifying the effects of my medical condition and the impact of this on studying, determining my specific needs in relation to studying requirements, IT and study materials that would enable me to carry out research. There was a recognition of how my reliance on others to type or send/read emails restricts my independence. I greatly appreciate the way this session was done.

### 11 June 2003

Had the EEG. What a contrast with my needs assessment last week! Twenty-two electrodes attached to my scalp, technician asked lots of questions. Halfway through, stopped and drew diagram of holes and crevices on my skull. Asked girl on work experience if she wanted to feel it. Felt like object. He answered her questions, but clearly didn't want me to hear what he said. I sensed discomfort in his voice and something slightly evasive in his tone. So I asked my own questions. I persevered and pushed with my questions. I said: 'What does that mean? You mentioned spiky patterns in that region – why is that significant? Why did you say to her: "I'll tell you later"? Why did you use the word episode?'

I know that when I'm in the position of patient and very anxious, I react/protect myself by engaging my intellect. It's an assertion of power when I feel helpless. I ask sharp and pertinent questions and push for answers. It is part of my need to assert myself as a person and to be related to as a person. I hate the passivity of the patient role. I'm also aware that since it is *my* brain which is being investigated I feel a strong need to show I can use it. To show that it is not a physiological object – it is part of who I am. (I watched an *Everyman/Horizon* programme which suggested idea that brain acts as a *receiver* of consciousness.) It isn't all of me but it acts to locate my 'self' within my body. I know that my questions put him in a difficult position. I know he's not supposed to comment but I still reserve the right to question someone who is sticking electrodes on my scalp and observing the patterns of electrical activity in my brain. So pissed off that I decided not to mention my spatial problems. Anyway, I had already told Dr Anderson. I gave technician quite enough information. But when I left the room, I turned left instead of right. Felt stupid.

### 12 June 2003

Very aware of how I use defiance as a way of living with my condition – I don't deny it, I do acknowledge it and I will *live* with it. I am aware that rationally my life expectancy may be limited, but I still have a feeling I'll live for some time yet. I might be wrong – but actually I don't doubt it. I feel quite strong as well as frightened. Just got to wait for MRI – still no appointment. Must ring.

I am aware that doing academic work/writing on my own loss is part of the way I deal with the uncertainty. As I still experience the symptoms and wait for my MRI scan, my writing is a way of acknowledging its presence but a way of maintaining a degree of distance. In a sense I am working with it, not just doing work about it.

Am so excited – we've converted spare room into workroom for me – love it – can work undisturbed, look out at trees and sky; it's my space – feels good, really precious, can't say how important it is to me.

### 13 June 2003

Ring MRI unit – ask if they can give me any indication when it will be. Say they've had no paperwork. Ring Dr A's secretary – says she delivered it personally in May, and in any case there's a 10-month waiting list. Ring MRI Centre again. Say they've received nothing. Ring her again. Says she'll do another letter. Worried. Know he's retiring next Friday.

### 30 June 2003

Ring MRI unit. Still not on list – say they haven't received the paperwork! And that his secretary is new. Ring secretary again:
'I'm one of Dr A's patients. I...'
'You were – he's just retired.'
'I know that', I snapped. 'He told me'. But thinking, I know he's gone because of this stupid fucking government, but it could equally be because of this stupid fucking secretary. I didn't say that, of course. I was the model of restraint. 'I'm ringing to inquire about the MRI he requested. The MRI Centre have still not received any paperwork.'
'Well, there's a 12-month waiting list.'
I think: 'I know, but I wouldn't mind being on it!' But I say: 'Can a duplicate be sent down?'
'Well, I'll have to get the registrar to sign it.'
Think of Arthur Frank's phrase – 'Something else to get done' – or not – in this case. How, when we are in the system, we become invisible, how we can't be sure we won't get lost or overlooked, disappear from view. Mortality beckons but none of *them* can see it.

### 3 July 2003

Finally I'm on waiting list. Twelve months long but at least I'm on it. So what about the fact that the EEG will be out of date by the time the MRI comes through? I give up. This is ludicrous. What is the point? I'm feeling OK at the moment. This goes on the back burner. If I have any more symptoms, then I'll ring...

### 8 July 2003

Comment from doctor character on *Holby City*: 'I do operations, I don't have them.' Awareness from scriptwriters of the divide – suggests shift in popular culture in postmodern times. Use of stories to address issues of power, role, positioning.

★    ★    ★    ★

My intention in including these extracts from my journal has been to give a sense of my journey/process as not linear, nor coherent nor on a steady gradient, but unsteady, at times polarized or contradictory, but ultimately a journey with meaning and purpose, even if most of the time I am not sure what that purpose is. I'm sure that anyone starting a new project/job/life-stage will feel insecure, doubtful, daunted, as well as excited, and hopeful.

I want to conclude by saying that I have produced this account 'all by myself'. I no longer have to rely on the goodwill and kindness of my family to type my hand-written scrawl. Since August, and as a result of my DSA needs assessment, I now have a laptop with an LCD screen which I find easier to read, voice-activated software, a touch-pad (rather than a mouse) which I find easier to use with my non-dominant right hand. I am sitting in my 'study' now, surrounded by the chaos of my books, files and papers, looking out at the autumn sunshine filtering through the trees and I have a sense of liberation and independence that, when I came round from my six-hour brain operation, I never thought I would have again.

*Chapter 15*

# Too Close To Home

## A Dilemma of Involvement

The researcher owns up to his or her perspective on the study and may even track its evolution by keeping a critical reflective journal on the entire research process and the particular role of the researcher.

(Janesick 2000, p.385)

## Jeremy's story

Jeremy's background is in social work and community development. Before training as a social worker he worked in the voluntary sector in hostels and night shelters, and was involved in writing business plans, organizational reviews, funding applications and policies. He also worked for a while for an agency involved in helping to develop the voluntary sector so that social work students could get a placement there. In 1994 Jeremy began a PhD, funded by the ESRC for three years. His choice to study parents who had been wrongly accused of child abuse was influenced by his involvement with friends who were accused of killing their baby in the early 1990s. The couple's other children were removed from home and later returned to them with the proviso that they would have 24-hour supervision, so Jeremy and some of his social worker friends moved in to provide that supervision. After six months of living under a cloud of suspicion his friends were cleared of any charges and allowed to care for their children once again. Until then Jeremy had had no involvement with child abuse but this personal experience led him to explore the topic for an MA.

Jeremy submitted his MA at a time when there was a lot of public interest in child abuse accusations that were later dismissed, and his application to the ESRC for funding to do a PhD was successful. His proposal was to examine how different narratives compete for acceptance: a narrative of guilt being written by the professionals – that the parents did whatever the professionals alleged, and another narrative of innocence written by the parents – two stories with apparently no meeting ground (Plummer 1995). When narratives compete, they can either find a neutral coexistence or agree not to talk about these things – in the case of child abuse this is not possible. So he was examining how two very fundamentally opposed stories, both of which sounded equally plausible, compete, and how ultimately one story manages to fend off the opposition.

I first met Jeremy at a conference when I heard his presentation based on his narrative PhD. Afterwards I spoke to him and he generously offered to send me a copy of his PhD. On reading his work I noticed that he seemed to be hinting at his own interest in the topic while avoiding doing so explicitly. I emailed him, asking about this apparent discrepancy. Everything he said seemed to indicate his belief in reflexivity but, in practice, there was little evidence of any. This correspondence led to me inviting Jeremy to join me in a conversation about these matters for this book, and it was not until then that I realized just how problematic this whole issue had been for him. He passionately believes in the values upon which reflexivity is based but he was constrained by the needs of the expectations of his examiners. Initially he had included his reflexive process, but when he was required to re-write his thesis he removed those portions.

When I asked Jeremy about his attitudes to being a reflexive researcher he explained how these beliefs had been partly based on what his involvement in a Jesuit community had taught him about the value of contemplation, reflection on personal values, finding God in everyday life, and discernment. For six months he had lived with three Jesuits in a their community as a social work placement, and over several years he had been on retreats and engaged in spiritual direction.

However, Jeremy became very personally entangled with the topic of his PhD research and the stress made him severely ill. I wanted to understand why, when Jeremy had received good support and supervision he had ended up almost becoming the very problem he was researching. His own child was removed from home. His complicated story cannot be more fully reported here for legal reasons – and it was suggested that his work in some way supported child abusers. I explored with him how he came to use a reflexive methodology.

Jeremy:   The choice of research topic very directly emerged out of my own story. I would never have chosen it had my friends not been accused and I'd been involved, and it's not only the choice of *what* you choose to research that depends upon personal biography, it's also *how* – so at some point it must resonate. I have great difficulty understanding people who view [their research topic choice] as very detached, as merely a piece of research that's interesting. To me there isn't anything inherently interesting: it only becomes interesting if it resonates at some level, and that might be in your head, it might be in your heart, it might be emotionally, it doesn't really matter, but there's always something I think… And similarly *how* you do your research depends… I could have done a nice statistical… I could have done a much more theoretical piece or a much more abstract piece.

Kim:   Mmm, a distant objective observer?

Jeremy:   Yes, rather than actually getting involved in listening to people's stories at length and writing them up. There's two chapters of my PhD, two long chapters, which are all about the stories, and then I go on to look at how different they compete or whatever. But there were lots of other ways of doing it.

Kim:      So using your self seemed very natural? It's almost like you're saying that you couldn't have *not* done it because that's...that was where your interest lay. It was *your* interest and you as a person affected that in some way, and were affected *by* it.

Jeremy:   That's right, because reflexivity is about how the research impacts on the researcher as well. Philosophically I don't go down this line of 'if there's a world out there...', a positivist world which you just can't...even positivists spend lots of angst ruling out the observer. I just don't go that way. Certainly in my research it was about processes; and an awful lot of work went into keeping people [participants] on board. These parents were very vulnerable at times, very damaged from what had happened and it was sometimes difficult just trying to keep them on board so that I could write it up and submit. *I* impacted on the process.

Kim:      Yes, absolutely. But there was a huge impact on *you* at the same time. I mean obviously that's been a very painful process for you, the whole of that, and producing a dissertation; having it knocked back; having to do it again; all of those personal things happening in the meantime; and your health being severely affected by the process. What part has your supervisor played in all this?

Jeremy:   Oh, he was great. He spent ages telling me to do less, and he would go through drafts and look at it, and we talked ages and ages when I was writing these stories for the thesis around whose voice is it: is it me, is it them? So that was just so useful to clarify, because sometimes I got so involved in it.

Kim:      That's one of the dangers of being reflexive and using a research topic that we are personally connected to in some way, isn't it? There's the usefulness and the richness of that – but there's also the danger that because it *is* personal we do get caught up and involved in it.

          I suppose one of the things that I'm thinking is: we encourage our students to work in this way in the counselling field, but we supervise them in ways that I think are very supportive and challenging, and ways that open up the transferences and counter-transferences that are potentially around and might otherwise complicate things. Also there's the fact that they would themselves have been in therapy and have a reasonably good awareness of their own part in what they're doing. I'm wondering if that's something that you had, and if you did, what *kind* of supervision you had? Was it personally supportive – not exactly therapeutic you know, but that kind of input?

          I was wondering also if you found ways of supporting yourself. Have you had counselling or therapy as part of this process? Yours is a different field, so I'm interested in how you managed that.

Jeremy:    I don't view the supervisory relationship as a therapeutic one, although it might have therapeutic spin-offs.

Kim:    That's the sort of thing I meant really.

Jeremy:    That's not what it's designed for.

Kim:    No. Exactly.

Jeremy:    No, it is a work-oriented thing. But he was very supportive, very personally supportive of me and, if I was unwell, giving me permission to say 'Well fine, you're well ahead with it, don't worry.' And we'd talk about how I felt about my work – what was good and bad, and all of that. And he continues to be supportive, like with the court case.

Kim:    So he's been beside you all along, all the way through?

Jeremy:    Oh yes, I'm sure he didn't particularly approve of what I had done, but certainly in the latter court case, he's been very supportive. He's been horrified at what's happened. Over many years I've been to spiritual directors, which again is partially therapeutic. It isn't psychotherapy but it is about being reflexive on how you're feeling and what's making sense – in a religious, spiritual framework. And I've also been to individual and group therapy.

Kim:    Do you have any regrets about your choice of topic or your way of working?

Jeremy:    Life would have been a lot simpler if I'd chosen some other topic. I don't know if it would have been any better. With child abuse there's this cloak of orthodoxy and I'm not alone in…there's a couple of guys in the States who wrote the first book that came out challenging professionals' decisions about child abuse. It was interesting to read in their preface, they're saying 'We are not in favour of child abuse' – the same problems had obviously come up for them.

Kim:    So it's like you have to make that statement first.

Jeremy:    Mmm, even to be allowed to challenge something. It's given me an insight into the lack of reflexivity in medicine, in social work, in law and how those narratives are constructed. And I'm all the more convinced now that legal narratives…the big thing about law is it's based on fact. Bollocks! It's as much an invention as any other story and it enters into the same procedures I was analysing. So I think I have got a lot out of it. And at some point I need to say to myself, 'Leave that subject behind' and move on. But it is painful. I was asked relatively recently to write an expert's report for somebody on what had happened in their case. Well, it was the aftermath thing – she was suing the local authority.

Kim:    This is the first time I've really heard of this happening [a researcher 'becoming' the very problem they were examining] and I suppose I'm wondering if there's anything that you understand about what happened that you could pass to others. When you reflect back now on what's happened to you, is there anything that you would have been able to put in place to ensure that you wouldn't have had to go through such a painful process? Is there anything *you* could have done differently? I know that you can't take responsibility for what other people have done. But with hindsight is there anything you could offer as a guide to other people who might follow on – doing this kind of reflexive research.

Jeremy:   I think there's a need for distance, at *some* level. Listening to the parents' stories, you have to be able to say somewhere: 'This isn't my problem.' I do feel it with the people I am researching now. They come out with these *awful* tales of how they've been treated really badly, and you have to say at some point: 'This ain't my problem.' I think there's also the need for someone outside the research relationship and the research environment, such as your supervisor, or others.

Kim:   A sort of anchor point?

Jeremy:   Yes, and my guess is that we should talk to the anthropologists – they have the classic story of when they end up 'going native'…

Kim:   Yes, it's like you got sucked into becoming one of the subjects of your own research.

Jeremy:   …or people who do participant observation, where they *have* to be part of it, in order to do the research.

Kim:   So in a way, the fact that it happened to your friends and you were so closely involved… Do you think that it might be contra-indicated, that it would be better to choose something as your research topic that you weren't quite so closely touched by?

Jeremy:   (Long pause) The difficulty for me was not the subject but *how* I approached it, and my stance that the orthodoxy may not be right. The usual stance in a lot of the professions, certainly social work and medicine, is that the professionals are *right*, you don't dispute what they say: they're the experts, whatever. And the social work profession states their position as one of 'disinterested application of expert knowledge'. I think a lot of my problems arose when I said: 'No, that's not true, we *all* have biographies and interests and desires, and there's an underbelly to even the best of practice.'

I used to say some of this on the social work course, that in even good social work practice there's a negative underbelly. So you might have solved this problem for this one person, but part of the underbelly is that there is a residual belief that 'you need professionals to sort out your problems'.

…But in answer to your question: What can I or other researchers do to protect themselves against that sort of thing? Two things come to mind. One is, when I wrote my research protocol, I had this great section on cost/benefits risks to the participants, and looking back on it, there's no mention of risks to the researcher. I think that's fairly standard: when people write research protocols they say what the risks are to the participants. Like when I was doing the one for carers, there was a whole section on 'How are you going to protect your participants?' and sod all on how you're going to protect yourself. I mean it's very low risk and we did say, 'Because I'm a lone worker…' but you know, there's nothing in there about 'What are you going to do if you find out one of your carers is abusing their mother?': elder abuse. Nothing about how you are going to deal with it yourself. And I don't think that's unusual…

Kim:     So if you *had* thought of that…, if you had been able to reflect on the possibilities…? I can't imagine that you would have ever dreamt of anything like this happening, but if that had been the case, now with the benefit of wisdom and hindsight, what might you have done to protect yourself?

Jeremy:   I think it would have been a good idea to have been more diligent in writing up my notes of interviews: not just about my impressions of them but about what was going on in me at that time. I did it sometimes: sometimes I did it immediately afterwards, sometimes later, sometimes I didn't do it. But to be more diligent around that and to set time to actually review that… And what I mean by review isn't simply about reviewing in the context of each interview, but reviewing the research log as a whole to see where I was at this point, at the beginning, and where I am now. I used to keep a personal journal and write the day's events and how I felt and look for patterns and things – but to be more diligent about that.

Kim:     How d'you think that would have helped in this instance?

Jeremy:   Because I think you then start seeing the processes and changes over time, and certainly you've got somebody outside who's looking at that as well. They may see…because a lot of stuff is very gradual, incremental. I mean the analogy with the carers' interviews I'm doing now. Day to day they don't notice much decline, even though the decline is there, but it's the people who go in once every three months who notice and say, 'Oh no, your wife's deteriorated a lot'.

Kim:     You're so close you don't see it?

Jeremy:   You don't see the small movements and most of us don't remember. You might remember highlights or lowlights but I don't think you remember all the stuff in the middle. So to have that… I used to keep a journal every day and I don't now. I regret that in some ways: it's very hard to pick it up again because it takes several months before you've actually got anything to work with.

Kim:     So looking back on that now, what d'you think you might have noticed if you'd been more diligent? What d'you think *might* have been brought to your attention?

Jeremy:   I think I had a tendency to accept too easily that some of the bizarre behaviour of some of the people I was interviewing was explicable by reference to what had happened to them rather than…some of the people I interviewed were odd.

Kim:     So you think you might have noticed yourself thinking, 'That person is a bit odd.'

Jeremy:   Well, I might have noticed my tendency to put down the odd behaviour to what had happened to them, which may or may not be right, but to notice that...

Kim:      And what difference would that have made d'you think if you'd noticed that?

Jeremy:   I think it would have given me that little bit more distance. I'm very concerned that telling one's own story can be, and I believe should be, a sort of empowering experience. I was interviewing people who'd been very disempowered, maybe hit with sledgehammers by the state, and were very damaged by that. And I wanted to give a voice to people who don't get heard. And for me, I'm not sure where the line is. I suppose it's also tied up with trying to keep people on board – and as a researcher, do I challenge it [odd behaviour] or do I just keep it to myself? But then, if I include it in anything I write up, that could be a betrayal of the relationship as well. But noticing that... I think noticing that some of their behaviour may have been there before [they were accused of child abuse] gives slightly more distance: that maybe these people are not totally victims.

Kim:      So you can suspend your judgement and not particularly get caught up with their victim position and...

Jeremy:   Yes, I mean I did try to do that, and I was asked to do that in various places, including the court. My stance is that I try to be agnostic, that it's not my place to decide what did or didn't happen but my work is to listen to the stories and look at how they compete. But I think, yes, looking back, I have more of a tendency to sympathize with the people who have been traumatized and it comes back to 'whose side are you on?'
          Now sometimes 'whose side are you on' allows you to gloss over some of the difficult things. No, that's not right, it didn't feel like glossing over difficult things because the incremental bits weren't difficult, but having that time-line so that you could identify 'well actually this is what I'm doing', and then you can make an adjustment if necessary.

Kim:      And you didn't interview the medical people, or the people on the other side did you, so the stories that you were involved with were one side of the story?

Jeremy:   Yes, with access to all the documentation from both sides of the story, obviously.

Kim:      It was very interesting reading it. I read the mother's story and was outraged and completely sucked into that awfulness and totally on the side of the angels, and then when I read all the other reports I thought 'My god this is a completely other story and I could feel completely with *this* story.' I think what you did was to demonstrate extremely well how there were two very different and incommensurable stories.

Jeremy:   And equally believable.

Kim:     And equally believable. I wondered what it would be like if I'd read them the other way round, and maybe it's because you put the mother's story before the professionals' story you were seen to be on that side?

Jeremy:  Because what normally happens, of course, is that the professional story comes first.

Kim:     Absolutely.

Jeremy:  Otherwise the mother wouldn't have to tell her story at all!.

Kim:     This might be an unfair question, and you can tell me to shut up if you want, but there's a little bit of me, the 'counsellor me', wondering if there's any part of that 'identification with the victim' that belongs somewhere else in your life that may have seduced you in there. And as I say, you don't need to answer that.

Jeremy:  One of the things I know I get from my mum and dad, which I treasure, is this sense of being on the side of the underdog. My parents weren't militant working-class activists, but they always did some sort of voluntary work in addition to their paid work.

Kim:     Very socially minded.

Jeremy:  Yes, they always stuck up for me in big things and little things. The local authority ran a Saturday school club, to help people learn musical instruments, and I said I'd like to go. And I wasn't very good. I'd only just started and so I strummed my three chords as best I could and they said I wasn't good enough, and my mum laid into them. She said: 'Look, you know, this thing has been set up to teach people to play, the fact he can't play now is irrelevant.' And they've always done that. When I've been depressed I've said some awful things about my mum and dad but they have always stuck up for me. And in FA cup finals, it's always the underdog they supported: if Tranmere is the underdog it's Tranmere they'd support.

Kim:     That's something you've been brought up with really, isn't it, and you became a social worker.

★    ★    ★    ★

As Jeremy and I spoke together I became aware of some of the potential dangers in researching topics about which we are passionate. We all have our biases, and being aware of them might not in itself sufficiently guard us from their allure, especially when researching in the field of abuse.

As I reflected upon this story I found myself thinking about the concept of 'abuse dynamics' – a reference to behaviours that are sometimes adopted (maybe unwittingly), particularly within relationships or organizations concerned with child abuse. Most counsellors who work with organizations or clients dealing with abuse are familiar with this concept and are aware of their need to monitor critically their propensity to become entangled, especially in the triangular dynamic roles of victim–persecutor–rescuer roles. However, as researchers we may be less aware or vigilant than we are as counsellors.

When researching incommensurable stories we might find ourselves wanting to take sides or having a particular opinion that supports one set of stories over another. In these situations it is all too easy to get drawn in.

In retrospect Jeremy offers suggestions about how to avoid some of the pitfalls that may be encountered when researching with people who have been victimized: namely, keeping a careful record of our relationships with them, and being able to acknowledge the reality and fullness of our responses. This will allow us to examine our relationships over time and as they develop.

One of the feminist values underpinning narrative approaches to research is to provide a platform for the voices of those who have been marginalized or victimized by society or other individuals. There is a danger that we report the voices of participants, either as powerless victims incapable of acts of resistance or as heroic stories of innocents who have overcome powerful destructive forces. The difficulty might be in maintaining a balance that acknowledges that we are all capable of being victims *and* perpetrators and that these are not positions to be judged, but rather to be seen as adaptive to circumstances that evoke those roles and behaviours. When we let go of judgements we may find it easier to document behaviours we notice without fear of 'betraying' our participants. Fine *et al.* (2000, p.125) suggest that, when we write our research stories,

> We stretch toward writing that spirals around social injustice and resilience, that recognizes the endurance of structures of injustice and the powerful acts of agency, that appreciates the courage and the limits of individual acts of resistance but refuses to perpetuate the fantasy that 'victims' are simply powerless.

As researchers we have an ethical responsibility towards our participants, the organization under whose name the research is being conducted and our profession and colleagues. We need therefore to pay attention to the specific ethical principles of professional practice (BACP 2002) and uphold them with integrity from the first to the last contact with participants.

The ethical principles related to research are concerned with informed consent and a person's right to withdraw from the research at any time:

- *Fidelity:* honouring the trust placed by the participant in the researcher
- *Autonomy:* respect for the participant's right to be self-governing
- *Beneficence:* a commitment to promoting well-being
- *Non-maleficence:* a commitment to avoiding harm
- *Justice:* the fair and impartial treatment of all participants
- *Self-respect:* fostering the researcher's self-knowledge and care for self

The principle of self-respect shows that we not only have a responsibility towards participants in research but also towards ourselves, especially when researching areas related to abuse in which complicated dynamics can abound and/or when we involve our selves reflexively in the research and not as distant 'neutral' observers. We need to promote our own well-being; to avoid doing harm to ourselves; to have respect for our own rights to be self-governing; to be treated fairly and impartially; and to trust our participants to take some responsibility for themselves and their part in the process. This, of course, can be challenging for those of us who are more used to thinking of the needs of others, but as researchers we need to find ways to balance caring for participants while also meeting our own needs in the research. No easy task!

*Chapter 16*

# Reflexive Embodied Research

It is through my body that I understand other people.

(Merleau-Ponty 1962, p.186)

In my view, Merleau-Ponty's quote tells only part of the story for it has been through my body that I have come to know *myself* as well as other people. In my most recent book, *Trauma, the Body and Transformation*, I explain how my complex relationship with my body led me to explore my own and other people's stories through researching those topics. So I have come to view my body and its responses as important, not only in my personal life but also in my professional life.

The body has increasingly become recognized as a source of wisdom and knowledge, as well as an important tool for therapists in their work with clients (Shaw 2003). The frequently quoted remark, 'the body does not lie', is something we take for granted without thinking too much about what it might mean to us as researchers. We speak of 'gut feelings' when our bodies respond to emotions instinctively: shivering with fear, blushing with shame, tears falling when we are saddened, fearful or enraged, connecting us with our feelings and thoughts, consciously or unconsciously in a dynamic dance between body and mind that might have as much to do with our past history as it does with the present. Braud (1998, p.218) suggests that our bodily responses, though often ignored, can, like any other tool for research, introduce error as well as truth:

> Bodily reactions also, however, can accurately reflect present realities in ways that are sometimes less filtered, distorted, or biased that those of intellect. Albert Einstein (1954, p.36), for example, noted that in the creative moments of his research, 'the words or the language, as they are written or spoken, do not seem to play any role'; rather, the elements in his 'thought' were 'visual and of some muscular type'. In his creative moments, Einstein apparently thought with aspects of his body (his muscles) other than his discursive intellect. Bodily reactions could contribute not only to discoveries but also to validity assessments of the larger body of one's work.

We can experience these responses in our relationships with research participants, as we read or write research ourselves, and we can evoke those responses in others who read what we have written.

Taking these kinds of ideas a few steps further, transpersonal researchers have begun to address topics that could not be researched using traditional methodologies. They have allowed and documented the results of how their research, clinical experiences and personal psychospiritual developments happen

> simultaneously, mutually informing one another, playing off and reinforcing one another. Our own 'lived world' experiences – including a variety of transpersonal experiences – were more fully informing and being incorporated into our research projects. Research suddenly became much broader, more relevant, and more exciting. (Braud and Anderson 1998, p.xv)

One of my participants, Dori Yusef, had been trained in biosynthesis and begun a PhD in April 2001 entitled *The Body as a Universal Gateway*. In her previous MA study, *The Body as a Gateway*, she had used a co-operative inquiry group which met four times as a method. After analysing the data from these group meetings, the group met again and Dori collected further data before going into retreat for four days to allow her self to remain in close touch with the data without the distractions of her daily life. She called this her 'examined life': a time when she focused entirely on her own experience of what was being evoked in her body through the process of research.

She began her story of becoming a reflexive researcher by remembering and re-telling the story of her MA research, which was embedded in her earlier experience of her biosynthesis training. This story was a precursor to her PhD story that followed.

## Narrative analysis

Narrative analysis views life as constructed and experienced through the telling and re-telling of the story (Bruner 1987, 1990, 1991; MacIntyre 1981), and the analysis is the creation of coherent and resonant stories. The analysis does not seek to find similarities across stories, and is not interested in conceptual themes, but instead values the messiness, depth and texture of experienced life. I present Dori's stories as *constituting* her reality and knowledge in themselves (Bruner 1991; Frank 1995; Ochberg 1994; Riessman 1993) and leave them to speak for themselves. I have arranged her spoken words in stanza form; it seemed no other representation could capture the quality of our conversation. My own interventions are placed at the right-hand side of the page.

Dori's interest in 'embodiment' was at the centre of everything she said: transpersonal experiences related to death and existence, and the threads that coalesced through her body and her research.

## 'The question was there inside of me'

It just seemed that the question was *there*
inside of me,
my question,
my topic was there already.

My background is in painting.
I went to Art School many years ago
so I was a very visual person.
I was very airy – and spiritual
and I needed to embody those parts of myself,
to bring them into the world.

The feminine part was very well established
with ideas and imagination
but I wasn't embodying it.

The MA, for me,
was a way to bring all my interests together,
visual, imaginary, transpersonal, body,
all together
and this now (the PhD)
is an extension of that
only much more focused
    a richer deeper one
     I hope.


## 'A more urgent journey'

But this is a more urgent journey for me.
It became more urgent
Because
when I was doing my MA
my mother became quite ill.
    She was ill anyway.
     14 odd years ago she'd had a liver transplant.

It was all tied up
a gift
in a way.

But when I started my MA
a cousin of mine was going through the process
of dying.

She was a young woman
and
eventually she died of cancer.

So it was almost like an initiation
into my MA: embodying this body.

Very much about the body
and what we hold;
and how the body holds *us*
for a measured time and space in this world;

and our boundary in this world is within the body
    or that's how it seems

that was as I was beginning my MA.

And as I was finishing my mother was quite ill
and my grandfather died;
and I was there at the process of his dying too.

I remember somewhere through that,
when I took my mother to hospital,
she said: 'You have to finish this.'
I was writing notes for my group.

There I was,
    sitting in an A/E dept with her,
writing this down,
and she said:
'You have to finish this for the family.'

And I just thought: 'Wow!'

It felt like an inherited purpose
or something that's been handed down to me
to deal with
    for women.

It felt – like a feminine role
and the [research] group happened to end up
an all-female inquiry group
and the story became
a story of shame.

And when I actually went into my little retreat
    on my own,
I had a dreadful headache,
I felt awful.
I thought: 'What am I doing here?'
This is all nonsense – it's all daft.

And on the 4th morning
    the last day
I had this kind of vision, or dream
    or whatever it was called.

As I was waking up,
it was almost like I saw my cousin
and she threw me something in imagination
and what she threw me I held in my hands

– and I didn't quite know what it was –
even as I'm dreaming this
I'm thinking: 'What might it be?'

One of the things I thought was:
'It's my little brooch.
It's a tiny, tiny brooch.'

And the brooch was a little metal angel
with a gold baseball bat.
Because she died in NY
and I went to NY to see her when she was very ill,
before she was dying.

And then I went back when she died.

Just after the funeral
we went to this hotel
    and I'd just sat down on a seat
    and looked down on the floor
    and I saw what looked like a roll of foil
    and I picked it up
    and I was just astonished
– it was this metal angel –
only about so big and it had a baseball bat.

I said to her brother: 'God look at this,'
and he said: 'That's her.'
I said: 'Do you mind if I keep it?'
and he said:
'No, no that's for you.'

I felt like it was her gift to me.
And then I lost it
I came home and lost it.

So in this vision it was like she was throwing this to me.
It didn't feel right in my body.
I thought. 'She's throwing me a crystal,'
and then I thought: 'No, its not that either,
I know what it is – it's light.'

(I feel quite moved saying this.)

I remember getting up from the bed,
    it was just incredible.
I just stood like that
and I said: 'I know what it is.'

It was like light filled me,
as if I became a conduit for light.
And when I looked at this in my therapy
I'm really like a prism in a rainbow.
    That is the key really.

The source of light comes through me
and then it disperses
into the spectrum.

I go through all these experiences
and then it comes back
and the body is the gateway.


## 'Heuristic research'

So for me heuristic research
is very appropriate
because it's what emerges
and what comes out of it.

We allowed it to just develop.

I didn't have any particular direction for it
I had some ideas and then we…

One thing I did was using postures
and
shamanic journeying
as part of it.
    That was just an offshoot
    and it's that offshoot that's taken my interest more.

The postures that we sat in
initiated similar experiences
    which I thought was fascinating.

So that was the heuristic experience for all of us,
And then there was one
(a heuristic experience)
of my own that was a wavy line
between what I was doing
    and what the group were doing
    and how I was responding
    and reacting to it back again.

So I suppose the method,
the logistics of doing it
was to have the group do those particular tasks
    and then write it up
    and then go into retreat.

When I describe the methodology
I use the example of painting
because I am traditionally a painter.

The canvas is there and I'm looking at it
and making a drawing
or whatever

it's as though I see it;
then I take it inside.

I may paint something and then I have to leave it
and then,
whatever cooks inside, incubates –
    does whatever it needs to do –
then I come back and I see it slightly differently
    and then something else emerges from it
it becomes more explicit.

It's that creative process that I described
    exactly the same as painting
    even if I'm doing something figurative
I still take it in
    I still have to absorb it.

I didn't realize I was doing that.
I absorb it and it does things in there
and takes on my personality and my experience of it
and then it's regurgitated.

                        I notice that you refer to the 'feminine'.
                        I have talked about scientific research
                        as masculine, white coats, etc.
                        the image of researcher
                        as traditionally masculine.
                        What you are describing is a feminine process – 'a
                        taking in'.

When I had all this material
I thought: 'What do I do with it now?
How do I analyse it – what do I look at?'
I thought it just seemed that some of it
I didn't have to explain.
    I didn't have to explain it.

This is what I discovered
this is what I found.
And it's a bit like the spectrum
    there are lots of facets and colours to it.
It's neither good nor bad, it's just different.

And of course that was what (my supervisor)
was saying:
    There's a way of using this material
    and finding your own voice.

Of course I'm reading around
    trying not to read too much
so that it doesn't then influence
how I explain it.

But then I suppose
you can't *not* be influenced.
You can't ever be truly fresh.

He said:
'Go in and find your own voice.'
And that's what I'm doing
– maybe that's the feminine part.

> Why are you trying not to be influenced?

Because if it's a heuristic way of doing it
there is an unknown quantity
but if I read everything
am I not going to know the answers
before I've found them?

So I'm reading some
    and then seeing what I've come up with
    and then perhaps going back
    and saying:
'That matches that
and this is what I've found.'

> A struggle with positivist thinking? We must not
> contaminate the evidence?

When you say that I'm thinking.
So what if I read it all – so what?
We know it anyway somewhere inside us.


## Reflexivity?

Well I hadn't heard of it until you explained it.

How I understand it
– it's me observing me doing my research,
    as I am doing it.

That's very much how it was when…
it was me observing how I was on that retreat.

Observing and reading what we had done as a group
and the feelings that were coming up for me
as I am reading it
and the feelings I had about the group experiences,
and my experiences as well.

Sometimes they came as dreams
– they could come as a dream
– or in the retreat group for example
almost as though this dream was watching me
watching myself waiting for something to emerge
when I was too interested in my headache.

In reflexivity it's almost like
the witness is speaking as well.

                        So both voices are heard?

Yes
whereas reflectivity
is more my experience right now
– reflecting on what has just happened.
But the witness watches how you are doing this as well
it feels sacred, almost sacred.

It feels a profound space to be in.
I feel quite moved even saying it.

It's almost like a very profound privilege
to be there
like there's a part of you…
– perhaps the 'soul experience' (laughs)

I sometimes think:
    'Oh gosh – is this mainstream?'
But it's almost like the soul watching
and saying: well done, well done.

                    You are worried about how
                    the mainstream might see you?

## 'A very lone journey'

Well because
with the MA it was really quite off the wall.

My old tutor from my MA
    – I had a struggle with him.
I felt very much on my own.
It was a very lone journey.
More so than this PhD.
I am quite *amazed* that we meet each month:

because there were three months
when I never even saw my MA tutor.
It was all new
    – we had hardly any guidelines.
We had a research methodology
For a couple of weekends,
wrote the proposal
and that was it.

I hardly saw him again.
Just some emails and that.
When he was there, he *was* there.

I never even got a criteria sheet to say what was required.

In a sense I was very angry
about a lot of it because
– perhaps that was the masculine bit –
my colleague, my close friend
did have a criteria sheet
and I said to my tutor: 'Should I have one?'
    (as he was head of the programme).
He said: 'Oh no, don't worry about that.'

So I didn't have the sheet
    and I just went on in my own sweet way
    and said: 'Gerald is this OK?'
and he said: 'Yeah.'

I went on in my own way
    non-mainstream I suppose
    although I had my chapters,
    and everything I needed to do.

I got a B,
B something.
My friend got a distinction.
What she had done was to look at her sheet
and say to her tutor: 'If any of those are not fulfilled
– let me know.'

Of course I didn't have that
and I couldn't refer back.
And somehow what it's taught me is
that I'm looking for some kind of accreditation
from outside when I really need
to get it from in here
(points to her chest).

And even though I went through
a real struggle with that
    and was very upset and hurt
I actually don't need to prove to myself.
I went through a lot of that;

## 'The PhD, is about my life'

I think what I'm doing now,
the PhD,
is about my life.
It's much more about my purpose in life than to get a degree.

At the beginning of this
– in the midst of me going for the PhD
I talked to Richard

he phoned me one day
   'cos I'd emailed him
   we emailed each other
and when he actually telephoned me
I'd just come home from College.
My brother had rung
and said my mother was worse.

I said: 'Thank you so much for ringing,
I really appreciate it;
but I can't speak to you right now
because my mother is very ill
and I need to leave.'

And then there was that whole
long, long
process of her dying
and
her actual death.

And it was after that
when I eventually got to see Richard
it became urgent for me to do something
– to do this (PhD)
almost as though I'd find her in it,
as though she's going to speak,
that her voice will come through in it.

And lots and lots of things
are happening in my life
and to me physically.

I've got a strange thing happening in my body.

And in thinking about the research
I'm thinking: 'Do I have another enquiry group again?
Do I do the same thing again?'
And I haven't gone down that road yet.
It's as though people just come
and things are happening.
With this colleague,
this friend of mine,
we sat down together to look at why I'm doing this
– quite similar to what we're doing now –
I'm going to be transcribing that
because it's all part of the process – and related to my questions.

So the environment does live through me.
Something *is* being expressed through me
maybe this is my mother's expression through me.

I've got strange things happening in my hands;
I've got numbness in my face,

stress-related
but it's also about me looking and watching.

During the summer,
I went with a friend to Iona
and we went to Skye.
I drove down through Peebles,
the borders.
I've never been before…
and the environment in Iona
    the island weather –
it was almost like
    any minute now I'd see my mother.
It was like I was in another realm
and I could just slip into the sea,
and become part of it.

And when I went to Skye
the landscape was me as well
– the landscape was inside me
and there's something about me *being* that
and *that* being me.
That's really powerful for me.

It seems things are presenting themselves to me
– so perhaps that's the feminine –
and it's for me now to see where it's going
and what to look at,
to see the direction
and see how it's informing me.

This illness
or whatever I've got
is informing me.

I'm fascinated by space and the big bang and time
So, I'm not sure where it's going to take me.
Quite a challenge for me too.
It's about my purpose.

                Finding some sort of meaning?
                It feels like it's something
                to do with your mother's body leaving
                and that giving you a purpose
                – a renewed purpose?

Renewed – yes!!
It was always there
– it's renewed purpose about life and why we are here.

One of the questions my friend asked me was:
What is it you want to know from the PhD?
And I laughed and said:

The purpose of life I suppose.

And she said: 'Well, what would be
your biggest disappointment?'

I said: 'That I'd find out there's no meaning.' (laughter)

I'm wanting to know what the meaning is
and the big disappointment would be
that there is no meaning
    but that could *be* the meaning
    that there doesn't have to be!

So there's a lot of amusement around it too
but for me –

I remember talking to the Director of the Diploma
at that time about this being
the kind of thing people could have done in the East
    I imagine mostly males
perhaps when they've got to a certain stage in their lives
and they've decided they don't want to work anymore
and they give up their worldly goods
    and go into retreat.

                      Going into the wilderness?

Yes, it's that for me.
But I don't choose to do it like that
because I choose to be at home.
I choose to be with my children
and still be employed
because I need to live
and I am choosing to embody it in the West,
in the world, in my way
so in a sense that's my search.

                      Can I ask how old you are?

I'm just 50.
I finished my MA a couple of years ago.
I thought: Gosh, why do I do this?
By the time I'm finished I'll be about 60 – so what?

It seems to me it's about my life.
It's not about getting a better job
'cos I'm not interested.

Well, there's no point.
University lecturers get their PhDs
when they are much younger.
It's not about gaining kudos.
But I am in awe of it,
I can't believe it.
I'm in awe that I'm doing it.

When I was going to do the MA I couldn't even *say* PhD.
I couldn't even utter it.
It's extraordinary.
(She whispers)
It's almost like: Who am I to do such a thing?

That's quite sad.

So that thing with the MA
– not getting a distinction
   perhaps fired me on.

But for me it's a long retreat.

> A long retreat –
> that's certainly a way of describing
> doing a PhD I've never heard before.

Interestingly just a couple of months ago
I actually ended a relationship.
I think it's preparation for going on this long journey

(too quiet to hear)…

## 'Wanting to wake up in this life without having to die first'

There's been a lot around death.

There are two people in my family
who are both terminally ill
– whether it's now or later I don't know.
But there's a lot about being in the body
and out of the body.

I am also interested in out-of-body experiences
– my mother used to have them a lot
particularly when she became ill a couple of years ago.

So it's very interesting
that I'm interested in the 'embodied experience'
but I am also interested in space and 'out there',
being out of the body.

What is this energy, this pulsation.
Is this the medium?

I don't know where it will take me
– that's what is exciting.

The joy of doing this research
is that it stretches me.
I can allow it to take me wherever it goes.

*Chapter 17*

# Ethical Relationships
# in Reflexive Research

> And if we abandon the traditional goal of research as the accumulation of *products* – static or frozen findings – and replace it with the generation of communicative process, then a chief aim of research becomes that of establishing productive forms of relationship.
>
> (Gergen and Gergen 2000, p.1039)

## Relational participants and power

When we enter into relationships with our research participants it is inevitable that issues of power come into focus and require us constantly to scrutinize and interrogate our own positions, views, and behaviours, turning back onto ourselves the same scrupulous lens through which we examine the lives of our participants, always looking for 'tensions, contradictions and complicities' (Olesen 2000, p.236).

Power is a word that often evokes discomfort. If we accept that we *are* powerful when we write about other people's lives, we can constantly monitor the ethical issues that emerge as the research unfolds. Ruthellen Josselson (1996, p.70) reflects:

> ...I would worry most if I stopped worrying, stopped suffering for the disjunction that occurs when we try to tell the Other's story. To be uncomfortable with this work, I think, protects us from going too far. It is with our anxiety, dread, guilt, and shame that we honor our participants. To do this work we must contain these feelings rather than deny, suppress, or rationalize them. We must at least try to be as aware as possible of what we are doing.

## Intimate stories

Being in reflexive relationships with our participants creates a level of intimacy that might invite them to reveal previously unarticulated, deeply personal stories. Storytelling in research can lead to new understandings, insights and revelations in ways that can that parallel the therapeutic encounter. However, these new insights may be entirely unexpected by the participants, who may have had an altogether different expectation of a relationship between researchers and themselves (Birch and Miller 2000).

Making different sense of our lives through reconstructing stories can lead us to construct new identities (Bruner 1995; Giddens 1991; Josselson and Lieblich 1993; Riessman 1989) and increasingly the parallels between therapy and research have been drawn (Birch and Miller 2000; Etherington 2001a, 2001c; Gale 1992; Hart and Crawford-Wright 1999; Skinner 1998; Wosket 1999). However, as researchers we need to take responsibility for the skills and knowledge we hold as therapists: if we stumble carelessly into intimate personal research relationships we take the risk of leaving participants worse off by our encounters with them. When we are clear about the differences in our roles as therapist and researcher, and make that part of the information provided to participants in the early stage of negotiating 'informed consent', we can bring these ideas into the open and explore a plan of action should painful or difficult memories arise as a result of participation in the research (Etherington 2000). For researchers who are not trained in therapeutic roles, this raises different and equally important issues for training.

## Writing about others

Negotiating relationships within rigorous ethical principles is complicated enough, but re-presenting this reflexive process can create even greater concerns about the impact on participants of reading what we have written about them and about ourselves in relationship with them. Reflexivity enables the researcher to recognize their point of entry and interest in the other's stories and that this is subjectively chosen. However, the stories that we pick up on may not be those that participants might have struggled to bring out into the open, after wrestling with denial, shame or fear. Without the benefit of an open and ongoing relationship with them as the research develops, this may only become apparent to the participant when they read what we have written it, or even published it. By then it may be too late; they may feel too ashamed or embarrassed to tell us how they feel and may be left alone to deal with their pain (Josselson 1996).

## Who is in control?

Reflexive researchers have sometimes been criticized as narcissistic or self-indulgent but rarely do we hear the view that participants might also carry narcissistic wounds that drive them unconsciously to offer their stories for research. Josselson (1996, p.65) warns us that in choosing people to write about we run the risk of aggrandizing them.

In fact we have aggrandized our participants – we regarded them as important enough to write about. But the experience of the grandiose self is always accompanied by shame and by an unconscious conviction of being in complete control of the Other, and this, I think, complicates people's experience of being written about...

Researchers therefore tread a delicate pathway between their own possible narcissism and need for control, and that of their participants. The tension thus created can be a healing for both at best, or the cause of an additional layer of betrayal at worst.

When our participants are those whose stories have been ignored, dismissed or silenced (by themselves, society or others) we must do more than attempt to encourage them to speak out or write about their lives; we must also share with them the power to discuss the *form* as well as the content of their communication (Houston and Kramarae 1991). This can challenge the researcher's ability to balance the ethical principles of non-maleficence, beneficence and autonomy in respect of the participant with principles of trustworthiness, honesty and personal freedom with respect to themselves (BACP 2002).

The following story raises many of these issues. It was written by Peter Martin, who is currently a senior lecturer at Roehampton University and a doctoral candidate exploring *therapists' life events and how they change their practice.* His story of learning to become a reflexive researcher, written especially for this book, shows the healing potential for ourselves as researchers (Grafanaki 1996), and others who are co-researchers or participants, when we allow ourselves to care about and be touched by them.

## Peter's story

I always wanted to be reflexive; it's just that I wasn't allowed. As a person who sometimes appears overconfident but is inwardly very doubtful of his intellectual and academic abilities, I tried to learn the 'rules' of talking posh. I had only done two years secondary schooling so I thought I ought to master the 'tests' that permitted you to get heard by others, especially those in academic circles. The trouble with this strategy was that I didn't get to hear myself, and what I discovered lost its personal resonance. So I responded for a while by being unawarely sneaky.

This underhanded strategy was in evidence in my first major piece of research. I now realize that when I did my grounded theory research for my Masters I was operating on two levels. At one level I was working with a kind of 'espoused theory' to please my academic masters and one part of myself. I also had, secretly stowed away, a potent parallel 'theory in use' (Argyris and Schon 1974). The 'theory in use' while doing my Masters research won hands down. I did do all the 'espoused theory' stuff about open coding and axial coding that Strauss and Corbin (1990) obligingly prescribed, and I suppose I did it well. But what I *really* did was to *relate* to what I found out from the questionnaires. I cared about the people who had responded to my questionnaires, and cared less about the methodology which was supposed to release and analyse their thinking. I wanted to emphasize their value. I surprised some of the participants by sending them a copy of the findings. I wanted most to honour my relationship with them, although ostensibly I was setting out to generate theory.

So when I began my heuristic inquiry for my PhD into life events of therapists I was determined to find a way of relating to my sources all the way through. I didn't want to hate my study part way through. I'm over half way through now and I am enthusiastic about what I am doing and most of all deeply absorbed with the people who are providing me with their stories. I don't necessarily 'take to' all of these storytellers straight away, but I do relate to them. They are *people*, and for me research has to be about people or it doesn't connect with what I call my soul.

My job at the time involved a lot of travelling. Driving in my car listening to tapes of the 15 people I had interviewed again and again has been a saga of small discoveries. I remember driving in Wiltshire when I discovered that a woman I once could only relate to as a helpful informant gradually became a fellow traveller. She and I were slowing down for yet another traffic calming scheme. Her voice was playing loudly above the surface noise and I found I was still 'conversing' with her. Then there was the time, negotiating a dark and narrow route when I had a 'conversation' with my ex-client, now a co-researcher. She gently yielded the sure knowledge that she had grown beyond the role of a client to her full stature, to her heritage as a mature woman in charge of her world.

Then there was another epiphany, this time about me. As I listened over and over again to the tape, I was aware of wondering 'Who is that disciplined, skilled and kindly man enabling people to speak so eloquently about their lives?' Of course, intellectually I knew it was me, but in that moment and subsequently, the self that I saw as me and the abused part, who I had seen as an impostor, became one entity. I no longer needed the metaphor of charade. What I heard was for real and it was me.

A darker side of listening to the tapes was the sure knowledge, indeed evidence, that sometimes I did not want to co-construct with my co-researchers. I wanted to impose. My respect for the robust humanity of one co-researcher grew and grew as we wrestled like Jacob and the angel until the dawn of an understanding that we could both live with emerged. But I also learned to be more forgiving of myself. The narcissistic notion that others depended on my unfailing benignity began to break down. And I listened to and heard them fighting their own corner, for their own definition, sometimes with silence, but sometimes simply telling me that I had got it wrong. Even in the ethically delicate space of a respectful conversation, there was still room to believe that dignity of others can negotiate its own story.

Another dent in the unhealthy but magnificent defence of narcissism has emerged from the reflexive process inherent in co-construction. I began my study because I wanted to understand better the changes in my own therapeutic practice following a breakdown some years ago. Yet, as my work has deepened and my focus has changed, I find that I am far less interested in my own story and much more interested in the 'other': another break in the narcissistic structure, which seems to me relates to early damage in the form of some kind of abuse. I feel warmly towards my co-researchers as a body, and often towards them individually. Freed of the need to be therapeutic within the interviews I am less interested in the effect I might be having on their story and much more interested in these people as 'others'. In fact many of the people have told me that they felt the interviews *were* therapeutic, but the point is, I suppose, I was able to be there without the same kind of attachment I would have had as a therapist. Reflexivity has allowed my co-researchers to *contribute* something, instead of in some way serving my needs. I see their stories, in the main, as a gift which I am privileged to hold for a while.

There is another side to this. Some of the tapes have almost been too much to bear. After some time I had to admit to myself that I was suffering a degree of secondary trauma. I looked after myself from then onwards with more supervision. I was moved to find that when I reported to the storytellers my reluctance to even pick up some of the stories, each person told me that my pain had affected them powerfully, giving significance to a story that they had been taught to see as unimportant. My vulnerability has never been in question to me. But I feel I have learned to use it differently, by sharing it and expressing it so that another level of communication is possible.

There has also been another experience that reflexivity has given me. The extended period of my study has enabled me to work through much of what psychodynamic people call 'countertransference'. I believe that there are many forces that stand in the way of seeing people as they are, and that many of them come from inside us. That is certainly often true for me. Living with my sometimes negative feelings, staying with them, and trying not to judge myself for having them, has offered me a boon. It has enabled me to see more lucidly the other person as they see themselves, but also with some sense of the emotional truth that they are speaking, in spite of the discomfort their truth may initially cause me. In order to let this happen, I had consciously to eschew the supervisor, the ethicist, the gatekeeper in me to let them be whoever they are to themselves – a bit like Husserl's notion (1931) of 'bracketing' I suppose. That discipline seemed to open a pathway to compassion that did not have to be forced. It grew within me as I drew closer to the experiences they proffered.

I remember seeing a person for a second interview and wanting to communicate something of what I felt. Her story had been gruelling and I had used some of our differences to protect myself from the harrowing nature of her tale. So our first meeting had been coloured for me by our different value systems. When we met again I said, 'Each time I listened to your tape I grew fonder and fonder of you.' I meant it. I am glad I said it because she has subsequently died and the opportunity to communicate would have been gone forever had I not seized the moment. This perhaps gives a clue to the existential meaning of doing reflexive research for me. I catch a moment in the lives of others. I ponder on it and respond to it. Meanwhile, their lives have moved on in a thousand different ways. Yet for me the fleeting moment has become a kind of aeon, and I am changed in some way.

I suppose the greatest gift I have gained from reflexivity is a healing of the split between research and practice. I am the same person, with the same mind and the same heart wherever I am. The discipline of research is just that. It can help me to be rigorous but it doesn't need to privatize my brain or to sequester my heart.

Part 4

# The Postdoctoral Stages

*Research journal: 23 November 2003*

I'm really struggling to write the last part of this book and I'm not sure why. I'll try writing it out – a way that often frees me up when I feel stuck – and see what happens.

Why does this part of the book seem so difficult when the other parts didn't? Well, it's about what it's like for people once they've achieved a doctoral degree. I have talked to six other people at this stage and, of course, it's where I am myself.

As I think about it I feel a kind of sadness inside. What is that about? I think some of it is a response to realizing that I am nearing the official retirement age for a university employee, and it feels as if I've only just really got going! But on the other hand, I know that if I were to ask my head of department to extend my contract beyond 65 then the indications are that I could. I'm not sure though if that is what I really want to do. I *would* like to extend the research part of my contract (and maybe some of the teaching) but not the administration that goes with course co-ordination. Can I do one and not the other? Is it to do with me being biologically and physically at my age and stage – ready to let go on one level, but intellectually I'm still trying to catch up and make up for all the years I spent 'in the wilderness'? I feel as if I've still got a lot to say!

So I *am* wondering about my own life; but I think I'm also responding to what I heard from other people too. Of course we're all different ages – they're mostly late forties to mid-fifties (I'm the oldest by quite a long way at 63) – but in terms of stages: most of us have been awarded doctorates in the last ten years. John, who is a professor now, had reached this postdoctoral stage much earlier than the rest of us, having studied for his PhD virtually straight after his first degree. That seems to be one of the differences between people who studied psychology for their first degree and those of us who come to counselling or psychotherapy later in life, maybe as a second or third career.

From this position, looking back at the earlier parts of this book, it seems that there is a great deal of 'youthful' excitement when people are at the Masters stage – it really sounded like people were on a voyage of discovery. At the doctoral stage it felt a bit more serious, a bit more like hard work in some ways, a bit more 'grown up', and then at this stage…

All that reminds me of theories of life stages and ego development that Erikson and others have proposed. Am I struggling to develop wisdom as an outcome of the struggle between 'integrity vs. despair', and is that what I'm hearing from some of the others? People knowing the kind of work they want to do – reflexive, contextualized, meaningful research – while also being constrained by the barriers that hold them back from doing that? Are we trying to make some kind of meaning out of our lives as researchers so far?

But maybe that struggle is not true for everyone. I guess it was mainly two of the men I spoke with who seemed to be facing something of a crisis point in their academic lives. Both of them talked about wanting more of a sense of 'community': to be with people who share their values and beliefs about research. One of the others talked about that too, recognizing that in his previous university reflexivity wasn't really valued and how that was part of the attraction when he relocated to a new university – knowing that some of those already working there really valued reflexive research.

Most of those working in universities indicated that they wanted to step back from the burdens and responsibilities that came with the territory in order to have more time to do the work they were really interested in – to write and spend time with themselves. But universities have other agendas too, and sometimes we have to compromise.

I think as I write this I am realizing it *does* seem to be a struggle for integrity – wanting to live the whole of our lives in tune with what we value and believe in, and not wanting to compromise on that.

I was also hearing about creativity or 'creation' as William called it. That's a more hopeful theme in their stories. But alongside that there seems to be a kind of frustration that things could be even better for students and for educational establishments (and maybe even for society) if we could do research that felt more meaningful and had relevance in our personal and professional worlds.

As I read the transcripts of these conversations over and over, and listen again to the tapes it feels like I'm on a roller-coaster. One moment I feel raised up and the next moment cast down. So I think maybe it's not really surprising that I am struggling.

*Chapter 18*

# Being a Reflexive
# Postdoctoral Researcher

Conscious beings make Dust – they renew it all the time, by thinking and feeling and reflecting, by gaining wisdom and passing it on.

(Pullman 2000, p.520)

In this last part of the book I focus on the stories of men and women who have reached the postdoctoral stage in their journeys. Having achieved a doctorate, researchers' lives can take many different routes.

My participants at this stage were a full-time Professor, a Reader, two Senior Lecturers at universities, a senior NHS practitioner, a social science researcher and myself. I am mainly a private practitioner in counselling, supervision, consultancy and training with a small academic role at a university as a Senior Lecturer.

## Backgrounds

These were the people I talked to who were all interested in using reflexivity in research, even though few of them were actually writing reflexively. John McLeod, who gained his PhD in 1977, having switched from a mathematics degree to psychology during his early twenties and later undertaking counselling training, does not currently practise as a counsellor. Tim Bond gained his doctorate in 1997, having trained and worked as a social worker in the early 1970s, and as a counsellor in the mid-1970s, when he was in his twenties. He currently limits the number of clients and supervisees he sees because of the pressure of other academic and professional commitments. William West, who currently supervises a few counsellors but has no clients himself, originally gained a degree in computer science and later worked as a Reichian therapist and international trainer in that field before undertaking an MA in counselling studies. After this he was encouraged to do a PhD, which he completed in 1995. Jane Speedy, who gained a first degree in history in the 1970s, worked as a teacher before training as a counsellor in the 1980s. She gained an MSc in 1992 and a PhD in 2001 and now has a small practice in counselling and supervision alongside being a full-time academic. Nigel Copsey was awarded his Doctorate in Psychotherapy in 2001. For the last 16 years he has worked in the NHS, where he has developed a department of spiritual and cultural care within the mental health services. Currently he leads a multicultural team promoting spiritual care. Prior to this work he was a minister in the docklands area of East London. Jeremy, some of whose story is told in Chapter 15 is now a full-time social researcher employed by a research institute.

Within this range it can be seen that a doctorate is sometimes part of a natural progression within academia and usually a requirement for promotion. A professional doctorate like Nigel's can also influence career progression outside of academia: in education, health or other statutory or commercial services. For others, doing a doctorate is not connected with their career pathway but rather a means of gaining confidence in themselves and their academic ability, and/or credibility within their professional role, or it may provide a framework for studying a topic of interest in depth over a period of years.

In 1995, at the age of 55, I was awarded a PhD, and on reflection I can now see that it provided me with a sense of being taken seriously academically – something I had always longed for as a female born into a patriarchal family and society.

## Stories

As I re-read the transcripts of our conversations over and over again, I became aware of themes emerging. I have tried to capture some of the stories that illustrated those themes in stanza form below. The themes I noticed will probably be different from those you might have noticed because you and I bring to our work the influences of our histories and our contexts: our families, culture, gender and the era through which we have grown and developed, personally and professionally. So in the end these themes and stories are mine and do not imply a 'Truth'. In this chapter I have limited myself to four themes but there were others for which there is no space within the pages of this book and I will use them in work that follows from this study.

The four themes I have focused on for this part of the book relate to links between reflexivity in research and:

- gender
- academics' lives
- creativity
- life stages.

It is my hope that the meanings you create as you read these stories, and their significance to the topic of how people experience becoming reflexive researchers, will provide you with new understandings, challenge your taken-for-granted assumptions and/or confirm what you already know.

## Gender

Apart from myself and one other, all of my participants for this last part of the book are men. I found myself wondering a great deal about this, especially as all except one of us are in a professional field that is heavily weighted towards female membership. I was also aware that participants in earlier parts of this book were mostly women too. At various points throughout the book different participants commented on reflexivity being more in tune with female ways of knowing and being (see Chapters 3 and 4 in particular). Perhaps this is unsurprising when we think about the influence of feminist researchers on how we conduct research (see Chapter 2). Feminists, being concerned with power relations, challenged researchers to make their values and beliefs more transparent so that readers could see how their subjective experiences influenced their interpretations. This required a shift from the objective voice of 'the researcher' to the subjective 'I'. It also meant that researchers had to emerge from behind the secure barrier of anonymity and own up to their involvement (Crotty 1998). These practices *do* seem to be more in tune with women's ways of communicating than men's.

Chancellor, a journalist for *The Guardian* 'Weekend' (2003, p.9), writes about a computer programme developed by a team of Israeli scientists after an exhaustive study of the differences between how men and women use language (booklog.net/gender/genie.html). He points out that one of their findings is that women are far more likely than men to use personal pronouns in their writing, and that men prefer words that identify and determine nouns (such as 'the', 'that') or that quantify them (two, one, more). The reason they give for this is that women are more comfortable thinking about relationships and people, whereas men prefer to think about things. Although sceptical about the scientists' claims that in 80 per cent of cases the programme correctly guesses the gender of the writer, Chancellor does admit to being impressed by 72 per cent of his checks turning out to be correctly identified. However, I tried putting some of this book into that computer programme and discovered that I'm a man!

Although an increasing number of females within the field of psychotherapy and counselling are appointed to senior academic posts, I can think of few (in the UK) who might be seen as 'reflexive researchers', although there are some who write reflexively (Clarkson 1998; van Deurzen 1998). Indeed an exploration of the literature concerning reflexivity across the social sciences in the UK reveals few female writers. This seems somewhat different in North America where there are many female researchers using reflexivity in their work, although not specifically within the field of counselling (Ellis 1995; Lather 1993; Richardson 2000, 2003; Riessman 2002; Ronai 1995; Weingarten 2003 – to name only a few).

Towards the end of my conversation with the only other female participant for this part of the book (apart from myself) I asked Jane if there was anything else she would like to say. She responded: 'I think it's very hard being a woman researcher'. She went on to talk about how, at a recent research conference, a man had presented one piece of reflexive research and, even though there were several women presenting reflexive research on the same day at the same conference, the man's work received a great deal more recognition than the women's. So, my first story is called:

## Being a woman researcher

I don't know what the difficulties are
about being a man researcher, obviously.

It's like,
    this is no disrespect to men
    some of whom have got into
    lots of these things in great ways,
but it's fascinating how thrilled people are
when a man dips a tiny little toe into
a tiny little very safe couple of paragraphs
in his entire life of what might be called
reflexive narrative research.
    It's not that I want the praise,
    but the recognition,
god if I got that amount of recognition from a toe dipping
I'd be covered in milk chocolate by now.

So there's that aspect of it,
and maybe that's about being a woman researcher,
but it's also something about…
because we're women…(pause)

> D'you mean:
> because we're women it's sort of expected
> that we all do that sort of thing?…

It comes easily to us.

> … 'And anyway, you can't help it
> because you're a woman,
> it's not that you have to work at it,
> it's just the way you are.'

Exactly!

> But if you're a man
> then you're doing something fantastic,
> something quite counter-cultural
> and kind of brave,
> and that needs to be seen in larger lights
> than a woman
> who's just doing what comes naturally.

It reminds me of when a man recently
Left a meeting, had to pick up his kids from school,
And everybody thought it was totally wonderful.

And it has another impact on me as a woman because
there's always a little voice
inside my head saying:
are they going to see this as me
being a kind of foolish woman…

Girlie researcher.

All this touchy feely stuff,
and is that in some way
going to discount the value that's put on it,
because this is just another of these women
who's catharting
all over the place.

(laughter)

That's it!
I want to say to them:
'We didn't do this because we're girls,
we've done thematic research
and we've done adding up
and we've done…,
and now we're doing this,
because we've really thought about it
and we're bright and intelligent, sentient beings
and we think this is what we want to do.'

So there's that.

But it's interesting isn't it,
because I do think that women are
more comfortable with reflexive research.
They don't have to worry about
being seen to be touchy feely creatures
because it's OK in a way,
it's what's expected –
judged maybe as lesser –
but that's how women fit
into the scheme of things.

On the other hand, perhaps it is equally difficult for men who want to be taken seriously as reflexive researchers within a society that still views men's strengths as 'logic, objectivity and rationality' and their weaknesses as anything that verges anywhere near stereotypically feminine qualities (Etherington 1995). Using personal pronouns or focusing on relationships might be seen as 'stepping out of line' for a man. One of my participants, Tim, talked about what it was like for him when he presented a piece of autoethnographic research at a conference. He began by talking about the need for courage. So I have called this story:

## The courage in stepping out of line

Now, how courageous I can be
I don't know.
I think there are two levels of courage:
One is that I'm already…

It's rather like being a painter:
if you've established your painting in a certain style
and been fairly successful in it
and have quite a lot of income and investment
    in terms of resource type,
it's quite a risk to walk away from that.
because you antagonize people.

It's one thing stopping doing it,
it's another thing if you re-create yourself to do something different.
And I've had a certain amount of that kind of response from
[my presentation].

I've had people say:
'Have you gone stark staring bonkers?'
I've had one or two people phone me up.
I've had all sorts of interesting projections, like:
was I in love with the client;
did I always like being rescued by my clients?

A whole range of some quite loopy stuff.

Researchers who include themselves in their stories often struggle with anxieties about how this might be viewed by others. A commonly felt anxiety for both men and women seems to be a reluctance to be 'seen'. I have described my own expanding use of reflexivity in writing as a process of 'coming out'. William used this same phrase in his story. He had questioned the wisdom of me being 'seen' in my writing, and I asked him what it was about this that worries him. He reflected on my questions for some time and then said:

## 'Coming out as a reflexive researcher'

What's kind of coming up for me
is a sort of ambivalence
about my *own* exposure
    and my *own* hiding,
that, yes I want to be in print
and, no I don't,
    you know?

It's like I want to be seen
and I don't want to be seen
    and, yes,

I want to be on the stage
and I want to be hidden under the chair
at the same time.

My coming into print,
    and coming out as a reflexive researcher
    and coming out heuristically,
has been a gradual process of:
is this going to be OK?
And then pushing it a bit further
and selecting the media,
    the journal
    or the conference,
where I can go that next step.

Yes, it's all a risk
and it's all a kind of a question
of knowing what I can...,
knowing what I can get away with.

Another of the concerns expressed by people about including themselves in their research writing is that sense of not being interesting in their own right. Tim also expressed some of these concerns as he explained that much of his reflexive process was not previously included in what he wrote:

I find it hard to believe
they'd be as interested in *me* as an individual,
as they are about,
    you know,
whatever it is I'm writing about.

So all through this,
what I did with it would largely remain private
and outside the realm of the research reporting.

It'd be something I'd discuss with friends;
I might discuss it in therapy;
I might discuss it with colleagues.

And that, in part, was perhaps in the context
of where I was then working.
I was already slightly pushing the boat out.
There was a limit to how far a boat could be pushed
before someone decides to haul in the anchor
or to cut the rope and send you out to sea,
let you drown, there were certain...

The culture I was in then was not reflexive.

Being a male (having been socialized to believe that men should be logical, rational and objective) might make the inclusion of personal responses seem more of a risk than it might for women. Andrew Sparkes (2003, p.73), a postdoctoral reflexive researcher, writes:

> Making public my fears, fragilities, and vulnerabilities has not endeared me to a great many scholars, particularly males. I have also been hurt by the trivializing charge of self-indulgence that is so readily levelled by mainstream academics against such work. Even though I have learned to recognize the anxieties and mis-understandings that fuel this charge, and so gained the confidence to reject it, this charge still has the power to sting and undermine my confidence.

If traditional research is seen as 'masculine' then personal intimate relational research could be seen as 'feminine' – a word that many men reject in relation to themselves. I believe that what is needed is a 'marriage' between the masculine and the feminine, and a valuing of both. We need the logical, analytical, rational, thinking voices as well as the relational, intimate voice that values feelings, sensation, symbols and metaphor – to create a richer tapestry and bring research alive for all.

## Academics' lives

This leads me to the second main theme that emerged as I was listening: the diffi-culties experienced by academics who value using themselves in their research. Academics within universities often do research alongside training, lecturing, course co-ordination or direction, which involve heavy loads of administration, attendance at committees and meetings, supervising students at masters and doctoral levels, conference attendance and examining students.

As full-time academics, in theory, their working life is divided between teaching, research and administration but, in reality, many of them complain that there is little time for them to do their own research.

Research funding is difficult to find, and there is increasing competition for travel costs and conference fees. But nonetheless full-time academics do receive an annual salary that supports them whether they are away at conferences, examining theses, on holiday or off sick. For myself, whose main role as a private practitioner runs alongside a minor academic contract, life is complicated in terms of trying to balance both. Although when I attend a conference I am paid by the university for one and half days during that week, any additional times (which would be the case if the conference was in another part of the world) would lead to loss of earnings and mean that I was not available for my clients.

However, many of my fellow academics see my situation as ideal, and in many ways it is. I have the freedom largely to manage my own working life while also having the benefits that affiliation with a university of high standing can bring. I have often been asked why I want to be part of a university, especially when I have felt exploited, undervalued and mistreated (for example, when I have been expected to work many hours beyond those for which I am contracted, to the point of exhaustion and at severe cost to my income as a freelancer), and in writing this chapter I have become more aware of those reasons. Being affiliated to the University of Bristol, and a department of education that has the highest rating in the UK, gives me a sense of pride and provides me with credibility in the eyes of the public in a way that simply being a private practitioner might never bring. I have a forum for creativity, colleagues and friends whose conversations stimulate me, and with whom I can sometimes have fun. Being *so* part-time, however, lessens those opportunities for contact while also relieving me of some of the unwelcome involvement in committees and responsibilities that are sometimes experienced as burdensome by full-time colleagues. So there are costs and consequences for everybody.

In theory, my full-time colleagues in academia have more opportunity to meet with others and discuss research than I have as a sole researcher, working mostly from home in comparative isolation. The reality, however, appears to be experienced somewhat differently: rather as a lack of a community in which to share ideas about research and receive the kind of stimulation good conversation with colleagues can provide.

Some full-time academics in the counselling field manage to contract with the university for a small portion of their time to be given to practice, if only so that they can remain close to the reality of client work to inform their teaching and research. This is not always the case in other disciplines. For instance, many colleagues in teaching and education spend no time teaching in schools. This leaves academics open to charges of being out of touch with the real world and contributes to the widening of the research–practice gap. For some, like John, this is a something they want to change.

## 'Well, I'm not primarily a practitioner'

I'm much more of an academic
who does some practice.

I can feel the stirrings
of wanting to be more of a practitioner
and getting free
from a lot of the academic things.

I was very interested
in what another research group were doing.
They were getting this steady stream of grants,
but they were killing themselves to do it.
And they were constantly asking
   'How do we get more money
   to employ somebody who has been working with us
   but is not on a permanent contract?'

And I thought: I don't want to go there
because I want to pursue my own ideas.
And it seemed to me

that to actually get serious research money
you had to produce political proposals.

And I'm deeply sceptical
about the possibility of getting money
to do some things that you and I would be interested in doing.

It would be great but...

> I find that kind of depressing.
>
> Wanting to do what you believe in and that you *know*
> to be a useful contribution to the development of the
> counselling field, and yet...
> it's kind of a hiding to nothing.

Yes. I share that
and I don't let myself go there
because I will get too upset about all that,
because
    (this is probably going to sound very grandiose)
but at this point
I feel very able to do really good research
but I've got loads of university responsibilities
and all sorts of things.

So the only way that I would do research
is to get a fairly substantial grant
with enough money to buy me out.

And I keep working away on that sort of thing,
but I just don't think it's ever going to happen.

I can't afford financially to retire
    because of the children,
so I probably won't ever do something like that.

But that's personal...

It seemed almost like an apology for including his personal view, which was, after all, exactly what I was seeking.

John's story seems to indicate a belief that reflexive, contextualized research will not be funded as long as funding organizations continue to privilege the dominant paradigm. He went on to talk about his hopes:

## 'What keeps me going through dark nights'

I think the psychotherapy research establishment
is like a bubble that could burst.
    I mean the mainstream...,
    all that crap,
randomized control trials and all that

is a bubble that could burst
because it's not actually producing useful knowledge.
It's producing political knowledge
    but that is important too
introducing knowledge the Department of Health wants to see
and so forth.

I think that the new qualitative reflexive type methodologies,
    collaborative research and so on,
have got such a lot to offer
and could produce such interesting things to read.

There's a chance
that within quite a short space of time
there will be a shift away...
[from RCT's etc.].

I mean,
just a couple of weeks ago
we had a national counselling research conference,
which was a day with about 11 papers
and everybody was speaking personally about their research
    and everybody thought it was great,
    it was just great –
a bit like the BACP research conference.

And that research is actually
offering something to people.

I suppose what I'm saying is
that people are going to see through that,
or I hope people are going to see through that.

What keeps me going through dark nights is
that I think there could be quite a shift but...

This kind of shift will only happen if we risk presenting, writing and publishing reflexive research and, as Andrew Sparkes reminds us, this is not without its perils, 'as well as pleasures, possibilities and potentials' (2003, p.74).

Sparkes (*ibid.* p.61), quotes Bochner (2000, p.421), who observes, 'Academic life is impersonal, not intimate. It provides a web of distractions. The web protects us from the invasion of helplessness, anxiety, and isolation we would feel if we faced the human condition honestly.' Sparkes responds to this by saying, 'Over the years, perhaps like many men, I have often found it easier to cloak myself in the "web of distractions" and maintain a gulf between my academic and personal world.' He goes on to say that through using himself as the subject of his autoethnographic research he has begun to accept and nurture his different 'voices'. 'Whereas before, I called upon separate voices to engage with these divided worlds, suppressing one at the expense of the other, I now feel more willing and able to combine them in the same writing arena.'

At a conference in 2002 Tim, who is an influential figure in the counselling world, presented an autoethnographic account that asked the question: is this research? In his introduction he stated: 'This is a research conference. What I am about to do challenges the accepted boundaries of what is research.' He went on: 'I may be about to make the biggest fool of myself in my career to date' (Bond 2002, p.134). In taking this risk Tim is both sheltered by his reputation as an established and bona fide person, and risking judgement. It may well be that it is only when we have the security that comes with having a position of 'authority' or influence, that we can take the risk to challenge the dominant paradigm (see Chapter 10).

Academics are also teachers of the new generation of researchers, and all of those I spoke with reflected on the value of reflexivity in learning, not only about research but also about practice. William told me of his sadness that the richness of this kind of work is not available to all:

## 'This could be so much better'

And there's a real sorrow that
I can feel for other people:
that sense that this could be so much better,
    not just for me
but for the department I work in
or my students or the world.

It doesn't have to be like this.
We could do this differently,
we could make this so much…

There's also got to be something in what we're saying
that's profoundly important for practice.
You could say like:
if we're taking ourselves seriously in this way
and modelling that,
that's great for our clients and our students.
    'You matter.
    I'm treating myself as if I matter
    and treating you as if you matter
    and you can treat yourself as if you matter.'

That's wonderful.

This sense that what we do and teach as researchers and academics can influence our own and our students' practice was also taken up by Jane as she reflected on the impact of becoming a researcher on her own practice:

## 'An accidental spill-out of being a researcher'

The way I work with clients is transformed.
That was primarily the accidental spill-out of being a researcher
that led to me uncovering
a whole different body of practices
that I've become fascinated with
and that I didn't even know about before.

The narrative therapy thing?

The narrative therapy thing.
It's all come out of...
the result of trying to find a way of interviewing people:
exploring ethical ways of staying curious as a researcher.

So it's been a huge process.
In terms of what's different now and,
and what I think about it,
is that it's also made me different as a teacher
because I was very committed to experiential learning
and now I'm not against that *or* for it
but I'm much more interested in creating a climate
for people to be questioning and curious,
than I am for them to 'experience' things.

I used to think it was enough
for them to experience themselves.
I have a wholly different construct
of what's important and ethical now.
So there's quite a lot of difference really.

## Creativity

Innovative and non-traditional methodologies that encourages us to use our selves in research writing provide us with many opportunities to be creative. In earlier parts of this book I have demonstrated how reflexive research encourages us to use our creativity, and how it often leads to personal development and growth, so I was not surprised to find that creativity was also an important theme in people's stories at this stage.

When we write in traditionally academic ways, we tend to 'privilege rigour over imagination, intellect over feeling, theories over stories, and abstract ideas over concrete events' (Sparkes 2003, p.61), which often results in limiting opportunities for freer and creative thinking. When we use all aspects of ourselves in research, including imagination, feeling, and stories that include concrete events, the free flow of interactions between all parts can spark creative ideas and their expression.

The idea that research can be a creative process might be surprising, but only when we limit our thinking about research to more traditional methodologies. Jane expressed how surprised she was to discover that research and 'writing as a form of inquiry' became an important focus for her own creativity:

## 'One of the most creative parts of my life'

If you'd have said to me ten years ago
you're going to end up being a researcher in a university,
I'd have said: 'Oh Christ, I'll have sold out
on my creativity:
    Oh my god! Doom strikes, she's dead.'
you know?

Whereas, in fact, I think it's one of the most creative,
    if not *the* most creative part of my life,
and that's kind of odd.
I would never have thought that, never.

> There's something about…
> the relationship with yourself
> that somehow allows you to…
> have time for you,
> time to be with that part of yourself,
> that creative part of yourself?

Well yes.
How can I put this?

I would associate losing myself
    or selves or whatever,
with painting, art of some kind, possibly poetry –
    and I think of those as 'arty things',
that losing myself, and suddenly realizing:
bloody hell it's dark outside!

And actually I find that happens with *researching*,
    well I don't know what researching means
but with *writing*,
writing from the perspective of being a researcher.

I have exactly that experience
of wrestling with these ideas
and wanting to get something across in a particular way,
or discovering in the writing…

Of course because the re-writing and the re-writing…,
    and that's the other thing,
    I've realized that I take a hell of a long time to write things.

But I don't care.
I used to really care,
it used to bother me.
I thought: I can't be a writer in this field, I take too long.

But I love it,
that struggle to capture the bit you want to say,
and then *knowing*…,

## Life stages

All of my postdoctoral participants have reached the stages in life that involve them in creative work and passing on to others what they have produced. So 'life stages' became my fourth theme in this chapter.

As I noted in my journal at the beginning of Part 4, I recognized a parallel in the journey towards becoming a researcher with the life-stage theories I learned in counselling training (Erikson 1950; Jung 1953–78; Sugarman 1986). I sometimes find those concepts helpful as I think with clients about the issues they bring to their counselling (seeing them as frameworks for enabling understanding and not as 'truths'), but this is the first time they have appeared in my thinking as I immersed myself in research data. Like any theory, these ideas are simply stories of their time and culture, and not to be used as straightjackets for our thinking, but rather as ideas to play with that might inform our thinking and help us make sense of our own, and other people's, experiences.

As I first began to play with the idea of these parallels, Erikson's eighth stage came into my mind and, as I explored this thinking further, I began to realize that perhaps the struggle I am experiencing is somewhat different from other participants because they are younger than me. Are they more concerned with the tasks of Stage 7, than 8 or somewhere in between? However, I do not see these stages as linear but simply as ways of thinking about our passage through life.

## Erikson's seventh stage

During my middle adulthood (between 45 and 60), I too was taken up with some of the tasks Erikson associated with his seventh stage, concerned with 'generativity vs. stagnation or self-absorption' (Harder 2002). His theory proposes that once the conflict between these states is successfully resolved this will lead to the development of strengths of 'production and care'. Erikson observed that during this stage we tend to be occupied with our families, and with creative and meaningful work. It is also a time when we can expect to be 'in charge' – something we might have envied in others and wanted for ourselves.

The significant task of this stage is to transmit values of the culture – perhaps of our family or our profession – and to work to establish stability in our environments. The thinking is that we will gain new strength through our care of others and by producing something that contributes to a better society. Erikson calls this 'generativity'. Anxiety may be created during this stage by our fear of inactivity, lack of productivity and a sense of meaninglessness in our lives.

During this stage our concerns (for those of us who have children) are about children leaving home, or our parents becoming elderly, infirm or dying. These transitions create space for us to reconsider our relationships, roles, and goals – in the workplace, our community and our family. We might be faced with major life changes, leading to what has become known as 'the mid-life crisis', as we struggle to find new meanings and purposes. The danger is, according to Erikson, that if we do not successfully negotiate this stage we can become self-absorbed and stagnate.

Jung named the process occurring at this stage of life 'individuation', which he described as:

> an expression of that biological process – simple or complicated as the case may be – by which every living thing becomes what it was destined to become from the beginning. (quoted in Stevens 1990, p.187)

He saw two possibilities for people at mid-life: either they changed or they became rigid:

> one's cherished convictions and principles, especially moral ones, begin to harden and grow increasingly rigid until, somewhat around the age of fifty, a period of intolerance and fanaticism is reached. It is as if the existence of these principles were endangered and it were necessary to emphasise them all the more. (in Stevens 1990, p.187)

Pope John XXIII put it more briefly: 'Men are like wine. Some turn to vinegar, but the best improve with age.'

All of my participants have indeed reached positions of 'being in charge' in some form or another, and have produced work that contributes to their professions (one of the requirements of a doctoral thesis). Most have also produced children. All of them have been/are passing on the values of their culture through teaching, supervision, writing and research. And indeed, all of that work is in the caring professions. So it can be seen that the tasks of Stage 7 are being/have been undertaken.

As I reflected on this theory I began to wonder if the two men I had experienced as 'struggling' were still involved in these tasks. William seemed to be experiencing a 'mid-life crisis' as he searched for a pathway to follow from this point on. He had had a similar struggle when he was doing his PhD but the framework provided by the task of completing his doctorate had held him through that struggle. Now it seems that he has less structure to hold him in his present crisis. Indeed he is now holding others in a way that he needs for himself:

## A personal change crisis

The weird thing at the moment
is that I'm going through profound…,
    what can I call it?

For about 18 months I've been in a kind of crisis
that's a bit like a low-key crisis,
a bit like the one I went through when I did the PhD.

By the time I came out of the PhD
I was…,

I'd become an academic.
I hadn't started as one or intended to be one,
but I'd just become one.

I'm having echoes of a lot of the same feelings these last 18 months
and I've got to move on,
and I don't know how I'm going to do it
because it's not like…
    what am I saying?
I'm saying that I think I'm still meant to be working academically
but more spiritually,
which is a strange combination
because I don't know many
spiritual academic institutions in this country.

But it feels like there's some shift that's being asked of me.
There's a process I'm in which is pushing me in various ways
and I don't know where to,
and I have to trust that that push
and that process is both healthy and kind to me
and it's not just that I'm washed up or that I've lost it.

It's a closing down
but actually, it's a push into the next phase,
but I can't see it or understand it, or name it,
and it may not exist until I'm ready for it to exist
and then it'll be obvious.

But it's a bugger.
And it requires a lot of self-trust.

It's something about creation,
it's about the wonder of creation,
this strange business of…,
it all seems to come from nothing.

## Erikson's eighth stage

My own experiences seem to resonate more closely with Erikson's eighth stage of 'late adulthood', which is said to occur between 55 and 65. But of course the research upon which his theories were based was undertaken in a different era, when men's and women's lives were lived differently. Taking that into account, there is still some value in his ideas.

Erikson suggested that we spend the greater part of our lives preparing for Stage 7, when we pass our knowledge on to the next generation from a position of some authority, experience readjustments and maybe even crises – and that we spend the rest of our lives recovering from it!

During the eighth stage, at best, we may be able to look back on our lives with a sense of contentment and fulfilment, believing that life has some meaning and that we have made a useful contribution. Erikson names this 'integrity' and sees the strength that comes from resolving the struggle between integrity and despair as wisdom – the wisdom of becoming ourselves and knowing that we are but a small part of a very large universe, that we are not the centre of it but have a somewhat detached concern for the larger picture, eventually accepting that death is the completion of life (Harder 2002).

Those who have not successfully negotiated the earlier tasks of adulthood may despair as they reach this stage, believing they have failed. They might struggle to find meaning and purpose in their lives, or they may defend against the anxiety created by such thoughts by becoming dogmatic, and believing they have all the answers and are always right.

Jung also saw the goal of this time of life as the achievement of wisdom: a stage when we reflect on our lives, assimilate the past, search for meaning and move towards wholeness (Stevens 1990). He urged us to remain creatively alive during older age and to continue to make a contribution – something that has become recognized in more recent times by such movements as the 'University of the Third Age'. I know that as I have become older it has become more important to me that I should live more fully in tune with my values and beliefs, express myself as I really am, and defend the dignity of my own lifestyle, while also acknowledging the legitimacy of others. These are the values that underpin my use of reflexivity in research.

I have chosen stories to illustrate the lived experience of two researchers who seem to be speaking about how their research activities create space to allow them to connect with themselves. Jane, although a bit uneasy with the term 'reflexive researcher', is nonetheless someone pursuing narrative co-research and a range of forms of writing as inquiry, which she describes as 'constitutive and transforming of both myself and others'. Her stories focused on how being a researcher had led her to value a deeper connection with herself through writing as a form of inquiry. William's stories, which follow Jane's, show how reflexivity and research connects him with his sense of spirituality.

## 'Being with me'

I think that I have become
a lot more solitary and reclusive in my ways as a person,
because I think that,
    and this has to do with writing research,
but those sorts of work are different from the work of
being in conversation with people all the time,
in teaching and therapy or whatever.

And so, instead of my days being to do with people all the time,
my days,
    I use the term 'my days' loosely,
    it's mostly my nights actually,
have been to do with being with me,

much more being with me,
    not me with my therapist
    or me with my…,
    but me, on my own,
because there's quite enough conversation
going on between me and…,
me and the project
    let's put it that way,
    whatever the project is,
and so in that sense…,

    and my family would say:
    'Oh she's in her cave, on her own,'
as opposed to:
    'She's counselling,' or, …

and I've loved it
so given a choice of going out with my mates to the theatre,
    I love going to the theatre so it's a good example,
or staying in
and thinking about that thing that's been really nagging at me
and perhaps doing a bit of writing,
I might well prefer…,
    I'm not saying which one I'd do,
but I might well really prefer to be staying in
with that thing that's been nagging at me in that book, etc.

So it's putting myself in a different position…
about what I want to do with my life.

Jane's words echoed some of the same changes I have noticed in myself. Writing has become for me a way of working myself out as I go along. Like her, I take great pleasure in spending solitary time grappling with concepts or ideas that challenge me. As counsellors and psychotherapists we are never at a loss for such intellectual or emotional material.

I have called William's stories: 'spirituality and connectedness'.

## Spirituality and connectedness

For me that is a huge philosophical
and spiritual question,
to do with truth and meaning.

I can never…
let me try…

I can never transcend being human,
I can never step outside of being human.

The universe to me is spiritual,
I experience…,
I have times of experiencing an inter-connectedness
that I regard as spiritual.
I cannot *not* be having that experience
but there's a sense in which
I can't step outside that and look at it,
because that's…,
    perhaps I could, it feels like I can't,
    that I can't stand somewhere
*outside* of being a human spiritual being.

And so everything I do, I'm *in*.
And I can't get out.
So it's not just reflective, reflexive…

                       You *are* a reflexive being?

Yes, and I'm wrestling quite a lot with that as life…
So I think quite a lot about that,
that inner reflexive being,
and the philosophy of it.
About the philosophy underlying my researching and my living,
yes.

And in terms of my personal growth and development,
I'm attempting to be as fully myself as I can be,
in the sense of being fully present
and that that feels like…,
just like a spiritual task or injunction
to actually be fully myself
and that challenges a Christian current
that's strong in our culture
    and particularly strong in my family of origin
but I feel that if I *don't* push that one
I'm going to really regret it,
going to wake up one day and think:
well, why didn't I, why was I so…?
Yes.

Am I doing it, am I getting on with my life?

                    Am I living fully out of me?

Yes, yes, yes.

                    What you just said at the end there
                    is something I resonate with quite strongly.
                    That's what it's about for me.
                    The spirituality…
                    is about honouring my wholeness in a way.

Yes, and then for me as well,
honouring my talent, if you like,
my god-given talent or
what I'm created for,
and to do less than that is,
I feel…I could say
it's not right.

William's words touched me deeply. His wisdom in trusting himself, in spite of how difficult that might be, and his continuing search for ways to live out his academic and spiritual life in coexistence, resonated with my own struggles at this stage in my life and career.

## Heuristic process

This chapter is one example of how heuristic inquiry can unfold. I am often asked 'How does it happen?'. But this is simply an example and no more. How this process might be for you will, almost certainly, be different from how I describe it. But the stages outlined by Moustakas can usually be followed as they emerge through most creative research. I have highlighted some of the words that indicate a heuristic journey in the following text.

I began this chapter in a state of '*not knowing*', aware of something *tacitly* that I was curious about, and feeling uncomfortable with. Some months previously I had *engaged* with this part of my wider inquiry, and *immersed* myself in the tasks of listening to the tapes and reading the transcripts of postdoctoral researchers who were interested in using reflexivity. But more recently I had avoided them, distracting myself instead by going back over earlier parts of the book, re-writing, fiddling about with fonts and layout, collecting the references and organizing them, doing anything, it seemed, *except* thinking about how I was going to use the data for this chapter. Whenever I tried to think about it I felt helpless, confused and troubled, and eventually I realized I simply needed to start writing. I had (for the first time) gone over my publisher's deadline for submitting the manuscript. So I did the only thing I know that helps to free me when I am stuck: I wrote in my *journal* describing my experience of stuckness. And as I wrote, a glimmer of understanding began to emerge.

When I look back from where I am today, with some slight distance, I can see how the stages of a heuristic process had unfolded and I can make sense of my experiences in a different way. What I had judged as 'avoidance' was, I now believe, the stage of *incubation*: I had put this part of the work on the back burner while I did other things. Writing in my journal, I was *filtering my participants' experiences through my own*, and gradually light began to dawn – the *illumination* stage. I tried tentatively talking to people as my ideas began to emerge from a fog of confusion and, through articulating my thoughts, and through telling and re-telling my stories, the fog began to clear. I was able to begin a process of constructing new meanings from the data: *the explication. Intuitively* I had known this process needed more time.

Through writing my *analysis* (creating themes or finding meanings), and as I began to arrange the stories on the page, further insights developed that fed into what had gone before and shaped what followed. After a spell of writing (which is intermittent because ordinary life goes on – clients and supervisees to see, students to teach and tutorials to give, spending time with family and friends, reading novels and Christmas preparations to complete) there is space for reflecting again on what has emerged, and further ideas and shapes are formed. This is a continuous loop that feeds back on itself.

As I write this now I begin to imagine how I will construct the *creative synthesis*, and begin to experiment with pasting quotes onto the page – quotes that appear as snatches of the conversations, overheard along the way as I have constructed this study. I am not sure how that will come to fruition but if you turn the pages of this book you may come across whatever those ideas have turned into by the time my work is finished.

As I come to the end of this chapter (and this book) I feel a sense of release and letting go. Perhaps the ambivalence I expressed earlier about being ready, on one level, to let go of my university role, while also wanting to continue with the work I really enjoy, has been played out through this chapter.

Like William, I sense an unknown future and wonder where my path will take me from here on and I know now that I am ready to wait and see – to trust.

# A Dream

*31 December 2003 (the night after writing the previous pages)*

I am in a single bed (with an iron bedstead) in a street that runs between two rows of shops. It reminds me of being in Jerusalem many years ago. Suddenly there is a fierce gust of wind and I realize that each side of my bed is attached by a long, thin, string to a large silver helium balloon, and the gust of wind takes the balloons away, high up above the roof tops into the sky. My bed is lifted precariously into the air and carried along. The patchwork quilt falls to the ground from quite a height. It feels dangerous, terrifying (and a bit exhilarating) to be swept along higher and higher into the air. The thin string bites into my hands as I cling on and I try to wrap it around my knuckles to make it easier to hold on. I know that I will be lost if I don't do something to bring myself back down to earth. Then I notice there are two or three people hanging onto the sheets trailing beneath my bed and they too are being carried along. Gradually their weight lowers me to the ground. As I come to rest I feel a mixture of relief that I have been saved from disappearing into the stratosphere and a slight reluctance to let go of the balloons, knowing that once I do so they will fly off without me and I will have given up my chance of ever flying again.

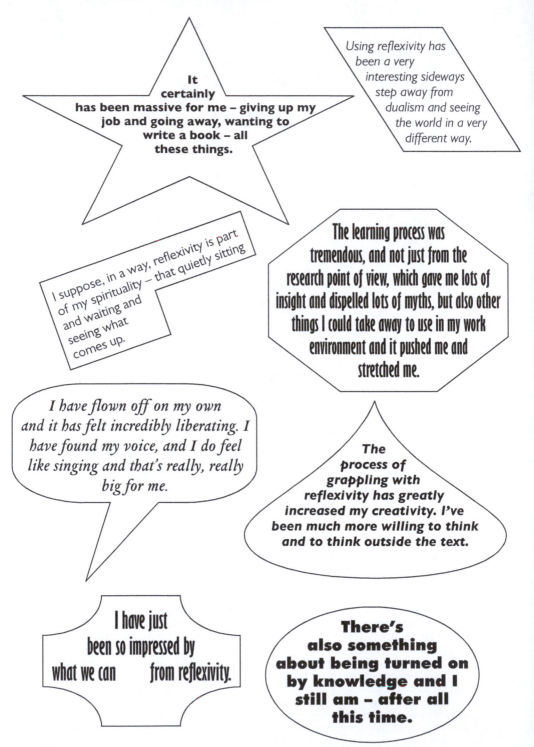

It certainly has been massive for me – giving up my job and going away, wanting to write a book – all these things.

Using reflexivity has been a very interesting sideways step away from dualism and seeing the world in a very different way.

I suppose, in a way, reflexivity is part of my spirituality – that quietly sitting and waiting and seeing what comes up.

The learning process was tremendous, and not just from the research point of view, which gave me lots of insight and dispelled lots of myths, but also other things I could take away to use in my work environment and it pushed me and stretched me.

I have flown off on my own and it has felt incredibly liberating. I have found my voice, and I do feel like singing and that's really, really big for me.

The process of grappling with reflexivity has greatly increased my creativity. I've been much more willing to think and to think outside the text.

I have just been so impressed by what we can        from reflexivity.

There's also something about being turned on by knowledge and I still am – after all this time.

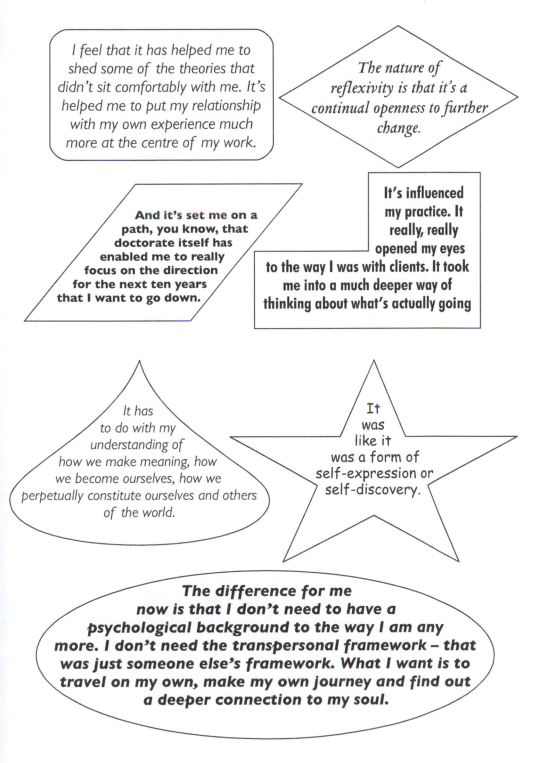

I feel that it has helped me to shed some of the theories that didn't sit comfortably with me. It's helped me to put my relationship with my own experience much more at the centre of my work.

The nature of reflexivity is that it's a continual openness to further change.

And it's set me on a path, you know, that doctorate itself has enabled me to really focus on the direction for the next ten years that I want to go down.

It's influenced my practice. It really, really opened my eyes to the way I was with clients. It took me into a much deeper way of thinking about what's actually going

It has to do with my understanding of how we make meaning, how we become ourselves, how we perpetually constitute ourselves and others of the world.

It was like it was a form of self-expression or self-discovery.

The difference for me now is that I don't need to have a psychological background to the way I am any more. I don't need the transpersonal framework – that was just someone else's framework. What I want is to travel on my own, make my own journey and find out a deeper connection to my soul.

It's on the fringes of what's accepted academically, and yet the more I think about it, the more I watch myself in interactions in various research projects I'm involved with, the more incredible it seems to me that so much research has chosen to exclude it. If you don't have any sense of the researcher, you're deprived of a major way of understanding what you're looking at.

For me there's never been a separation between that kind of work and who I am, which causes me enormous problems now, because I've got a family and other things in my life and I can't just get lost in that.

In my training of others there is a kind of respect for my experience. It's as though they recognize the journey – they know they can come and talk to me.

There are things I've written that have got glimpses of my process, but there's also things I've taken out of published papers, because I've felt too shaky about it. A lot of it is about me, about the idea of being known and so on.

# References

Alcoff, L. and Potter, E. (1993) 'Introduction: When feminisms intersect epistemology.' In L. Alcoff and E. Potter (eds) *Feminist Epistemologies*. Routledge: New York.

Alvesson, M. and Skoldberg, K. (2000) *Reflexive Methodology*. London: Sage.

Angoff, C. (1994) 'Preface.' In A. Lerner (ed.) *Poetry in the Therapeutic Experience* (2nd edition). St Louis, MO: MMB Music Inc.

Aptheker, B. (1989) *Tapestries of Life: Women's Work, Women's Consciousness, and Meaning of Daily Experience*. Amherst, MA: University of Massachusetts Press.

Argyris, C. and Schon, D. (1974) *Theory in Practice*. San Francisco: Jossey-Bass.

Atkinson, P. and Hammersley, M. (1998) 'Ethnography and participant observation.' In N. Denzin and Y.S. Lincoln (eds) *Strategies of Qualitative Inquiry*. London: Sage.

BACP (2002) *Ethical Framework for Good Practice in Counselling and Psychotherapy*. Rugby, UK: British Association for Counselling and Psychotherapy.

Barnes, C., Mercer, G. and Shakespeare, T. (1999) *Exploring Disability: A Sociological Introduction*. Cambridge, UK: Polity Press.

Barnett, R.L. (2003) 'Angels nesting in the mind.' In K. Etherington (2003) *Trauma, the Body and Transformation*. London: Jessica Kingsley Publishers.

Baron, J. (1991) 'The many promises of storytelling in law.' *Rutgers Law Journal 23*, 1, 79–90.

Behar, R. (1996) *The Vulnerable Observer: Anthropology that Breaks Your Heart*. Boston: Beacon Press.

Berg, D.N. and Smith, K.K. (eds) (1988) *The Self in Social Inquiry: Researching Methods*. London: Sage.

Birch, M. and Miller, T. (2000) 'Inviting intimacy: The interview as a therapeutic opportunity.' *International Journal of Research Methodology 3*, 3, 189–202.

Bird, J. (2000) *The Heart's Narrative: Therapy and Navigating Life's Contradictions*. Auckland, NZ: Edge Press.

Blom, L.A. and Chaplin, L. (1988) *The Moment of Movement: Dance Imporvisation*. Pittsburgh, PA: University of Pittsburg Press.

Bochner, A.P. (2000) 'Criteria against ourselves.' *Qualitative Inquiry 6*, 2, 266–272.

Bochner, A.P. and Ellis, C. (eds) (2002) *Ethnographically Speaking: Autoethnography, Literature, and Aesthetics*. Oxford: AltaMira Press.

Bochner, A.P. and Ellis, C. (2003) 'An introduction to the arts and narrative research: Art as inquiry.' *Qualitative Inquiry 9*, 4, 506–514.

Bolton, G. (1999) *The Therapeutic Potential of Creative Writing: Writing Myself*. London: Paul Chapman Publishing.

Bolton, G. (2001) *Reflective Practice*. London: Jessica Kingsley Publishers.

Bolton, G. (2003) 'Around the slices of herself.' In K. Etherington (ed).) *Trauma, the Body and Transformation*. London: Jessica Kingsley Publishers.

Bolton, G., Howlett, S., Lago, C. and Wright, J. (2003) *Writing Cures: Therapeutic Writing in Therapy and Counselling On- and Off-line.* London: Brunner Routledge.

Bond, T. (2002) 'Naked narrative: Real research?' *Counselling and Psychotherapy Research 2*, 2, 133–138.

Boyatzis, R.E. (1998) *Transforming Qualitative Information: Thematic Analysis and Code Development.* London: Sage.

Braud, W. (1998) 'An expanded view of validity.' In W. Braud and R. Anderson (eds) *Transpersonal Research Methods for the Social Sciences.* Thousand Oaks, CA: Sage.

Braud, W. and Anderson, R. (1998) *Transpersonal Research Methods for the Social Sciences: Honouring Human Experience.* London: Sage.

Bridges, N. (2003) Review of *Narrative Approaches to Working With Adult Male Survivors of Childhood Sexual Abuse* by Kim Etherington. Unpublished MPhil Essay, University of Bristol, UK.

Bridges, N. and Etherington, K. (2003) 'Contracting the MPhil/PhD student–adviser relationship.' Conference presentation, University of Bristol, *July 2003.*

Bruner, E.M. (1993) 'Introduction: The ethnographic self and the personal self.' In P. Benson (ed.) *Anthroplogy and Literature.* Urbana, IL: University of Illinois Press.

Bruner, J.S. (1986) *Actual Minds, Possible Worlds.* Cambridge MA: Harvard University Press.

Bruner, J. (1987) 'Life as narrative.' *Social Research 54*, 1, 11–32.

Bruner, J. (1990) *Acts of Meaning.* Cambridge, Mass: Harvard University Press.

Bruner, J. (1991) 'The narrative construction of reality.' *Critical Inquiry 18*, 1, Autumn, 1–21.

Bruner, J. (1995) 'The autobiographical process.' *Current Sociology 43*, 161–77 (special issue: Biographical Research).

Budd, J. (2003) 'Less than super supervision.' *Guardian Education*, Tuesday 18 March, 2.

Burgess, R.G. (ed.) (1994) *Postgraduate Education and Training in the Social Sciences: Process and Products.* London: Jessica Kingsley Publishers.

Burr, V. (1995) *An Introduction to Social Constructionism.* London: Routledge.

Butler, A., Van Cleave, C. and Stirling, S. (1994) *The Art Book.* London: Phaidon Press.

Carr, D. (1986) *Time, Narrative and History.* Bloomington: Indiana University Press.

Chancellor, A. (2003) 'Sometimes it's hard to be a woman.' *Guardian 'Weekend'*, 8 November, 9.

Charmaz, K. and Mitchell, R. (1997) 'The myth of silent authorship: Self, substance and style.' In R. Hertz (ed.) *Reflexivity and Voice.* Thousand Oaks, CA: Sage.

Clandinin, D.J. and Connelly, F.M. (1994) 'Personal experience methods.' In N.K. Denzin and Y.S. Lincoln (eds) *Handbook of Qualitative Research.* Thousand Oaks, CA: Sage.

Clandinin, D.J. and Connelly, F.M. (2000) *Narrative Inquiry.* San Fransisco: Jossey Bass.

Clarkson, P. (1998) 'Writing as research in counselling psychology and related disciplines.' In P. Clarkson (ed.) *Counselling Psychology: Integrating Theory,Research and Supervised Practice.* London: Routledge.

Clements, J., Ettling, D., Jenett, D. and Shields, L. (1998) 'Organic research: Feminine spirituality meets transpersonal research.' In W. Braud and R. Anderson (eds) *Transpersonal Research Methods for the Social Sciences: Honoring Human Experience.* Thousand Oaks, CA: Sage.

Cooper, L. (2001) *Re-searching Myself: An Auto-ethnography of my Personal Experience of Work-related Stress, Drawing on Personal, Professional and Research Narratives.* Unpublished MSc dissertation, University of Bristol.

Cooper, N., Stevenson, C. and Hale, G. (eds) (1996) *Integrating Perspectives on Health.* Buckingham UK: Open University Press.

Cortazzi, M. (1993) *Narrative Analysis.* London: Falmer Press.

Crossley, M.L. (2000) *Introducing Narrative Psychology: Self, Trauma and the Construction of Meaning.* Buckingham UK: Open University Press.

Crotty, M. (1998) *The Foundations of Social Research: Meaning and Perspective in the Research Process.* London: Sage.

Cushman, P. (1992) 'Psychotherapy to 1992: A historically situated psychology.' *American Psychologist 45,* 599–611.

Cushman, P. (1995) *Constructing the Self, Constructing America: A Cultural History of Psychotherapy.* Reading MA: Addison-Wesley.

Danforth, S. (1997) 'On what basis hope? Modern progress and postmodern possibilities.' *Mental Retardation 35,* 93–106.

Denzin, N. (1989) *Interpretive Interactionism.* Newbury Park, CA: Sage.

Denzin N.K. (2000) 'The practices and politics of interpretation.' In N.K. Denzin and Y.S. Lincoln (eds) *Handbook of Qualitative Research* (2nd edition). Thousand Oaks, CA: Sage.

Denzin N.K. and Lincoln Y.S. (2000) *Handbook of Qualitative Research* (2nd edition). London: Sage.

Derrida, J. (1981) *Positions.* Baltimore: Johns Hopkins University Press.

Devereux, G. (1967) 'From anxiety to method in the behavioural sciences.' In P. Reason and J. Rowan (eds) *Human Inquiry – A Sourcebook of New Paradigm Research.* Chichester: Wiley.

Dingwall, R. (1997) 'Accounts, interviews and observations.' In G. Miller and R. Dingwall (eds) *Context and Methods in Qualitative Research.* Thousand Oaks, CA: Sage.

Douglass, B. and Moustakas, C. (1985) 'Heuristic inquiry: The internal search to know.' *Journal of Humanistic Psychology 25,* 3, 39–55.

Einstein, A. (1954) *Ideas and Opinions.* New York: Crown.

Ellis, C. (1995) *Final Negotiations: A Story of Love, Loss, and Chronic Illness.* Philadelphia: Temple University Press.

Ellis, C. (1996) 'On the demands of truthfulness in writing personal loss narratives.' *Journal of Personal and Interpersonal Loss 1,* 151–177.

Ellis, C. (2001) 'With mother/with child: A true story.' *Qualitative Inquiry 7,* 5, 598–616.

Ellis, C. and Berger, L. (2003) 'Their story/my story/our story: Including the researcher's experience in interview research.' In J.F. Gubrium and J.A. Holstein (eds) *Postmodern Interviewing.* Thousand Oaks, CA: Sage.

Ellis, C. and Bochner, A.P. (eds) (1996) *Composing Ethnography: Alternative Forms of Qualitative Writing.* Oxford: AltaMira Press.

Ellis, C. and Bochner, A. (2000) 'Autoethnography, personal narrative, reflexivity: Researcher as subject.' In N.K. Denzin and Y.S. Lincoln (eds) *Handbook of Qualitative Research* (2nd edition). Thousand Oaks, CA: Sage.

Ellis, C. and Flaherty, M. (eds) (1992) *Investigating Subjectivity: Research on Lived Experience.* Thousand Oaks, CA: Sage.

Ely, M., Vinz, R., Downing, M. and Anzul, M. (1997) *On Writing Qualitative Research: Living by Words.* London: Falmer Press.

Engel, G.L. (1977) 'The biopsychosocial model and the education of health professionals.' *Annals of the New York Academy of Sciences 310,* 169–181.

Erikson, E. (1950) *Childhood and Society*. New York: Norton.

Etherington, K. (1992) *Fathers and Daughters: A Study of the Relationship and its Effects on the Lives of Adult Women*. Unpublished MSc Dissertation, University of Bristol.

Etherington, K. (1995) *Adult Male Survivors of Childhood Sexual Abuse*. Brighton: Pavilion Publishing.

Etherington, K. (2000) *Narrative Approaches to Working with Male Survivors of Sexual Abuse; The Client's, the Counsellor's and the Researcher's Story*. London: Jessica Kingsley Publishers.

Etherington, K. (2001a) 'Writing qualitative research – a gathering of selves.' *Counselling and Psychotherapy Research 1*, 2, 119–125.

Etherington, K. (2001b) *Counsellors in Health Settings*. London: Jessica Kingsley Publishers.

Etherington, K. (2001c) 'Research with ex-clients: An extension and celebration of the therapeutic process.' *British Journal of Guidance and Counselling 29*, 1, 5–19.

Etherington, K. (2001d) 'Supervising counsellors who work with abuse.' *Counselling Psychology Quarterly 13*, 4, 377–389.

Etherington, K. (2002a) *Rehabilitation Counselling in Physical and Mental Health*. London: Jessica Kingsley Publishers.

Etherington, K. (2002b) 'Working together: editing a book as narrative research methodology.' *Counselling and Psychotherapy Research 2*, 3, 167–176.

Etherington, K. (2003) *Trauma, the Body and Transformation*. London: Jessica Kingsley Publishers.

Fine, M., Weis, L., Weseen, S. and Wong, L. (2000) 'For whom? Qualitative research, representations, and social responsibilities.' In N. K. Denzin and Y. S. Lincoln (eds) *Handbook of Qualitative Research* (2nd edition). Thousand Oaks, CA: Sage.

Flemons, D. and Green, S. (2002) 'Stories that conform/stories that transform: A conversation in four parts.' In A.P. Bochner and C. Ellis (eds) *Ethnographically Speaking: Autoethnography, Literature, and Aesthetics*. Oxford: AltaMira Press.

Fontana, A. and Frey, J.H. (2000) 'The interview: From structured interviews to negotiated text.' In N.K. Denzin and Y.S.Lincoln (eds) *Handbook of Qualitative Research* (2nd edition). Thousand Oaks, CA: Sage.

Foucault, M. (1980) *Power/Knowledge: Selected Interviews and Other Writings*. Brighton, UK: Harvester.

Frank, A.W. (1995) *The Wounded Storyteller: Body, Illness and Ethics*. Chicago, IL: University of Chicago Press.

Freedman, J. and Combs, G. (1996) *Narrative Therapy: A Social Construction of Preferred Realities*. London: W.W. Norton.

Freedman, J. and Combs, G. (2002) *Narrative Therapy with Couples...and a Whole Lot More! A Collection of Papers, Essays and Exercises*. Adelaide: Dulwich Centre Publications.

Freeman, M. (1993) *Rewriting the Self: History, Memory, Narrative*. London: Routledge.

Freire, P. (1972) *Pedagogy of the Oppressed*. Harmondsworth: Penguin.

Freire, P. (1985) *The Politics of Education: Culture, Power and Liberation*. London: Macmillan.

Gadamer, H. (1975) *Truth and Method* (2nd edition). New York: Continuum.

Gale, J. (1992) 'When research interviews are more therapeutic than therapy interviews.' *The Qualitative Report 1*, 4, 31–38.

Gee, J. (1991) 'A linguistic approach to narrative.' *Journal of Narrative and Life History 1*, 15–39.

Geertz, K.J. (1973) *The Interpretation of Cultures: Selected Essays*. New York: Basic Books.

Geertz, K.J. (1983) *Local Knowledge: Further Essays in Interpretive Anthropology.* New York: Basic Books.

Gendlin, E.T. (1969) 'Focusing.' *Psychotherapy 6,* 4–15.

Gendlin, E. (1978) *Focusing.* New York: Everest House.

Gendlin, E. (1981) *Focusing.* New York, London: Bantam Books.

Gergen, K. (1985) 'The social constructionist movement in modern psychology.' *American Psychologist 40,* 266–75.

Gergen, K. (1994) *Toward Transformation in Social Knowledge* (2nd edition). London: Sage.

Gergen, K.J. (1999) *An Invitation to Social Constructionism.* London: Sage.

Gergen, K.J. and Gergen, M.M. (1986) 'Narrative form and the construction of psychological science.' In T. Sarbin (ed.) *Narrative Psychology: The Storied Nature of Human Conduct.* New York: Praeger.

Gergen, K.J. and Gergen, M.M. (1991) 'Towards reflexive methodologies.' In F. Steier (ed.) *Research and Reflexivity.* Newbury Park: Sage.

Gergen, M.M. and Gergen, K.J. (2000) 'Qualitative inquiry: Tensions and transformations.' In N.K. Denzin and Y.S. Lincoln (eds) *The Handbook of Qualitative Research* (2nd edition). Thousand Oaks, CA: Sage.

Gergen, M.M. and Gergen, K.J. (2002) 'Ethnegraphic representation as relationship.' In A. Bochner and C. Ellis (eds) *Ethnographically Speaking: Autoethnography, Literature, and Aesthetics.* Walnut Creek, CA: Mta Mira Press.

Giancola, J. (1992) 'Multi-representation techniques in research: The rise and descent of the rain dance video collective 1968–1973.' Paper presented at the Southern Sociological Society, New Orleans, LA. In C. Ellis (1995) *Final Negotiations: A Story of Love, Loss and Chronic Illness.* Philadelphia: Temple University Press.

Giddens, A. (1991) *Modernity and Self-identity: Self and Society in the Late Modern Age.* Cambridge: Polity Press.

Ginsberg, A. (1956) *Howl and Other Poems.* San Francisco: City Lights Books.

Glaser, B. and Strauss, A. (1967) *The Discovery of Grounded Theory.* Chicago: Aldine.

Godin, J. and Ooghourlian, J-M. (1994) 'The transitional gap in metaphor and therapy.' In J.K. Zeig (ed.) *Ericksonian Methods: The Essence of the Story.* New York: Brunner/Mazel.

Grafanaki, S. (1996) 'How research can change the researcher: The need for sensitivity, flexibility and ethical boundaries in conducting qualitative research in counselling/psychotherapy.' *British Journal of Guidance and Counselling 24,* 3, 329–338.

Gubrium, J.F. and Holstein, J.A. (1998) 'Narrative practices and coherence of personal stories.' *Sociological Quarterly 39,* 163–87.

Gubrium, J.F. and Holstein, J.A. (2003) *Postmodern Interviewing.* Thousand Oaks, CA: Sage.

Harber, K.D. and Pennebaker, J.W. (1992) 'Overcoming traumatic memories.' In S. Christianson (ed.) *The Handbook of Emotion and Memory: Research and Theory.* Hillsdale, NJ: Erlbaum.

Harder, A.F. (2002) *The Developmental Stages of Erik Erikson.* http://www.learningplaceonline.com/stages/organize/Erikson.htm

Hart, N. and Crawford-Wright, A. (1999) 'Research as therapy, therapy as research: Ethical dilemmas in new paradigm research.' *British Journal of Counselling and Guidance 27,* 2, 205–215.

Heidegger, M. (1962) *Being and Time.* Oxford: Blackwell.

Herman, J. (1992) *Trauma and Recovery.* New York: Basic Books.

Heron, J. (1996) *Co-operative Inquiry: Research into the Human Condition.* London: Sage.

Hertz, R. (ed.) (1997) *Reflexivity and Voice.* Thousand Oaks, CA: Sage.

Hockey, J. (1995) 'Getting too close: A problem and possible solution in social science PhD supervision.' *British Journal of Guidance and Counselling 23*, 2, 199–210.

Hockney, D. (1993) *That's the Way I See It.* London: Thames and Hudson.

Holliday, A. (2002) *Doing and Writing Qualitative Research.* London: Sage.

Holsti, O.R. (1969) *Content Analysis for the Social Sciences and Humanities.* Reading: Addison-Wesley.

hooks, bell (1989) *Talking Back: Thinking Feminist Thinking Black.* Boston: South End Press.

hooks, bell (1994) *Teaching to Transgress: Education as the Practice of Freedom.* New York: Routledge.

Houston, M. and Kramarae, C. (1991) 'Speaking from silence: Methods of silencing and of resistance.' *Discourse and Society 2*, 4, 425–437.

Howard, G.S. (1991) 'Culture tales: A narrative approach to thinking, cross-cultural psychology and psychotherapy.' *American Psychologist 46*, 3, 187–197.

Hunt, C. (2000) *Therapeutic Dimensions of Autobiography in Creative Writing.* London: Jessica Kingsley Publishers.

Hunt, C. and Sampson, F. (1998) *The Self on the Page. Theory and Practice of Creative Writing in Personal Development.* London: Jessica Kingsley Publishers.

Husserl, E. (1931) *Ideas: General Introduction to Pure Phenomenology.* London: George Allen and Unwin.

Inskipp, F. and Proctor, B. (1993) *The Art, Craft and Tasks of Counselling Supervision. Part 1: Making the Most of Supervision.* Twickenham: Cascade.

Janesick, V.J. (2000) 'The choreography of qualitative research design: Minuets, improvisation, and crystallization.' In N.K. Denzin and Y.S. Lincoln (eds) *The Handbook of Qualitative Research* (2nd edition). Thousand Oaks, CA: Sage.

Johns, H. (1996) *Personal Development in Counsellor Training.* London: Cassell.

Josselson, R. (ed.) (1996) *Ethics and Process in the Narrative Study of Lives*, 4. London: Sage.

Josselson, R. and Lieblich, A. (eds) (1993) *The Narrative Study of Lives*, 1. Newbury Park: Sage.

Jung, C.G. *The Collected Works of C.G. Jung (1953–78)* H. Read, M. Fordham and G. Adler (eds). London: Routledge.

Kagan, N. (1986) 'Interpersonal process recall: basic methods and recent research.' In D. Larsen (ed.) *Teaching Psychological Skills.* Monterey, CA: Brooks Cole.

Karma (2003) *A Mother's Account of Addiction.* Unpublished MSc dissertation, University of Bristol, UK.

Katz, A.M. and Shotter, J. (1996) 'Hearing the patient's "voice": Toward a social poetics in diagnostic interviews.' *Social Science and Medicine 43*, 6, 919–31.

Kiesinger, C.E. (1998) 'From interview to story: writing Abbie's life.' *Qualitative Inquiry 4*, 71–95.

King, E. (1996) 'The use of self in qualitative research.' In J.T.E. Richardson (ed.) *Handbook of Qualitative Research Methods for Psychology and the Social Sciences.* Leicester: BPS.

Kleinman, A. (1988) *The Illness Narratives: Suffering, Healing and the Human Condition.* New York: Basic Books.

Kneeshaw, J. (2000) *The Silence of Somatization: A Personal Exploration to Discover Whether Childhood Trauma had Manifested as Physical Illness Late in Life.* Unpublished MSc dissertation, University of Bristol, UK.

Kvale, S. (1996) *InterViews: An Introduction to Qualitative Research Interviewing.* Sage: Thousand Oaks.

Kvale, S. (1999) 'The psychoanalytic interview as qualitative research.' *Qualitative Inquiry 5,* 1, 87–113.

Lapadat, J.C. and Lindsay, A.C. (1999) 'Transcription in research and practice: From standardization of technique to interpretive positionings.' *Qualitative Inquiry 5,* 1, 64–86.

Lather, P. (1993) 'Fertile obsession: Validity after poststructuralism.' *Sociological Quarterly 34,* 673–693.

Lather, P. and Smithies, C. (1997) *Troubling the Angels.* Oxford: Westview Press.

Law, S. (2002) *Hope, Hell and High Water: An Autoethnographical Journey From Addiction to Recovery.* Unpublished MSc dissertation, University of Bristol, UK.

Leftwich, A. (1998) *But I Must Also Feel It as a Man.* Unpublished MSc dissertation, University of Bristol, UK.

Lerner, A. (ed.) (1994) *Poetry in the Therapeutic Experience.* St. Louis, MO: MMB Music.

Levine, P. (1997) *Waking the Tiger: Healing Trauma.* Berkeley, CA: North Atlantic Books.

Lincoln, Y.S. (1995) 'Emerging criteria for quality in qualitative and interpretive inquiry.' *Qualitative Inquiry 1,* 275–289.

Lincoln, Y.S. and Denzin, N.K. (1994) 'The fifth moment.' In N.K. Denzin and Y.S. Lincoln (eds) *Handbook of Qualitative Research.* Thousand Oaks, CA: Sage.

Lynch, M. (2000) 'Against reflexivity as an academic virtue and source of privileged knowledge.' *Theory, Culture and Society 17,* 26–54.

MacIntyre, A. (1981) *After Virtue.* London: Duckworth.

Mair, M. (1989) *Beyond Psychology and Psychotherapy: A Poetics of Experience.* London: Routledge.

Marshall, C. and Rossman, G.B. (1999) *Designing Qualitative Research* (3rd edition). London: Sage.

Martin, P. (2003) *A Critique of Heuristic Research Methods.* CLIO presentation at University of Bristol, UK, February 2003.

Martin, V. (2003) *Reflexivity.* Lecture notes for MSc in Counselling (Research Unit), University of Bristol, UK.

May, T. (1999) 'Reflexivity and sociological practice.' *Sociological Research Online 4,* 3. http://www.socresonline.org.uk/socresonline/4/3/may.html

Mayhew, G. (2003) 'Journey of a lifetime.' In K. Etherington (2003) *Trauma, the Body and Transformation.* London: Jessica Kingsley Publishers.

McAdams, D. (1993) *The Stories We Live By: Personal Myths and the Making of the Self.* New York: Morrow.

McLeod, J. (1994) *Doing Counselling Research.* London: Sage.

McLeod, J. (1997) *Narrative and Psychotherapy.* London: Sage.

McLeod, J. (2001) *Qualitative Research in Counselling and Psychotherapy.* London: Sage.

McLeod, J. and Balamoutsou, S. (1996) 'Representing narrative process in therapy: Qualitative analysis of a single case.' *Counselling Psychology Quarterly 9,* 61–76.

McMorland, J., Carroll, B., Copas, S. and Pringle, J. (2003, May) 'Enhancing the practice of PhD supervisory relationships through first- and second-person action research/peer partnership inquiry (65 paragraphs).' *Qualitative Social Research* (On-line Journal), 4, 2. Available at: http://www.qualitative-research.net/fqs-texte/2-03/2-03mcmorlandetal-e.htm (accessed 5.1.04).

Merleau-Ponty, M. (1962) *The Phenomenology of Perception*. London: Routledge and Keagan-Paul.

Mishler, E. (1986) *Research Interviewing*. Cambridge, MA: Harvard University Press.

Mishler, E. (1991) 'Representing discourse: The rhetoric of transcription.' *Journal of Narrative and Life History 1*, 255–280.

Mishler, E.G. (1999) *Storylines: Craft Artists: Narratives of Identity*. Cambridge, MA: Harvard University Press.

Morse, J. (2000) 'Editorial: Writing my own experience.' *Qualitative Health Research 12*, 9, 1159–1160.

Moustakas, C. (1975) *The Touch of Loneliness*. Englewood Cliffs, NJ: Prentice Hall.

Moustakas, C. (1990) *Heuristic Research Design, Methodology and Applications*. London: Sage.

Moustakas, C. (1994) *Phenomenological Research Methods*. Thousand Oaks, CA: Sage.

Moustakas, C. and Douglass, B.G. (1985) 'Heuristic inquiry: The internal search to know.' *Journal of Humanistic Psychology 25*, 3, 39–55.

Mykhalovskiy, E. (1997) 'Reconsidering "table talk": Critical thoughts on the relationship between sociology, autobiography, and self-indulgence.' In R. Hertz (ed.) *Reflexivity and Voice*. London: Sage.

Oakley, A. (1981) 'Interviewing women: A contradiction in terms.' In H. Roberts (ed.) *Doing Feminist Research*. London: Routledge and Kegan Paul.

Ochberg, R.L. (1994) 'Life stories and storied lives.' In A. Lieblich (ed.) *Exploring Identity and Gender: The Narrative Study of Lives*. Thousand Oaks, CA: Sage.

Olesen, V.L. (2000) 'Feminisms and qualitative research at and into the millennium.' In N.K. Denzin and Y.S. Lincoln (eds) *The Handbook of Qualitative Research* (2nd edition). Thousand Oaks, CA: Sage.

Oliver, M. (1993) 'Re-defining disability.' In J. Swain, V. Finkelstein, S. French and M. Oliver (eds) *Disabling Barriers – Enabling Environments*. Sage: London.

Parker, I. (1994) 'Reflexive research and the grounding of analysis: Social psychology and the psy-complex.' *Journal of Community and Applied Social Psychology 4*, 239–52.

Payne, M. (2000) *Narrative Therapy – An Introduction for Counsellors*. London: Sage.

Pearlman, L.A. and Saakvitne, K.W. (1995) *Trauma and the Therapist: Counter-transference and Vicarious Traumatisation in Psychotherapy with Incest Survivors*. London: W.W. Norton.

Pels, D. (2000) 'Reflexivity: One step up.' *Theory, Culture and Society 17*, 1–25.

Penn, P. (2001) 'Chronic illness: Trauma, language and writing: breaking the silence.' *Family Process 40*, 1, 33–52.

Pennebaker, J.W. (1988) 'Confiding traumatic experiences and health.' In S. Fisher and J. Reason (eds) *Handbook of Life Stress, Cognition and Health*. Chichester: Wiley.

Pennebaker, J.W. (1993) 'Putting stress into words: Health, linguistic and therapeutic implications.' *Behaviour Research and Therapy 31*, 539–48.

Picart, C.J.S. (2002) 'Living the hyphenated edge: Autoethnography, hybridity, and aesthetics.' In A.P. Bochner and C. Ellis (eds) *Ethnographically Speaking: Autoethnography, Literature, and Aesthetics*. Oxford: AltaMira Press.

Plummer, K. (1995) *Telling Sexual Stories: Power, Change and Social Worlds*. London: Routledge.

Polanyi, M. (1983) *The Tacit Dimension.* New York: Doubleday.

Polkinghorne, D.E. (1988) *Narrative Knowing and the Human Sciences.* Albany: State University of New York.

Polkinghorne, D.E. (1995) 'Narrative configuration in qualitative analysis.' In J.A. Hatch and R. Wisniewski (eds) *Life History and Narrative.* London: Falmer Press.

Pullman, P. (2000) *The Amber Spyglass.* London: Scholastic Children's Books.

Prosser, J. (1992) *Child Abuse Investigations: The Families' Perspective.* Stanstead, UK: PAIN.

Reason, P. (ed.) (1994) *Participation in Human Inquiry.* London: Sage.

Reed-Danahay, D.E. (1997) *Auto/Ethnography: Rewriting the Self and the Social.* Oxford: Berg.

Rees, M. (2001) *The Rainbow Journey: An Autoethnography of Personal Growth Through Addiction Recovery and Becoming a Counsellor.* Unpublished MSc dissertation, University of Bristol, UK.

Rennie, D. (1998) *Person-centred Counselling; An Experiential Approach.* London: Sage.

Richardson, L. (1990) *Writing Strategies: Reaching Diverse Audiences.* London: Sage.

Richardson, L. (2000) 'Writing: A method of inquiry.' In N.K. Denzin and Y.S. Lincoln (eds) *Handbook of Qualitative Research* (2nd edition). Thousand Oaks, CA: Sage.

Richardson, L. (2003) 'Poetic representation of interviews.' In J.F. Gubrium and J.A. Holstein (eds) *Postmodern Interviewing.* Thousand Oaks, CA: Sage.

Riessman, C.K. (1989) 'Life events, meaning and narrative: The case of infidelity and divorce.' *Social Science and Medicine 28,* 81–92.

Riessman, C.K. (1993) *Narrative Analysis.* London: Sage.

Riessman, C. (2002) 'Doing justice: Positioning the interpreter in narrative work.' In W. Patterson (ed.) *Strategic Narrative: New Perspectives on the Power of Personal and Cultural Stories.* Oxford: Lexington Books.

Rogers, C.R. (1951) *Client-Centered Therapy: Current Practice, Implications and Theory.* London: Constable.

Ronai, C.R. (1995) 'Multiple reflections of child sex abuse.' *Journal of Contemporary Ethnography 23,* 4, 395–426.

Rosenthal, G. (2003) 'The healing effects of storytelling: On the conditions of curative storytelling in the context of research and counseling.' *Qualitative Inquiry 9,* 6, 895–915.

Rossman, G.B. and Sallis, S.F. (1998) *Learning from the Field: An Introduction to Qualitative Research.* Thousand Oaks, CA: Sage.

Rothschild, Lord (1982) *An Enquiry into the Social Science Research Council.* London: HMSO.

Sarbin, T.R. (1986) 'The narrative as a root metaphor for psychology.' In T.R. Sarbin (ed.) *Narrative Psychology: The Storied Nature of Human Conduct.* New York: Praeger.

Sarup, M. (1996) *Identity, Culture and the Postmodern World.* Athens, GA: University of Georgia Press.

Schlosser, L.Z., Knox, S., Moskovitz, C. and Hill, C. (2003) 'A qualitative examination of graduate advising relationships: The advisee perspective.' *Journal of Counseling Psychology 50,* 2, 178–188.

Schneider, J. and Conrad, P. (1983) *Having Epilepsy: The Experience and Control of Illness.* Philadelphia: Temple University Press.

Schon, D. (1983) *The Reflective Practitioner.* New York: Basic Books.

Schon, D. (1987) *Educating the Reflective Practitioner.* San Fransisco: Jossey Bass.

Schwartz, B. (1999) 'Memory and the practice of commitment.' In B. Glassner and R. Hertz (eds) *Qualitative Sociology as Everyday Life.* Thousand Oaks, CA: Sage.

Scott-Hoy, K. (2002) 'The visitor: Juggling life in the grip of the text.' In A.P. Bochner and C. Ellis (eds) *Ethnographically Speaking: Autoethnography, Literature, and Aesthetics.* Oxford: AltaMira Press.

Shaw, R. (2003) *The Embodied Psychotherapist: The Therapist's Body Story.* Hove, UK: Routledge.

Silverman, D. (1993) *Interpreting Qualitative Data: Methods for Analysing Talk, Text and Interaction.* London: Sage.

Skinner, J. (1998) 'Research as a counselling activity? A discussion of some of the uses of counselling within the context of research on sensitive issues.' *British Journal of Guidance and Counselling 26*, 4, 533–540.

Smith, J.K. and Deemer, D.K. (2000) 'The problem of criteria in the age of relativism.' In N.K. Denzin and Y.S. Lincoln (eds) *Handbook of Qualitative Research* (2nd edition). Thousand Oaks, CA: Sage.

Smith, S. (2000) 'Sensitive issues in life story research.' In S. Moch and M. Gates (eds) *The Researcher Experience in Qualitative Research.* London: Sage Publications.

Smyth, J. and Shacklock, G. (1998) 'Behind the "cleansing" of socially critical research accounts.' In G. Shacklock and J. Smyth (eds) *Being Reflexive in Critical and Educational Research.* London: Falmer Press.

Sparkes, A. (1998) 'Reciprocity in critical research? Some unsettling thoughts.' In G. Shacklock and J. Smyth (eds) *Being Reflexive in Critical Educational and Social Research.* London: Falmer Press.

Sparkes, A. (2002) 'Autoethnography: Self-indulgence or something more?' In A.P. Bochner and C. Ellis (eds) *Ethnographically Speaking: Autoethnography, Literature, and Aesthetics.* Oxford: AltaMira Press.

Sparkes, A. (2003) 'Bodies, identities, selves: Autoethnographic fragments and reflections.' In J. Denison and P. Markula (eds) *Moving Writing: Crafting Writing in Sport Research.* New York: Peter Lang.

Speedy, J. (2001) *Singing over the Bones: A Narrative Inquiry into the Construction of Research and Practice Cultures and Professional Identities by Counsellor Educators at the University of Bristol and Within the UK.* PhD dissertation, University of Bristol, UK.

Speedy, J. and Etherington, K. (1999) *Personal Development as an Intended Consequence of an Experiential Counselling Research Programme.* Conference paper, BAC Research Conference, Leeds, May 1999.

Spence, D.P. (1982) *Narrative Truth and Historical Truth: Meaning and Interpretation in Psychoanalysis.* New York: W.W. Norton.

Spiro, H.M., McCrea, C., Curnen, M.G., Peschel, E. and St James, D. (eds) (1993) *Empathy and the Practice of Medicine: Beyond Pills and the Scalpel.* London: Yale University Press.

Stevens, A. (1990) *On Jung.* London: Penguin books.

Steier, F. (ed.) (1991) *Research and Reflexivity.* London: Sage.

Stainbrook, E. (1994) 'Poetry and behaviour in the psychotherapeutic experience.' In A. Lerner (ed.) *Poetry in the Therapeutic Experience.* St Louis, MO: MMB Music Inc.

Stiles, W. (1993) 'Quality control in qualitative research.' *Clinical Psychology Review 13*, 593–618.

Strauss, A. and Corbin, J. (1990) *Basics of Qualitative Research.* London: Sage.

Sugarman, L. (1986) *Life-span Development.* London: Methuen.

Swain, J., Finkelstein, V., French, S. and Oliver, M. (eds) (1993) *Disabling Barriers – Enabling Environments.* London: Sage.

Swinnerton-Dyer, P. (1982) *Report of the Working Party on Postgraduate Education.* London: HMSO.

Trahar, S. (2003) *Conversations Across Cultures: The Impact of Multi-culturalism on Postgraduate Teaching and Learning Practices in the Higher Education Learning Environment.* Paper presented at the 7th Oxford International Conference on Education and Development. Oxford, UK, 9–11 Septmeber.

Valle, R. and Mohs, M. (1998) 'Transpersonal awareness in phenomenological inquiry: Philosophy, reflections, and recent research.' In W. Braud and R. Anderson (ed.) *Transpersonal Research Methods for the Social Sciences: Honouring Human Experience.* Thousand Oaks, CA: Sage.

van Deurzen, E. (1998) *Passion and Paradox in Psychotherapy: An Existential Approach to Therapy and Counselling.* Chichester: Wiley.

Walsh, R.A. (1996) 'The problem of unconsciousness in qualitative research.' *British Journal of Guidance and Counselling 24,* 3, 377–384.

Weingarten, K. (2003) *Common Shock: Witnessing Violence Every Day: How We Are Harmed, How We Can Heal.* New York: Dutton.

Wengraf, T. (2001) *Qualitative Research Interviewing: Biographic Narrative and Semi-structured Method.* London: Sage.

West, W. (1998) 'Critical subjectivity: Use of self in counselling research.' *Counselling 9,* 3, 228–230.

West, W. (2001) 'The use of a heuristic approach to counselling research.' *Counselling and Psychotherapy Research 1,* 2, 126–131.

White, M. (1995) *Re-authoring Lives: Interviews and Essays.* Adelaide, Australia: Dulwich Centre Publications.

White, M. and Epston, D. (1990) *Narrative Means to Therapeutic Ends.* New York: Norton.

Widdershoven, G.A.M. (1993) 'The story of life: Hermeneutic perspectives on the relationship between narrative and life history.' In R. Josselson and A. Lieblich (eds) *The Narrative Study of Lives 1.* Thousand Oaks, CA: Sage.

Williams, P. (1999) 'Telling tales: The elusive power of stories.' *The Therapist 6,* 1, 18–23.

Winfield, G. (1987) *The Social Science PhD: An ESRC Enquiry on Submission Rates – The Report.* London: ESRC.

Winter, R., Buck, A. and Sobiechowska, P. (1996) *Professional Experience and the Investigative Imagination: The Art of Reflective Writing.* London: Routledge.

Wolcott, H.F. (2001) *Writing up Qualitative Research* (2nd edition). London: Sage.

Woolley, M. (1993) 'Acquired hearing loss: Acquired oppression.' In J. Swain, V. Finkelstein, S. French and M. Oliver (eds) *Disabling Barriers – Enabling Environments.* London: Sage.

Wosket, V. (1999) *The Therapeutic Use of Self: Counselling, Practice, Research and Supervision.* London: Routledge.

Wu, Su (2002) 'Filling the pot or lighting the "fire"? Cultural variations in conceptions of pedagogy.' *Teaching in Higher Education 7,* 4, 387–395.

Yalom, I. (1989) *Love's Executioner.* New York: Basic Books.

Yalom, I. (2001) *The Gift of Therapy: Reflections on Being a Therapist.* London: Piatkus.

Yalom, I.D. and Elkin, G. (1974) *Everyday Gets a Little Closer: A Twice Told Therapy.* New York: Basic Books.

Zohar, D. and Marshall, I. (2000) *Connecting with our Spiritual Intelligence.* London: Bloomsbury.

# Subject Index

# Author Index